New Labour and the new world order

MANCHESTER
1824

Manchester University Press

For Zach

New Labour and the new world order

Britain's role in the war on terror

Steven Kettell

Manchester University Press
Manchester and New York
*distributed in the United States exclusively
by* Palgrave Macmillan

The right of Steven Kettell to be identified as the author of this work has been asserted by him in accordance with the Copyright, Designs and Patents Act 1988.

Published by Manchester University Press
Oxford Road, Manchester M13 9NR, UK
and Room 400, 175 Fifth Avenue, New York, NY 10010, USA
www.manchesteruniversitypress.co.uk

Distributed in the United States exclusively by
Palgrave Macmillan, 175 Fifth Avenue, New York,
NY 10010, USA

Distributed in Canada exclusively by
UBC Press, University of British Columbia, 2029 West Mall,
Vancouver, BC, Canada V6T 1Z2

British Library Cataloguing-in-Publication Data
A catalogue record for this book is available from the British Library

Library of Congress Cataloging-in-Publication Data applied for

ISBN   978 0 7190 8136 1 hardback

First published 2011

Typeset
by Frances Hackeson Freelance Publishing Services, Brinscall, Lancs
Printed in Great Britain
by CPI Antony Rowe Ltd, Chippenham, Wiltshire

Contents

	Preface	*page* vi
	Acknowledgements	vii
1	Introduction	1
2	Old and new	6
3	Barbarians at the gates	25
4	Chaos	45
5	Above the law	71
6	A road well travelled	95
7	Brown's war	120
8	Elysian fields	146
9	Decline and fall	172
	References	185
	Index	196

Preface

The 'war on terror' has shaped and defined the first decade of the twenty-first century. Launched by the US in the wake of the 9/11 attacks, the declared objective of the campaign was to deal with the threat posed by a confluence of rogue states, international terrorism and weapons of mass destruction. The underlying dynamics, however, were conditioned by a shift in the US towards a new imperialist strategy of global reordering that had been set in train since the end of the Cold War. In this endeavour, Washington enjoyed staunch support from a New Labour government keen to elevate Britain's influence in international affairs. This included British participation in the invasions of Afghanistan and Iraq, support for extra-legal measures taken by the US, and a diminution of civil liberties through punitive anti-terror legislation. Ostensibly set within a political framework of promoting humanitarian values, the Labour government's conduct in the war on terror proved to be largely counter-productive. Eroding trust between the citizenry and the state, putting the armed forces under increasing strain, reducing Britain's global position and exacerbating the threat from radical Islamic terrorism, the consequences will be felt for many years to come.

Acknowledgements

This book owes much to a number of people. Thanks, first of all, to Pete, Nick and Heather for indulging my soliloquies on all matters relating to the subject, and thanks also go to all the students who have taken the module 'Britain and the War in Iraq' during the past three years, both for enduring similar monologues with fortitude and patience, and for their unfailingly persistent ability to discover new, awkward and challenging questions. Thanks, too, are extended to my colleagues in the Department of Politics and International Studies at the University of Warwick, and especially Trevor for his words of wisdom on the Bush administration and the innards of American political life. I am also grateful to the team at Manchester University Press for their help and advice in bringing the project to fruition, and to the comments and suggestions of their anonymous reviewers. Thanks, most of all, however, must go to my family, and especially to my wife, Marie, without whom none of this would have been possible. Any faults, inaccuracies, errors or omissions are, of course, entirely my own.

1

Introduction

In the early 1960s, with the sun dipping beyond its imperial horizon, the ex-US Secretary of State, Dean Acheson, famously remarked that Great Britain had lost an empire and had not yet found itself a role. By the early years of the new millennium, however, any sense of uncertainty had been firmly dispelled. Under a New Labour government keen to elevate Britain's position on the international stage, the country had found itself cast as the supporter-in-chief of the much-vaunted US 'war on terror'. Launched by the US in the aftermath of the 9/11 terrorist attacks, the overarching objective of this campaign was to advance a wide-ranging project of geo-strategic reordering designed to extend and enhance US global dominance. For the New Labour leadership, support for this endeavour was considered to be vital not only for securing Britain's national interests, but as a means of helping to forge and fashion a new world order for the twenty-first century.

Not surprisingly, the circumstances surrounding the war on terror have attracted an enormous amount of commentary and analysis. Typologically, this divides into several clear, if not discrete forms. By far the largest of these, again unsurprisingly, has focused on the role of the US. For most accounts the central aim has been to deal with these events via a broad examination of the US role in global affairs, or, conversely, to detail the specific actions and intentions of the Bush administration.[1] Beyond this, scholarly attentions have also centred on specific episodes or themes within the war on terror as a whole, such as the invasion of Iraq or the use of extra-legal practices,[2] while others have set out to explore the role played by the arch-enemy of the US in the conflict, focusing either on the al-Qaeda network, on its leader, Osama bin Laden, or on the phenomena of radical Islamic terrorism more generally.[3]

Set against this, analyses of Britain's role in the war on terror, though vastly smaller in number, have been similarly variegated. Generally speaking, the focus has centred on specific aspects of Britain's participation,

1

such as the nature of the 'special relationship' with the US or its involvement in Afghanistan or Iraq,[4] or has set out to consider the domestic consequences, typically focusing on anti-terror legislation, and the impact on civil liberties and social cohesion.[5] Still further, other studies have sought to examine these various matters less in their own right, but as part of a broader analysis of the New Labour governments in general, or the leadership of Tony Blair in particular.[6]

Although these respective accounts are useful for illuminating the numerous and varied issues involved in Britain's role in the war on terror, the existing coverage of these developments has been notable for its lack of holistic analysis. While focusing on specific aspects, issues and events by definition yields a partial understanding in terms of the overall picture, consideration of the wider context in which these elements are set enables their respective interconnections and underlying dynamics to be brought into clearer view. Such an analysis, then, is the central purpose of this book. The examination that follows is based on two main conceptual frames. The first, and more general premise, is that the unfolding dynamics and circumstances of the war on terror are best explained in terms of the underlying drivers and processes of 'new imperialism'. This reflects one of the dominant themes in scholarly analyses of contemporary international affairs; namely, the extent to which the actions of the US can be considered as manifestations of a broader imperial project. The second, and the principal frame of the book, sets out to examine the way in which Britain's role in the war on terror has been shaped both by these developments and by New Labour's approach to foreign policy, and to consider how these events, in turn, impacted upon domestic political affairs under the governments of Tony Blair and Gordon Brown.

Within this, one of the main themes of the book is that the events and conduct of the war on terror, in both its international and domestic spheres, have failed to effectively deal with the threat posed by radical Islamic terrorism. A central issue here is that the dynamics of Washington's broader geo-strategic manoeuvres, leading to military invasions of Afghanistan and Iraq, ensured at the same time that the content of both the US military effort as well as the post-war stability and reconstruction operations were limited to doing that which was deemed necessary to ensure a rapid victory and a quick withdrawal of US forces. The corresponding absence of substantive post-war planning in respect of Iraq, however, contributed directly to an outbreak of chaos and insurgency that commanded an ever-rising amount of US resources and attention, and which led ultimately to the abandonment of the initial limited approach in favour of an intensive troop surge. At the same time, a similar lack of engagement with the post-war situation in Afghanistan, in addition to the distractions of Iraq, allowed al-Qaeda, along with the deposed Taliban regime, to regroup and re-gather their capabilities. This led to an intensification of violence in the initial theatre of war, and to the adoption of another military surge in an attempt to gain a measure of control over the situation. Having also (if paradoxi-cally) served to undermine the credibility of Washington's willingness to use military power to enforce its will on the international stage, the im-pact of these events extended far beyond the Middle East, with ramifica-tions for the broader balance of power and stability in world affairs.

The impact of the war on terror on domestic British politics has also been profound. The controversies surrounding Britain's participation in the military conflicts in Afghanistan and (especially) Iraq have left deep and lasting scars on the political landscape, the consequences of which continue to resonate. Beyond this, the government's support for the US use of extra-legal practices in the fight against international terrorism, including a secret programme of extraordinary renditions and detentions at Guantánamo Bay and elsewhere, also proved to be highly contentious. So too was New Labour's domestic anti-terror strategy. The core elements of this, based on strengthening the security provisions of the state and on the adoption of a 'values-based' approach to dealing with the problems of domestic radicalisation, did little to address the underlying causes of radical Islamic terrorism. Indeed, on the contrary, much of this served to exacerbate and sustain its underlying factors while delimiting the pros-pects for effective action. In its legislative response, a significant portion of which was driven by party political considerations, a progressive ero-sion of civil liberties fostered growing levels of distrust and suspicion be-tween the citizenry and the state, and served to politicise and alienate many within Britain's Muslim community. This accompanied a broader political theme based on debates about 'Britishness' and the ascription of social identity along ethno-cultural and religious lines, which also did much to feed the conditions for radicalisation. In addition to this, a fer-vent rejection by New Labour of any notion that Western (and especially British) foreign policy could itself serve to promote terrorism, a political compulsion in the wake of the Iraq war and the 2005 London bomb-ings, was also problematic. In precluding any critical analysis of a causal role for foreign policy, this foreclosed any consideration of policy change, thereby allowing the list of grievances amassed against the British govern-ment to grow ever larger. In all of this, while the circumstances involved clearly changed, the strategic approach to the war on terror taken by New Labour differed little between the governments of Tony Blair and Gordon Brown. In their alliance with the US and their charge of the domestic stage alike, the bearers of the New Labour crown showed greater similarities than either would probably have cared to admit.

This book is structured as follows: Chapter 2 explores the course of British foreign policy since 1945. It considers the centrality of the US special relationship to New Labour's geopolitical strategy, and examines the utility of 'new imperialism' as a conceptual framework for analysing contemporary international affairs. Chapter 3 examines the underlying dynamics of the war on terror. The key elements of this involve the shift to a new imperialist trajectory by the US, the rise of New Labour in Britain and the emergence of radical Islamic terrorism during the 1990s. Detailing the US and British response to the 9/11 attacks, the events surrounding the invasion of Afghanistan as well as the government's initial legislative reaction are also considered. Chapter 4 covers the events surrounding the invasion of Iraq. The core themes in this centre on the political machinations behind the war, on the ineffective nature of the post-war planning arrangements, and on events in the aftermath of the conflict. Following this, Chapter 5 analyses the extra-legal dimension to the war on terror, and Britain's support for such measures. These included a US programme of extraordinary renditions and a policy of secret detentions at Guantánamo Bay and elsewhere. The chapter also considers the development of New Labour's domestic anti-terror strategy and its response to the increasingly prominent theme of radicalisation following the terrorist attacks in Madrid and London. Chapter 6 examines the transition from the final period of Tony Blair's rule and the initial phase of Gordon Brown's tenure as Prime Minister. While aspects of change concerning their approach to the war on terror were clearly evident, strong thematic bonds of continuity also remained. The central theme of Chapter 7 focuses on the rapid decline in Brown's political fortunes amidst a growing crisis of leadership authority from the latter part of 2007. Detailing the way in which the Prime Minister sought to deal with this by centring on the issue of national security and the war on terror, the chapter also assesses the extent to which this proved to be successful. Chapter 8, set against the Presidential transition from George Bush to Barack Obama in the US, examines the growing difficulties of the military campaign in Afghanistan, the unveiling of a new domestic anti-terror framework in Britain, and charts the final demise of New Labour in the General Election of 2010. Finally, chapter 9 sets out the overall conclusions of the analysis and suggests various ways in which some of the issues raised might be addressed.

Notes

1 From amongst the voluminous literature, see for example: Chomsky (2003); Ignatieff (2003); Kagan (2003); Todd (2003); Burrach and Tarbell (2004); Cox (2004, 2005); Ikenberry (2004); Shawcross (2004); Bello (2005); Blum (2006); Johnson (2006); Kiely (2006); Hopkins (2007).

2 See Ahmed (2003); Marsden (2003); Blix (2004); Chatterjee (2004); Diamond (2004); Rose (2004); Woodward (2004); Grey (2006); Smith (2007); Steele (2008); Sands (2009).

3 See for example: Burke (2004); Sageman (2004, 2008); Coll (2005); Rashid (2008); Roy (2008); Kepel (2009).

4 See Stothard (2003); Coates and Krieger (2004); Kampfner (2004); Riddell (2004); Azubuike (2005); Dumbrell (2006); Kettell (2006); Niblett (2007).

5 See for example: Haubrich (2003); Bamford (2004); Elliott (2006); Gove (2006); Oborne (2006); Shah (2006); Walker (2006); Brighton (2007); Croft (2007); Kirby (2007); Githens-Mazer (2008); Hewitt (2008); O'Duffy (2008); Saggar (2009).

6 For example see: Naughtie (2004); Oborne and Walters (2004); Stephens (2004); Seldon (2005).

2

Old and new

British foreign policy after 1945 evolved within a strategic context of progressive imperial and economic decline, Continental moves towards the integration of Europe, and the 'special relationship' with the US. One of its central aspects, as the post-war period unfolded, was a desire on the part of British governments to establish closer ties with the US as a means of compensating for Britain's decline as an independent Great Power. Yet relations with both Europe and the US remained variable during this time, and the problems of decolonisation and decline continued unabated. The coming to power of the New Labour government in 1997 portended a self-conscious attempt to resolve these issues by placing both relationships at the heart of British foreign policy. Framed as a transatlantic bridge strategy, the key aim of this was to elevate Britain's global influence by establishing mutually reinforcing ties with each side. The pursuit of this objective, however, was also shaped by a transformation of the international sphere in the form of a shift from an old to a 'new' imperialist context. Altering both the nature and the balance of power on the world stage, these changes proved to be crucial both for the success of the transatlantic bridge approach, as well as for the dynamics of the war on terror.

A special relationship

The course of British foreign policy after 1945 was shaped by several interrelated dynamics: the emergence and progression of sustained economic decline, the steady demise of the empire, the process of European integration, and the vagaries of the so-called 'special relationship' with the US. Taken together, these elements formed the strategic context within which successive governments sought to maintain a leading role for Britain on the international stage, and to enhance its position within

6

the global political and economic order. At the conclusion of the Second World War, the conditions for this appeared to be far from propitious. With the struggle against Nazism having left the country economically exhausted, and with the aftermath of the conflict being accompanied by the onset of a long process of decolonisation, starting with the independence of India in 1947, Britain found itself confronting an uncertain future and the prospect of irrevocable decline. Yet despite these problems, a central aim of governments during the early post-war period was to retain Britain's global reach and Great Power status. Attempting to sustain a position of imperial authority as the central hub in a Commonwealth of nations, ministers remained aloof and detached from the nascent process of European integration, an approach that was exemplified by Britain's refusal to participate in the establishment of the European Coal and Steel Community during the early 1950s.

The underlying fragility of Britain's position, however, was exposed by its newly established special relationship with the US. Although the term was not deployed publicly until after the cessation of hostilities in 1946 (with Britain's wartime leader, Winston Churchill, referring to a 'fraternal association of the English-speaking peoples', and 'a special relationship between the British Commonwealth and Empire and the United States of America'),[1] the high levels of military cooperation forged during the course of the conflict, as well as the close personal ties between Churchill and the US President, Franklin Roosevelt, were considered by many in senior political circles to have established a common and enduring bond that was unique among nations, both in kind and intensity. But the balance of power between the two countries was far from equal, and transatlantic relations were far from trouble-free.[2] Notable weak points centred on the issues of Palestine and cooperation over nuclear weapons technology (particularly following the US decision to cease bilateral collaboration in 1946), while the ongoing themes of economic and international rivalry complicated matters also. With the need for high levels of wartime assistance leaving Britain in a position of financial servitude to the US at the war's end, and with US plans for the creation of a new and liberalised world order being based, in part, on a desire to break up the British empire and to gain access to its markets and resources, US officials wasted no time in pressing home the advantage. In September 1945 the abrupt termination of the 1941 Lend-Lease agreement, through which the US had provided Britain with large amounts of financial and material support for the war effort, provoked an economic crisis and forced the newly elected Labour government to negotiate a fresh Anglo-American loan deal. The terms of this, though far more favourable to the US, led directly to an exchange-rate crisis in 1947 and soured prospects for closer financial cooperation.[3]

All the same, with Britain at this point still able to command extensive global influence, the competitive nature of transatlantic relations was tempered by an equivalent need to work together on a number of fronts. Prevalent here, despite differences over the precise details, were shared interests in preventing the spread of Soviet-style Communism, especially into Western Europe; a mutual desire to sustain Western influence in the Middle East, facilitating an orderly transition from British to US dominance of the region; and the pressing need to rebuild and reinvigorate the world economy, which had been shattered both by the war and by the depression preceding it. This common ground provided the platform on which many of the institutions that comprised the post-war international order were based. Amongst these, the creation of the United Nations (UN) in 1945 and the establishment of the Bretton Woods system from 1944 (based on the IMF, the World Bank and US-led monetary arrangements) helped to provide a broad framework for economic stability and regeneration, and a series of US loans to Western European countries under the terms of the Marshall Plan (or European Recovery Program) from 1947 to 1951 provided the basis for political stability and the reconstruction of the region, as did the establishment of the Northern Atlantic Treaty Organisation (NATO) in 1949, which formally integrated the US into Western European security and defence structures.

Notwithstanding an initial lull in the immediate post-war period, military and intelligence links between Britain and the US also remained close during this time. Britain's efforts to retain its status as a first-rank power and to assist Washington in policing the newly emergent world order ensured that levels of defence spending remained amongst the highest of all the advanced industrial nations and led to a series of foreign interventions alongside the US, most prominently in the Korean war of the early 1950s and in the fostering of a coup to overthrow the Iranian Prime Minister, Mohammad Mossadeq, in 1953. The machinations of the Middle East, however, also proved to be highly disruptive to Anglo-American relations. In 1956 a decision to nationalise the Suez Canal by the Egyptian President, Gamal Abdel Nasser, prompted the British Conservative government to launch a contrived military operation, along with France and Israel, in order to ensure continued access to what had become a site of crucial geo-strategic importance, and to prevent any further steps in the direction of state ownership. The response to this from the US, though, was both unexpected and unwelcome. Viewing the assault as a reversion to the imperialist practices of the nineteenth century, Washington declared itself to be ardently opposed to the invasion and called for an immediate withdrawal. To add extra pressure, the US also refused to lend any support to the pound sterling, whose exposure to financial volatility as a result of the intervention had left it perilously weakened, and threatened to drive its value down still further if Britain refused to pull out. Facing an unpalatable choice between financial crisis and ignominious retreat, the British government (following the resignation on health grounds of the Prime Minister, Anthony Eden) duly opted to take the latter course of action, brutally confirming the inequitable balance of power that now lay at the heart of the 'special' relationship.

Although the Suez debacle marked one of Britain's most disastrous foreign policy episodes of the twentieth century, the trauma did not lead to a deep fracturing of Anglo-American ties. Indeed, in the years soon after the crisis, the transatlantic relationship enjoyed a substantial improvement, even if its parameters were now increasingly shaped by the twin realities of US dominance and British decline. For the new Prime Minister, Harold Macmillan, the central strategic theme of the post-Suez period was based not merely on a desire to revive the special relationship with the US, but to place it at the forefront of Britain's pattern of international alliances. Notwithstanding a period of middling relations between the Prime Minister and the US President, Dwight Eisenhower, a fond personal connection between Macmillan and Eisenhower's successor, John F. Kennedy, helped chart a course to warmer climes. Significant dividends for the government soon followed, most notably in the field of nuclear weapons technology (with the US now agreeing to supply Britain with its Skybolt and Polaris systems), but the underlying problems of decline continued to raise important questions about Britain's place in the world. In particular, and despite encouraging the creation of the European Free Trade Association, in part as a counterweight to the process of European integration, by the 1960s the government had arrived at the belated conclusion that greater consideration now needed to be given to the European dimension. The key drivers for this strategic shift were twofold. Firstly, a closer relationship with the continent was now seen to offer increasingly evident benefits, with the creation of the European Economic Community (EEC) in 1958 raising the possibility of being able to secure greater access to markets with which to offset the impact of decolonisation and economic decay. Secondly, officials were struck by a growing sense of concern that continuing to remain distant from Europe would lead to diminishing influence in Washington as the importance of Continental political and economic institutions increased.[4]

Britain's hopes of gaining swift entry into the EEC, though, were undermined by the ongoing political fallout from the Suez crisis. With Anglo-French relations remaining strained, and amidst Gallic suspicions that British membership would serve as a Trojan horse for the promotion of US interests, Britain's application to join the Community (along with a subsequent application in 1967) was unceremoniously vetoed by the French President, Charles de Gaulle. Now excluded from European developments, and with a resurgent Germany assuming the role of the Continent's leading power, Britain's international position, already under significant pressure, began to look ever more exposed as the decade wore on. The point was underscored by events during the leadership of the new Labour Prime Minister, Harold Wilson, who succeeded Macmillan's replacement in office, Alec Douglas-Home, in 1964. Despite pledging to retain Britain's role and status as a Great Power, the new government found itself beset by deep and protracted economic difficulties, leading to the devaluation of sterling in 1967 and to a decision to withdraw from Britain's military commitments East of Suez starting in the same year. Relations with the US, too, deteriorated significantly during this period, as Britain's international retrenchment and the lack of any personal affinity between Wilson and the US President, Lyndon B. Johnson, took their toll. Reflecting this, the Prime Minister's refusal to provide military (and even at times moral) support for the US war effort in Vietnam, aptly symbolised the extent of the atrophy to which the special relationship had now succumbed.[5]

Influence is power

While Anglo-American relations never again plumbed quite the same depths as the Wilson–Johnson era, the respective fault lines between the two nations continued to widen during the course of the 1970s. With US geo-strategic interests now appearing to shift towards East Asia and away from Western Europe, and with the scale of British decline becoming increasingly pronounced, so the strategic dilemmas surrounding Britain's position within the world system became ever more pressing. The initial response to this, coming under the leadership of the avowedly pro-European Conservative Prime Minister, Edward Heath, was to realign Britain's pattern of international relations in a more Continental direction. However, despite finally managing to secure British entry into the EEC in 1973, the effects of this proved to be far from panacean. Throughout the rest of the decade Britain remained bedevilled by a progressively deepening sense of economic and political crisis, leading to the fall of Heath's government in 1974 and to the demise of its Labour successor in 1979.

In addition to this, domestic support for closer relations with Europe remained equivocal. The divided state of public opinion remained unsatiated by a positive referendum result on continued EEC membership in 1975, while the Labour Party's stance on the issue remained decidedly ambivalent prior to a pro-European conversion during the latter half of the 1980s. For the Conservatives, having ousted Labour from office in 1979 under the leadership of Margaret Thatcher, the move was decisively in the opposite direction, shifting from a pro-European position in the early part of the decade (on economic issues at least) to an increasingly hostile pitch as the process of European integration intensified. Although Conservative antipathy to Europe was somewhat eased following Thatcher's prime ministerial deposition in 1990, acute internal party splits on the issue, coupled with the negative experience of Britain's membership of the European Exchange Rate Mechanism during the early part of the decade, required sensitive and diplomatic handling of the subject by her successor, John Major. The result was to preclude a more positive engagement with Europe, and to once again leave Britain isolated and marginalised in its political relations with the rest of the continent.

While Britain's position in Europe remained problematic, Anglo-American ties improved dramatically during the 1980s. After a decade of generally lukewarm relations under the leaderships of Heath, Wilson and James Callaghan, the close personal chemistry between Thatcher and President Ronald Reagan brought a degree of warmth to the elite political level that had not been seen since the days of Churchill and Roosevelt. Despite several points of tension, particularly over the 1983 US invasion of Grenada (a British Crown colony), and Washington's initial equivocation over the status of the Falkland Islands following the Argentine invasion of 1982 (the US subsequently provided Britain with invaluable intelligence, as well as resources and logistical assistance in the ensuing Falklands war), the renewed vigour in the special relationship was clearly apparent. This was reflected across a broad spectrum of issues, including diplomatic and political unity in opposing the Soviet Union; an upgrading of Britain's US-supplied nuclear deterrent (moving from Polaris to the Trident missile system); the stationing of US nuclear missiles on British soil; support for the US Strategic Defense Initiative (otherwise known as the missile defence, or 'Star Wars' programme); and backing for US military action against Libya in 1986, in which US warplanes were permitted to use British airspace and bases in order to conduct bombing operations in retaliation for Libyan involvement in terrorism.[6]

Transatlantic relations in the post-Reagan era, on the other hand, were discernibly less buoyant. Notwithstanding the obvious continuance of military cooperation, most notably with Britain's involvement in the first Gulf war, the personal links between Margaret Thatcher and the new US President, George Bush Senior, were palpably cooler. At the same time, the fall of the Berlin Wall and the demise of Soviet-style Communism during the early 1990s ushered in an era of global uncertainty, accompanied by US proclamations of a 'New World Order' and a strategic preference towards Germany as its key partner in Europe, raising fresh questions about Britain's place in the international system.[7] The phlegmatic nature of the relationship between Thatcher and Bush continued into the premiership of John Major. Personal acquaintances between the two leaders remained formal and businesslike, as did relations with Bush's successor, Bill Clinton, for whom the absence of any individual connection was compounded by revelations of back-room Conservative partisanship in favour of the Republican Party during the 1992 Presidential Election.[8] Disagreements over political affairs in Northern Ireland, tensions over the Western response to the conflict in the former Yugoslavia, and, from the perspective of the US, Britain's increasingly peripheral status in Europe, were also detrimental to transatlantic ties as the twentieth century neared its end.[9]

The election of the New Labour government led by Tony Blair in 1997 augured a pronounced transformation in Britain's global positioning. Sweeping to power with the self-avowed aim of reversing Britain's postwar economic and political decline in both the domestic and the international spheres, the new government immediately sought to promote a more engaged, expansive and re-energised role for Britain in world affairs. One of the chief hallmarks of this, at least initially, was the claim that foreign policy would now include an overtly 'ethical dimension'. Announced as part of a new mission statement by the incoming Foreign Secretary, Robin Cook, the declared ambition was to lay down a marker about the progressive intent of the new administration, and to present a clear line of division from the activities of its Conservative predecessor, which remained tainted by high-profile controversies over the sale of arms to Iran, and particularly to Iraq. But rhetorical assertions about ethics soon clashed with the reality of the new government's approach to foreign relations. Disclosures about the sale of arms to countries with less-than-impressive ethical records, such as Zimbabwe, Sri Lanka and Saudi Arabia, provided live ammunition to critics, as did embarrassing revelations during the 1998 'Arms to Africa' affair, in which Foreign Office officials were found to have circumvented one of their own embargoes, and to have given tacit assistance to a private military firm supplying arms to supporters of the deposed President of Sierra Leone with a view to restoring him to power.[10]

But official claims to be acting out of ethical considerations remained secondary to the overall thrust of New Labour's foreign policy approach, the central strategic theme of which was an attempt to reposition the British state as a 'transatlantic bridge' between Europe and the US. The core objective of this was to establish a virtuous circle of mutually reinforcing influence that would elevate Britain's position on the world stage above that conferred upon it by virtue of its natural weight. The underpinning assumption here was that a closer proximity to Washington would enhance British influence in Europe, and conversely, that a greater engagement with Europe would improve Britain's standing in the US. In contrast to the strategic imperatives of Macmillan and Thatcher, both of whom remained committed to the special relationship for its own merits, and with limited reference to Europe, the approach adopted by Blair sought to maximise British influence in both spheres simultaneously as a means of increasing its overall capacity to shape world affairs. The overriding objective of the government's foreign policy, as the Prime Minister explained, was to uphold Britain's ability 'to exercise a role on the international stage', and to maintain its position as 'a global player'.[11] '[A] nation's chances', he proffered, 'are measured not just by its own efforts but by its place in the world. Influence is power is prosperity'.[12]

The practical results of this strategy were apparent in a number of areas. In terms of Britain's relationship with Europe, the wholesale negativity of the Thatcher and Major governments was now replaced by a markedly more positive approach. The appointment of a minister for Europe, the signing of the Amsterdam and Nice treaties, and support both for the Lisbon agenda and the process of enlargement provided a firm indication of Britain's willingness to play a more constructive role as a full partner in the politics of the European Union (EU) (the EEC's replacement from 1993), as did the adoption of a more positive stance, at least initially, on the possibility of joining the single currency. Signs of increased engagement on the issue of defence were also evident, most notably in the 1998 St Malo agreement on Anglo-French military cooperation and the future of European security. On the Western side of the bridge, relations with the US also found themselves on an upward curve, with Blair's close personal and political affinity with Clinton providing a stark and immediate contrast to the dour atmosphere that had afflicted relations with his predecessor.[13]

Beyond the nature of personal ties at the senior political level, which had been perspicuously diverse throughout the post-war period, the nature of Anglo-American relations during the New Labour era was also subject to a range of broader structural influences, all of which acted to solidify a pro-American stance. Amongst these, strong social and cultural links, including the much-hailed commonalities of shared linguistic and historical bonds, mutual interconnections in spheres such as travel, media and entertainment, and a similar sense of values and outlook in terms of a preference for free market capitalism and liberal democracy, provided a strong set of underpinnings in support of the political dimension.

Accompanying this, the enduring notion of a 'special relationship' itself, by now a long-standing and deeply entrenched axiom within the British political psyche (due not least to the status accorded to it by the media and political elites), also continued to exert a significant influence, the dominant assumption being that efforts to sustain the relationship were – and continued to be – in Britain's innate national interests and were essential if Britain was to play any kind of leading role in the world. Economic linkages, too, were important in upholding this perception. Mutually high levels of finance and trade, with the US forming Britain's top market for exports and investment, as well as providing the single largest source of investment into Britain, established a substantive material basis for close political ties. And in addition to this, enduring cooperation across a variety of military, security, diplomatic and intelligence issues, including the continued presence of US military personnel, hardware and bases within Britain, added a further layer of connectivity to the links that drew the two countries together.[14]

A major new development

New Labour's efforts to enhance Britain's international influence through the pursuit of a transatlantic bridge strategy, and hence the nature of its relationships with both the US and Europe, were also shaped by the broader dynamics of the global political and economic system. For most of the post-war period this had been fixed within the bipolar framework imposed by the pressures of the Cold War, forming a relative stable and predictable, if not an entirely auspicious operating environment. The latter part of the twentieth century, however, witnessed a dramatic reconfiguration of the international landscape, altering both the nature and the balance of power on the world stage, and transforming the very conditions on which the strategic development and conduct of British foreign policy was based. One of the main themes in scholarly analyses of these events is that this signified a shift from an era of old to 'new imperialism'. Central to this is the notion that the collapse of the Soviet bloc and the emergence of a unipolar world centred on the US as the sole remaining super- (or hyper-) power, transformed Washington into a 'New Rome', an empire analogous to the fallen Republic of antiquity, but one that now stood unparalleled in its reach, scope and power. As Magdoff and Foster put it, the situation heralded 'a major new development in the history of imperialism', or as Krauthammer famously exulted, the US was now 'no mere international citizen', but had become 'the dominant power in the world, more dominant than any since Rome'.[15]

Beyond an emphasis on unipolarity, debates about the nature and the implications of new imperialism are far from uniform, but comprise a diverse and eclectic field. In this, opinions range from assertions hailing a far-reaching and radical shift in international affairs, to those which claim that that there has, in fact, been no significant change at all from the dynamics of old imperialist practices. In broad terms, these various analyses tend to cleave into two main forms, principally focusing either on 'economic' or 'geopolitical' forces and motivations. The former of these is also characterised by two core themes. The first, is that the modus operandi of new imperialism, in contrast to its antecedents, no longer derives from control over foreign territories and states, but from the ability to exert control and influence over global markets.[16] The second defining theme is an emphasis on the notion of crisis, both within the US as well as the global capitalist system itself. Typically, this is framed in terms of a progressive decline in US economic dominance since the 1970s, coupled with the onset of a more generalised structural crisis (usually presented as one of overproduction, or overaccumulation) within the world economy.[17]

Within this thematic framework, various conceptual sub-divisions present a broader series of explanation. For some, the analytical emphasis is on the new-found dominance of global economic forces, the growth in the scale and the intensity of which in recent decades is now thought to have transformed the world market into a singularly ascendant form of sovereignty, putting it beyond the ability of any individual state or government to control and enabling it to impose its will with impunity.[18] Others, though, reject the notion that states are now powerless in the face of an all-powerful global capital, and instead argue that the relentless expansion of the world economy and the pursuit of market-friendly policies by the major industrial nations has been fuelled either by the hegemony of a US-based transnational capitalist class,[19] or has been orchestrated by national governments themselves in an attempt to extend their own wealth and influence within the international order.[20] Cutting through these various sub-streams, however, economic analyses concur in their interpretation of US militarism under the rubric of the war on terror, which is typically considered to be something of a rearguard action; as an attempt to address these various crises and to prop up the weakening international position of the US.[21] As Harvey explains, while military measures are but 'the tip of the imperialist iceberg', the use of armed force on the part of the US denotes a growing emphasis on what has now become its last remaining facet of undisputed supremacy.[22]

In contrast to economic accounts, geopolitical analyses of new imperialism view the key distinguishing features of the post-Cold War environment not in terms of markets, but as the emergence of increasingly disordered territorial zones (in the form of rogue or failed states) and the growth of moral, cultural and legal norms of human rights within the global political sphere. This also highlights the particular areas of difference between the eras of old and new imperialism. While the former was based on the exertion of raw military power, territorial conquest, direct metropolitan rule and the deployment of ideologies of racial and cultural supremacy, the latter is thought to be rooted in the use of informal methods of maintaining order, such as diplomacy, finance and trade, alongside an ideological commitment to notions of equality, democracy and self-determination.[23] Coterminous with this, geopolitical accounts also point to a heightened strategic imperative for the use of humanitarian arguments to justify and legitimise foreign interventions, and emphasise the pressures on such operations to be rapid and limited in scope in order to effect a return to normality with the minimum outlay of manpower, time and finance. As Ignatieff puts it, the situation is one of 'imperialism in a hurry: to spend money, to get results, to turn the place back to the locals and get out'.[24] Thus: 'the new empire is not like those of times past, built on colonies and conquest. It is an empire-lite, hegemony without colonies ... without the burden of direct administration and the risks of daily policing'.[25]

Another common feature of this approach is an assertion that the US embodies a distinctly anti-imperialist ethos, acting as a positive and beneficent force for good in the world. By providing international goods of peace and security, and by helping to promote the spread of democratic freedoms and human rights, the US, as Krauthammer maintains, is from this view seen to represent 'a uniquely benign imperium'. Or, as Kagan proclaims: 'the truth is that the benevolent hegemony exercised by the US is good for a vast portion of the world's population', and that, far from being a miscreant, the US exercises 'the kind of enlightened self-interest that, in practice, comes dangerously close to resembling generosity'.[26] Thus, while economic analyses view the actions of the US as an attempt to deal with the threat to its international position posed by economic decline and global capitalist crisis, geopolitical accounts maintain that its behaviour in the war on terror has been driven principally by a need to address problems of global disorder and to meet the humanitarian challenges posed by failed and rogue states. In this context, the use of military force is seen not as an indication of aggressive US expansionism, but as a form of 'defensive imperialism'; a necessary expedient for protecting the values of democracy, freedom and human rights in the modern world.[27]

Not all commentators, however, are so convinced that these assertions about new imperialism actually amount to anything really new. Rather, for those sceptical of such claims, the extent of historical difference and novelty that is attributed to the contemporary international landscape is considered to be grossly overstated. Central to the case here is a view that the anti-imperialist ethos of the US is, and has always been, nothing more than a rhetorical illusion masking more generic imperial ambitions and practices. As such, the increased levels of US militarism during the first decade of the twenty-first century are not considered to be a reflection of any wholesale change in US objectives, but are seen as evidence of a sustained continuity in terms of the overarching intentions of the US imperium to sustain its global position of power and dominance.[28] Typically, too, the various means by which this is to be achieved, in attempting to ensure control over global energy supplies (principally Eurasian and Middle Eastern oil), to secure political, economic and military leverage over potential challengers and rivals, and to support these endeavours through the creation of a new 'enemy narrative' (replacing the threat from Soviet Communism with one from Islamic terrorism), are also thought to expose a high degree of consistency with previous US practices.[29] The situation for sceptics then, is that old, rather than new imperialism remains the order of the day. As Callinicos explains: 'The world of imperialism, as it was portrayed by Lenin and Bukharin during the First World War – an anarchic struggle of unequal rivals – still exists, with the United States as first among unequals'.[30]

Recurring themes

The ubiquity of new imperialism as a scholarly framework of analysis is not matched by its consistency. Rather, with current approaches to the subject being characterised by an overly narrow focus on either the economic or the geopolitical dimension, a defining feature of the debate is its lack of consensus on many of the central issues. Core areas of disagreement include the causal and driving forces behind new imperialism, such as US economic decline, global capitalist crisis and humanitarian motivations; the timing of its emergence, with this being variously traced to the post-war period, to the economic crises of the 1970s, the collapse of the Soviet Union or the coming to power of George W. Bush; as well as the question of what exactly, if anything, makes new imperialism genuinely 'new', whether it be a qualitatively new form of imperialism itself, defined either by 'economic' or 'geopolitical' factors, or whether it be little more than a new strategy for achieving more generic imperial aims. Normative concerns, too, provide a source of disagreement, with commentators divided over whether the actions of the US should be seen as beneficial for the rest of the world, or whether they amount to little more than an ill-disguised attempt at global subjugation and control.

While these various issues make it impossible to speak of a single form of new imperialism, the notion of a new phase in imperialist practice, if not in the more general aims of imperialism itself, nevertheless remains a valuable one for examining contemporary global relations, and hence for analysing the strategic context within which New Labour's approach to foreign affairs developed. The effective use of this conceptual framework, however, requires a more holistic approach than has typically been deployed, bringing together relevant aspects from both economic and geopolitical analyses, as well as combining other features of the new international landscape. In so doing, it is possible to identify a number of core areas in which the dynamics, practices and novelties of new imperialism can be distinguished from those of earlier periods.

The first of these, as emphasised by economic accounts, concerns the scale and intensity of global market pressures. While economic forces have played a key role in all eras of imperialism, by the end of the twentieth century the centrality of the market had reached far higher levels than anything ever seen before. Fuelled in part by the rise of major new industrial economies such as India, Brazil and China, as well as by the pursuit of deregulatory practices in the West and the continuous internal drive for expansion present in capitalism itself, the results were to stimulate the growth of globally mobile financial capital (the defining *leitmotif* of 'globalisation'), and to place greater emphasis on the need for states to gain influence within international markets as the primary route to wealth and power in the modern world.[31] Similarly, a second key point of difference between the contexts of old and new imperialism centres on the degree of influence and control that is capable of being exercised by the world's leading power. While many previous eras have witnessed periods of unchallenged dominance by a single power (such as the Roman or British empires), as noted by geopolitical accounts, the extent of US dominance following the demise of the Soviet Union, backed by the unparalleled reach, scope and technological prowess of its military machine, was one that was simply unrivalled in world history.

A third defining feature of the contemporary era, and one that serves to limit the scale of US power, is the increased pluralisation of the international sphere. In comparison to the age of classical (European) imperialism during the nineteenth and early twentieth centuries, the world of today is a far more variegated environment. The greater size, intensity and (albeit to a lesser degree) multi-directionality of trade and capital flows, enmeshed with a proliferation of international organisations and agencies, non-governmental actors and pressure groups, as well as an increasing number of states themselves, have heightened pressures for inter-state and inter-agency cooperation (be it via multi- or bilateral methods), and have increased the number of institutional structures to which major states are obliged to engage with, or at least pay some form of lip-service to.[32] This creates a series of constraints which, though far from Lilliputian, can nevertheless impinge upon the direction and conduct of US geopolitical strategy. Regardless of the unparalleled degree of power at its disposal, a course of untrammelled unilateralism that rides roughshod over the rest of the world will, at the very least, undermine any claims to legitimacy that the US may seek to advance, exacerbate anti-American sentiments and activities, and, in so doing, endanger its prospects of success. To compound matters, technological developments, principally related to the revolution in information technology that has transformed global communications from the 1980s, and which has led to the emergence of new and 24/7 media outlets, have further added to these pressures. The main impact of this technological shift has been felt in the greater extent and avidity with which state officials in democratic societies must now seek to manage public opinion, shape the political agenda and direct the flow of sensitive or politically controversial information. The practical effects of this, though, are dual-sided: exposing state managers to information flows that fall beyond their ability to control and forcing them to present their actions in such a way as to be amenable to public concerns and values, but, at the same time, opening-up opportunities for officials to shape the discursive landscape and to frame key issues in ways that are ultimately favourable to the pursuit of their goals.[33]

These changes in the international context combine to produce another key feature of the contemporary era; namely (as is also highlighted by geopolitical accounts), increased pressure on state managers to adhere to a discursive framework rooted in humanitarian values and principles. While such assertions have long been a prevalent feature of imperial strategies, forming, as Eland notes, 'one of the recurring themes of empires throughout history',[34] a core difference today is the extent to which legal and cultural norms of human rights have become embedded in the landscape of international politics.[35] As such, the extent to which humanitarian justifications are now necessary for conferring legitimacy upon foreign interventions is far greater than at any previous point in history. The effects of this ideological transformation, as with the impact of technological change, are also dual-sided. On the one hand, effectively placing geo-strategic issues within a discursive framework of human rights and democratic norms can go a long way to ensuring acquiescence for other, less palatable and more contentious aims.[36] On the other, such an approach also contains inherent dangers, given that the ultimate objectives of any imperialist strategy are, by definition, designed to serve the national interests of the metropolitan centre. Since the practical results are thus unlikely to match the loftiness of any espoused humanitarian objectives, the eventual outcomes, should any discrepancies between rhetoric and reality emerge, are likely to undermine claims to ethical motivations, and to thereby erode and delegitimise the action taken.[37]

Yet another defining characteristic of the contemporary world order concerns the nature of the security challenges that are now faced by the US, and by the Western world in general. In contrast to the threats posed by territorially fixed and defined states, such as that presented by the Soviet Union during the Cold War era, the decentralised and dispersed threat now posed by radical Islamic terrorism, as well as by unstable territorial zones, is one that is both qualitatively distinct and unique. While the scale of such challenges may not be of the same order of existential magnitude as that posed by direct invasion or Cold War nuclear armageddon, the risks are nevertheless significant, and the available options for dealing with them remain highly problematic. Not least is this due to the fact that attempting to use military force in all possible countries, regions or scenarios in which an actual or potential threat to US or Western interests might conceivably exist would be highly unlikely to succeed, and, moreover, would be likely only to prove a costly means of exacerbating anti-American and anti-Western sentiments and of thereby fuelling further dangers. Indeed, as Ignatieff notes: 'The war on terror is risky because it appears to require the exercise of American power everywhere at once'.[38]

While these various factors signify a change in the nature and the exercise of power in the global sphere, one especially notable consequence has been to change significantly the way in which military power, in particular, is now wielded and used. Generating strong systemic pressures in favour of small, flexible, high-tech and limited military operations, the result has been a growing tendency towards a 'military lite' approach, in clear contrast to the large-scale and manpower-intensive forms of military operation characteristic of times past. The economic pressures of globalisation have helped to create a desire to avoid open-ended and expensive overseas projects (especially where these might involve assuming direct burdens of territorial administration); the dominance of humanitarian norms, along with the pressures of managing public opinion and the dangers of stoking greater levels of anti-American feeling have also mitigated against prolonged and overtly imperialist enterprises; while the dispersed and decentred nature of the threat to the West has placed a greater premium on retaining a capacity to effectively police the world system as a whole, as opposed to devoting resources too intensively to one particular country or region. Taken together, these conditions have also created a heightened strategic need for credibility in the use of military power. As the inability of the US to deal directly with every possible deviant, threat or challenger has grown, so too has the importance of being able to avoid having to engage in military operations by being credibly willing to do precisely that.

The analytical value of new imperialism, then, lies not in the idea of a clearly delineated break from the past. Rather, the context and conduct of global affairs in the twenty-first century contains elements of continuity with, as well as change from, previous eras. Indeed, many of the features highlighted as novel by economic and geopolitical accounts are not of themselves qualitatively unique and distinct, but are characteristics denoting an intensification, an extension and a sharpening of pre-existing trends and features from earlier periods. That said, while the sceptical claim that the actions of the US are designed merely to sustain its own dominance is not without more than a grain of truth, this should not be taken to mean that no significant change has taken place. Rather, what has been key in the global transformations since the mid-1970s has been the way in which these goals are achieved. In this sense, 'new' imperialism signifies a change in the means, if not the ends, of imperial practice in the modern world.

The implications of these developments for New Labour's attempt to promote a greater role for Britain on the world stage were no less significant. While many aspects of the new imperialist landscape, such as the need for market-friendly policies, an emphasis on humanitarian norms and the necessity of maintaining military credibility appeared to chime perfectly with the government's own political worldview, its ability to pursue an effective transatlantic bridge strategy was eventually undermined by a divergence between the US and Europe in a variety of fundamental areas. These included their perceived roles and interests in the post-Cold War era, their respective capacities for action, and the way in which either side was prepared to exercise these capacities in the pursuit of their aims. Despite possessing the world's largest internal market and an economy of comparable size to that of the US, the multilateral contours of the European sphere diminished the prospect of producing any clear, cohesive and unified 'European' position, let alone collective or decisive action, on foreign affairs. With a fragmentation of power between EU member states, an intergovernmental Common Foreign and Security Policy, limited military capabilities and no consensus between its constituent bodies as to its role in the world, the idea that a closer relationship with the European Union could form one of the keystones of British foreign policy was set to fare poorly when pitched against New Labour's outward-looking and more expansive ambitions.[39]

By comparison, the Western pole of the transatlantic bridge promised to be far more conducive to such ventures. Vastly more powerful than Europe in military terms, and notably more willing and able to pursue its interests through the use of armed force, the US offered a potential and ultimately more enticing channel through which the government's policy objectives could be advanced. While the ability to influence the direction of Continental politics, and hence the cultivation of close relations with the European Union, remained an essential commodity in Britain's dealings with Washington, the opportunity to capitalise on a special relationship with the greatest power on earth, and, through this, to seek to influence the direction of US efforts to shape world affairs, was one that senior figures proved unable to resist. These tensions at the heart of the transatlantic bridge approach, remaining for the most part submerged, or at least manageable during New Labour's early years in office, became increasingly pronounced following the onset of the war on terror. As the possibility of containing its internal strains diminished, the ramifications for the government's geopolitical strategy became ever more serious. With the dynamics of new imperialism directly shaping the contours of the war on terror, and with the course of subsequent events being driven by its strategic imperatives, New Labour's decision to bind its policy interests tightly to those of the US committed the government to a course of action that would both dominate the remainder of its time in office, and play a key part in its eventual demise.

Conclusion

New Labour's rise to power during the latter years of the twentieth century augured an approach to foreign policy that promised to resolve the dilemmas of the post-war period. While successive British governments had, at different times, sustained variable relations with both Europe and the US, typically tending to privilege one pole or the other (or neither as the case may be), the strategy adopted by the incoming Blair administration sought to overcome this dichotomy through the pursuit of a unifying transatlantic bridge approach. The central aim of this was to enhance Britain's ability to play a leading role on the world stage by establishing a virtuous circle of mutually reinforcing relations with both sides. The context within which this strategy was set, however, was defined by a broader reconfiguring of the global environment in terms of a shift from old to new imperialism. Altering both the nature and the balance of power within the world system, this created a pronounced divergence between the outlook and the capacities of Europe and the US, with the latter, as the centre of a unipolar world order, proving to be the only power, by some margin, able to exert a decisive, imposing and shaping influence on international affairs. The implications of this disjuncture for the efficacy of a transatlantic bridge approach would prove to be highly significant. Impelling New Labour to draw closer to the US as a means of satisfying the desire for an active and engaged foreign policy, the result, following the onset of the war on terror, would tie Britain to a course of action with unanticipated and far-reaching consequences.

Notes

1   'The sinews of peace' speech by Winston Churchill to Westminster College, Fulton, Missouri, 5 March 1946.
2   On wartime relations between Britain and the US, see Dimbleby and Reynolds (1988), Chapters 7–9; Dobson (1988), Chapters 2–3; Woods (1990); Dickie (1994), Chapter 2.
3   From amongst the broad literature on the special relationship, and for much of what follows in this section, see for example: Reynolds (1986); Dimbleby and Reynolds (1988); Dobson (1988, 1995); Louis and Bull (1989); Dickie (1994); Baylis (1997); Jones (1997); Dumbrell (2001, 2006); Gamble (2003); Riddell (2004); Wallace and Phillips (2009).
4   Dumbrell (2001); Ashton (2005); Wallace and Phillips (2009).
5   Reynolds (1986); Dickie (1994); Colman (2004); Wallace and Phillips (2009).
6   Dobson (1995); Wallace and Phillips (2009).
7   See for example, Coker (1992); Dickie (1994).
8   Party activists had examined Clinton's MI5 files in the hope of uncovering material from his student days at Oxford that could be of political benefit to the Republicans.
9   On Britain's US–European relations see Riddell (2004), Chapter 2.
10 Kettell (2006), pp. 34–7.
11 Speech at the Lord Mayor's Banquet, 10 November 1997.
12 Speech to the Labour Party conference, 1 October 2002.
13 Smith (2005).
14 For an overview see Foreign Affairs Committee (2010).
15 Magdoff and Foster (2002); C. Krauthammer, 'The Bush doctrine', *Time*, 5 March 2001; Also see Magdoff and Foster (2001); Ignatieff (2003); Burrach and Tarbell (2004); Cox (2004); Bello (2005); Johnson (2006). For a more nuanced and comparative approach see Murphy (2007). The literature on 'old' imperialism is typically divided into 'classical' and 'post-war' accounts. For the former see Kautsky (1914); Schumpeter (1918); Bukharin (1929); Luxemburg (1951); Lenin (1963); Hobson (1978); Hilferding (1981). For the latter see, for example, Gallacher and Robinson (1953); Fieldhouse (1966); Frank (1966); Baran and Sweezy (1968); Galtung (1971); Mandel (1975); Wallerstein (1975); Amin (1977); Doyle (1986).
16 See for instance, Ikenberry (2002, 2005); Barrow (2005); Coen (2005); Meiksins Wood (2005); Stokes (2005).
17 See Meiksins Wood (1999); Harvey (2003, 2007); Cox (2004); Beitel (2005); Kiely (2006); Chesnais (2007); Robinson (2007).
18 This is typically the position adopted by proponents of globalisation, but for a more direct link to new imperialism see Hardt and Negri (2000).
19 Robinson (2007); also see Sklair (2001); Kiely (2006).
20 Meiksins Wood (2005).

21 See Meiksins Wood (1999); Sklair (2001); Harvey (2003, 2007); Cox (2004); Beitel (2005); Coen (2005); Kiely (2006); Chesnais (2007); Robinson (2007).

22 Harvey (2003), p. 181.

23 See Cooper (2002); Ignatieff (2003); Reid (2005).

24 M. Ignatieff, 'The American empire: the burden', *New York Times*, 5 January 2003; also see Ignatieff (2003a); Bello (2006).

25 Ignatieff (2003), pp. 1–2.

26 See C. Krathammer, 'The Bush doctrine: ABM, Kyoto and the new American uni-lateralism', *The Weekly Standard* 6(36), 4/ June 2001; Kagan (1998). Also see Rieff (1999); M. Boot, 'The case for American empire', *The Weekly Standard* 7(5), 15 October 2001 (also Boot, 2003); Donnelly (2002); Maier (2002); Ignatieff (2003, 2003a); Rosen (2003); P. Bobbit, 'Better than empire', *Financial Times*, 13 March 2004; Ferguson (2008).

27 Cooper (2002), p. 16.

28 Callinicos (2002), p.319; Pilger (2003); also see Chomsky (2003); Bello (2005); Meiksins Wood (2005); Foster (2006); Khalidi (2006).

29 See for example: Magdoff and Foster (2001); Eland (2002); Chomsky (2003, 2008); Klare (2003); Pilger (2003); Spence (2005); Foster (2006); Johnson (2006); Pieterse (2006); Bose (2007). For a useful counter-argument to the 'oil thesis' see Bromley (2005).

30 Callinicos (2002), p. 319; also see Chomsky (2003); Pilger (2003); Bello (2005); Meiksins Wood (2005); Foster (2006); Khalidi (2006).

31 On this see Brenner (2001); Kettell (2004).

32 Kiely (2006).

33 On this see, for example, Savigny (2002).

34 Eland (2002), p. 3.

35 Cooper (2002).

36 Neep (2004); also see Heuer and Schirmer (1998); Ayers (2009).

37 See Bello (2006).

38 Ignatieff (2003), pp. 2–3; also see Eland (2002); Boot (2003).

39 See for instance Peterson and Sjursen (1998); Nuttall (2000).

3

Barbarians at the gates

The onset of the war on terror was shaped by both long-term and immediate factors. In the first of these, the geo-strategic dynamics of Cold War rivalry in the Middle East helped to create the conditions for the globally oriented threat of radical Islamic terrorism, while the subsequent collapse of Soviet Communism produced a discernible shift to a new imperialist strategy by the US during the 1990s. The second series of factors centred on the particular characteristics of the US and British governments during the early years of the twenty-first century. In the former, a Republican administration headed by George W. Bush sought to capitalise on the position of the US as the sole remaining superpower by launching an expansionary project of global re-ordering following the terrorist attacks of 9/11. In the latter, a New Labour government anxious to elevate the influence of the British state on the world stage provided a ready source of political and military support for this endeavour. The ramifications, involving an invasion of Afghanistan, the adoption of extra-legal practices and restrictions on civil liberties in the name of national security, would dominate international and domestic politics for the rest of the decade.

A new world order

The origins of the war on terror are to be found in three interlocking dynamics of the post-war period: the Cold War struggle between the US and the Soviet Union, US moves towards the adoption of a new imperialist strategy during the 1990s, and the emergence of a globally oriented form of radical Islamic terrorism. In the first of these, the main impetus for later events was bound up with the mutually antagonistic support given to client regimes in the Middle East by both the US and the USSR. By the 1980s, these pressures had wrought a profound influence over the political geography of the region, playing a key contributory factor in (amongst other things) the intractability of the Arab–Israeli conflict, the emergence of Islamic revolution in Iran and the ascendancy of the brutal Ba'athist regime in Iraq. Taken as a whole, the most significant developments to emerge from the region's Cold War rivalry, however, occurred in Afghanistan. In July 1979, with tensions between the US and the Soviet Union rising, the CIA sought to open up a new front against the USSR and to undercut its designs for regional hegemony by providing covert support for Afghanistan's Islamic Mujahideen in its domestic fight against Communism. In December the Islamic resistance was met with a Soviet invasion, triggering the start of a nine-year conflict. The eventual result, combined with internal political and economic degeneration along with a fierce and costly arms race with the US, was to drain the Russian empire of its vital resources, culminating in a chastened withdrawal from Afghanistan in 1989. This was shortly followed by the collapse of the Berlin Wall, and by the material demise of Soviet Communism itself.[1]

Freed from the shackles of the Cold War, consecutive US administrations sought to extend their country's new-found position of unchallenged global dominance. Marking the transition, the 1991 US National Security Strategy warned that it would be dangerous for the US to turn inward as Communism waned, and called instead for the 'inescapable' US global leadership to be turned towards the creation of 'a new world order'. The nature of this, it observed, would be centred on supporting the global spread of democracy and dealing with the emergence of varied and novel security threats (with the greatest danger of all being 'instability itself'), including cross-border flows of refugees and drugs, as well as the problems of terrorism and weapons of mass destruction (WMD) in the Middle East. At the same time, the Strategy also portended a shift away from the prevailing large-scale, manpower-intensive military structures of the Cold War period, and promoted the adoption of a smaller, more flexible and increasingly high-tech model. Observing that while 'the ability to project our power will underpin our strategy more than ever', the necessity, at the same time, was for 'deliberate reductions to no more than the forces we need to defend our interests and meet our global responsibilities'.[2] The following year the shape of US strategic thinking was outlined further in a document commissioned by Dick Cheney, the US Defense Secretary (and overseen, amongst others, by his under-secretary, Paul Wolfowitz), entitled *Defense Planning Guidance*. The central theme of this, set out in draft copy before being watered down due to political pressures, was that the US should capitalise on its military advantage 'to establish and protect a new order' based on an expansion of free markets and democratic systems of government, designed, not least, for 'anchoring the east-central Europeans into the west'. More specifically, a primary objective was to prevent the emergence of a 'potential future global competitor' and to avoid 'the domination of key regions by a hostile power'. A central concern here, of course, remained the Middle East; the declared goals towards which were to retain the US position as 'the predominant outside power', 'to preserve US and Western access to the region's oil', and to prevent 'a hegemon or alliance of powers from dominating the region'.[3]

Washington's willingness to use military power to shape the geo-strategic contours of the Middle East during this period was clearly evident. In August 1990 Iraq's decision to invade Kuwait transformed its President, Saddam Hussein, until this point one of the main regional allies of the US, into an international pariah of the first order and led to the gathering of a US-led coalition to secure the expulsion of Iraqi troops. However, while drawing on the still dominant, but decidedly pre-new imperialist Powell Doctrine (a post-Vietnam injunction that any military action taken by the US be based on the use of overwhelming force), the coalition's victory did not lead to moves to depose the Iraqi regime, but was instead followed by a policy of containment based on the imposition of sanctions, no-fly zones and UN weapons inspections designed to rid Iraq of its weapons of mass destruction. Tensions surrounding Iraq, though, remained persistent throughout the rest of the decade. The human cost of sanctions provided a constant and grim reminder that the matter remained unresolved, the need for continuous enforcement of the no-fly zones (being patrolled by British and US aircraft) raised issues of cost and practicality, while periodic crises in the UN inspections regime raised questions about the effectiveness and long-term viability of the entire containment strategy.[4]

The outlines of the US' shift to a new imperialist strategy became clearer under the Clinton administrations. This transition was notable, firstly, in the primary strategic thrust of the new US government, characterised by efforts to deepen and extend the parameters of the capitalist world economy, as well as US influence within it, under the guise of the neo-liberal globalisation agenda, with measures such as the creation of the North American Free Trade Agreement, the Free Trade Area of the Americas and the development of the World Trade Organization seeking to open up markets and enhance flows of trade and finance. The movement was also evident in military terms, with the shift towards quick, limited and 'arm's-length' interventions being clearly discernible in US operations throughout the rest of the decade. While the dangers of utilising a scaled-down military force were obvious in the inglorious involvement of the US in Somalia during 1993, the rapid and (initially at least) successful invasion of Haiti the following year, followed by the effective use of NATO air strikes in Bosnia during the mid-1990s, appeared to demonstrate the utility of a minimised and flexible military approach based on the use of advanced technology.[5] In December 1998 this approach was put to the test once more as Iraq's decision to terminate cooperation with the UN process of weapon inspections led to a four-day bombing campaign, ostensibly designed to degrade its WMD capabilities, known as Operation Desert Fox.

The attacks, which were carried out without UN approval and in the face of widespread global criticism, also marked the first use of military force by New Labour. Having readily committed to support the US-led action, Tony Blair's favourable predisposition towards geo-strategic re-ordering was also readily discernible. As the Prime Minister put it to the House of Commons during the course of the campaign, the pursuit of regime change via the removal of Saddam Hussein was 'a broad objective of our policy', with Blair adding that '[i]f we can possibly find the means of removing him, we will'. That such a policy was on this occasion not actively pursued, then, owed less to the disposition of the Prime Minister and more to the unfavorable legal, political and military practicalities of the situation.[6] Indeed, the following year these sentiments were further reflected in an internal memo, jointly written by the Foreign and Defence Secretaries, Robin Cook and George Robertson, which set out the government's policy towards Iraq in more detail. Noting that the long-term goal of the British government was 'to reintegrate a territorially intact Iraq as a law abiding member of the international community', the paper warned that while the policy of containment was problematic, no viable alternatives were currently available, and that 'a policy of trying to topple Saddam would command no useful international support'.[7]

By this time, however, New Labour's pursuit of an enhanced global role was also on display in Central-Eastern Europe, where Blair had placed himself firmly in the vanguard of an intensive NATO bombing campaign, ostensibly being conducted to force Serbian paramilitary forces to withdraw from Kosovo, an autonomous province of Yugoslavia, and to halt their programme of ethnic cleansing against the Albanian population. Here, strong new imperialist themes were also evident. While the Prime Minister's justification for the bombing (which, as with Desert Fox, took place without UN approval) was pitched in distinctly humanitarian terms, as the world's first 'progressive war' being waged for the universal values of human rights, a mixture of geo-strategic and economic drivers were also at work. These included the potential for the spread of political instability in Europe, a desire on the part of Western powers to integrate ex-Soviet states into the global capitalist system, and concerns about the credibility of NATO itself, an organisation facing an uncertain future in the post-Cold War world. As Blair himself explained, the issue of Kosovo was enmeshed within 'big strategic interests that would have justified intervention in their own right'. Any failure or inaction on the part of NATO, he maintained, would have left the region 'totally destabilised', would have given succour 'to dictators everywhere', and thus, 'the consequences would have been really immense, on the credibility of NATO, and on world stability'.[8]

The conflict also put the Prime Minister's transatlantic bridge strategy under noticeable strain. Highlighting the military shortcomings of the European Union, along with its lack of cohesive leadership on foreign policy issues, the crisis also raised tensions with the US following Clinton's refusal to countenance the use of ground forces in order to secure a decisive victory. As the war dragged on with no perceptible sign of a breakthrough, Blair adopted a more forcible approach, taking advantage of a high-profile speech in Chicago to unveil a conceptual framework, called the 'Doctrine of International Community', for determining the conditions under which military intervention would be permissible in contemporary global affairs. In this, the Prime Minister argued that old ideas about state sovereignty were no longer applicable in an increasingly interdependent world, and that interventions would sometimes be necessary for the purposes of maintaining or enforcing peace and order. Central to this, too, was the idea that the spread of human rights and democracy were crucial to ensuring security, and that a demonstration of credibility in Kosovo was vital 'to ensure that others do not make the same mistakes in the future'.[9]

Eliminate al Qaeda

The eventual Serbian withdrawal from Kosovo in the summer of 1999 owed as much to Russian diplomacy as it did to the military prowess of NATO, but was nonetheless seen to vindicate the new imperialist use of arm's-length military measures and humanitarian justifications.[10] The apparent success of the venture was also taken by Blair as an endorsement of New Labour's interventionist foreign policy. During the course of the next two years the Prime Minister's predilections for this were strengthened further by two key events. The first of these came within a matter of months of the Kosovo war, and coincided with a sharp decline in Blair's political fortunes. By the spring of 2000 the Prime Minister was facing the nadir of his political life to date, as public discontent with the government's preoccupation with media management, as well as with the apparent vacuity of the Prime Minister himself, combined to produce something of a mini-crisis for the New Labour project. Blair's response, a concerted drive to present himself as a strong, decisive and resolute leader, involved another (albeit small-scale) military intervention during the summer, deploying British troops in support of the government of Sierra Leone in its fight against internal rebel forces. The swift and successful outcome to this further entrenched Blair's belief in the efficacy of an activist foreign policy, and carried the Prime Minister further towards the field of foreign affairs as his preferred arena of operation. The second defining event, in contrast, emerged in a context of political success. In the summer of 2001 New Labour were returned to power following a resounding general election victory, making Blair the first Labour leader in history to secure a second full consecutive term in office. But the Prime Minister's strength was also shadowed by weakness. In a defining Cabinet reshuffle immediately after the election, Blair proved unable to extend his control over the government by dislodging the Chancellor, Gordon Brown, for fear of the political turmoil that would invariably ensue. With Blair's involvement in the domestic sphere now curtailed by Brown's ubiquity over huge swathes of economic and social policy (infamously secured under the terms of the 'Granita deal' on Blair's pursuit of the party leadership almost a decade earlier), his penchant for matters foreign would now become ever more apparent.[11]

Back in the US, the mantle of imperial responsibility had, by this point, been returned to the Republican right following the end of the Clinton Presidency and the election of George W. Bush in November 2000. But if the new administration's initial game-plan of asserting US power by withdrawing from multilateral agreements and institutions (such as the 1997 Kyoto treaty) reflected its political composition, an uneasy balance between moderates, nationalists and hard-line neoconservatives, the policy preferences of the latter camp lay in a more activist direction. For many, the neoconservative vision was succinctly encapsulated in a September 2000 report by an influential think-tank called the Project for the New American Century, entitled *Rebuilding America's Defenses*. Hailing the 1992 *Defense Planning Guidance* as a 'blueprint for maintaining US pre-eminence' in the world, this called for a 'grand strategy' designed to preserve US dominance 'as far into the future as possible'; its key aims being to expand the 'zones of democratic peace' and to ensure 'a favourable order in vital regions'.[12]

By the turn of the millennium another major theme in world politics had also emerged in the form of radical Islamic terrorism. This was fuelled, in part, by the failure of reformist political Islam during the postwar period, with hopes that decolonisation would lead to the creation of an Islamic state having been dashed, and by the forging of close diasporic links and an intermingling of political Islamist ideas with those of radical Salafist ideology during the course of the Soviet invasion of Afghanistan.

While the Soviet withdrawal was followed by a descent into civil war among rival factions and warlords, from which the radical (if nationally oriented) Islamic Taliban movement emerged to take control, the wider result was to give rise to notions of a Global Jihad, centring on the US as the leading power sustaining a Western-dominated world system that oppressed and divided Muslims. In what would become the most infamous manifestation of this new form of international Islamic militancy, during the early 1990s a hitherto unknown Saudi radical, Osama bin Laden, began drawing together a disparate network of associates under the aegis of al-Qaeda ('the Base'), its membership being bound together by grandly, if loosely conceived notions of driving out the Western crusader-Zionist presence in the Gulf, and of inspiring Muslims to rise up against the US and to establish 'true' Islamic regimes across the Middle East and beyond. At this point, the network comprised a small and inchoate collection of Islamic militants, functioning as a focal hub for channelling resources, contacts and expertise to like-minded affiliates, though by the middle of the decade much of this was now finding its way into a series of high-profile terrorist attacks. The most notable of these, the bombing of the World Trade Center in 1993, and strikes on US targets in Saudi Arabia, Kenya and Tanzania (the first al-Qaeda operations proper) were accompanied by a declaration of religious war against the US by bin Laden himself, who by now was heading-up the al-Qaeda network in Afghanistan as a guest of the Taliban regime.[13]

The response from the US to this emergent threat was limited and largely ineffectual. Air strikes against al-Qaeda bases in Afghanistan, along with a suspected chemical weapons factory in Sudan (which turned out to be a pharmaceutical plant supplying nearly all of the country's medicine), did little to dent either the terror group's organisational capacity or its resolve. An increase in covert anti-terrorist actions, including limited efforts to kill bin Laden, along with extra diplomatic measures, including the imposition of UN sanctions against the Taliban and numerous attempts to persuade its leadership to extradite bin Laden for trial, proved to be similarly unsuccessful.[14] The military options, however, were re-examined by the incoming Bush administration following an al-Qaeda attack on the *USS Cole* in October 2000, in which 17 US sailors were killed. While the weight of evolving plans at this point centred primarily on providing support for anti-Taliban groups rather than direct action by the US itself, momentum in support of a ground invasion was also starting to gain strength. According to Donald Rumsfeld, the new US Defense Secretary, '[i]t had become increasingly clear ... that we needed an approach that treated terrorism more like fascism – as an evil that needed to be not contained, but fought and eliminated'. Or, as Colin

Powell, the US Secretary of State, put it, '[f]irst and foremost, our goal was to eliminate al Qaida', an ambition that 'might well require introducing ground forces'.[15]

As things currently stood, though, the prospects for a full-scale military assault were constrained not just by new imperialist pressures, but by a lack of regional support and cooperation, as well as by a lack of public and political support, in part due to an absence of perceived legitimacy for such a dramatic step.[16] In July 2001, Washington's disquiet with this state of affairs was expressed at UN-sponsored talks on Afghanistan in Berlin, during which, according to Niaz Naik, a former Pakistan foreign secretary and member of the Pakistani delegation, those in attendance sought to persuade the Taliban of the economic and political benefits of establishing a broad-based national government, and of re-engaging with the international community. When the talks broke down, US diplomats allegedly turned to more forcible measures, raising the threat of a military operation by mid-October to overthrow the Taliban unless bin Laden was handed over to the US.[17] Making the point in colourful fashion, Tom Simons, a member of the US delegation and a former ambassador to Pakistan, is purported to have put the ultimatum in stark terms, that '[e]ither you accept our offer of a carpet of gold, or we bury you under a carpet of bombs'.[18]

While such claims are rejected by the members of the US delegation, Simons himself admitted that a threat may well have been issued outside of the official meeting rooms, and confirmed, in any case, that the US position was leaning towards 'a military answer' should 'solid evidence' of bin Laden's involvement in the USS Cole attack come to light.[19] As he put it, 'feeling in Washington was strong ... that military action was one of the options down the road', and that 'the drift of US policy was to get away from a single issue, from concentrating on Bin Laden as under Clinton, and get broader'.[20] Against this backdrop, a new three-phase plan for dealing with the Taliban, involving a final ultimatum for handing over bin Laden, covert support for anti-Taliban groups, and direct military action to overthrow the regime, was formally agreed by American National Security officials on 10 September.[21]

Not whether but when

The al-Qaeda attacks on New York and Washington on 11 September 2001 were presented by administration officials as a vivid demonstration of the dangers posed by a confluence of rogue states, WMD and radical Islamic terrorism. The historically unique and world-changing nature of these events was underlined by the practical US response; the launching of an overtly militaristic 'war on terror' ostensibly designed not just to annihilate al-Qaeda but to end all forms of international terrorism. As Bush put it, al-Qaeda were 'the heirs of all the murderous ideologies of the twentieth century', and the 'war on terror will not end until every terrorist group of global reach has been found, stopped and defeated'.[22]

Although the atrocity drew expressions of solidarity from around the world, including declarations of support from regional bodies such as the Association of South East Asian Nations (ASEAN) and the EU, and with NATO invoking its Article V for the first time, under which an attack on a member state is regarded as an attack on all members, the events of 9/11 led to a strengthening of Washington's unilateralist tendencies. Imbuing the Bush administration with a new and invigorating sense of purpose, the attacks tilted the balance of internal forces in favour of its more hard-line elements and provided them with the political space needed to pursue a wider and more aggressive policy of global re-ordering than had hitherto been possible. As Colin Powell noted, the attacks 'changed radically the environment in which we were operating', and the available options for dealing with terrorism had now 'expanded enormously'.[23] Donald Rumsfeld, too, was clear on the point. The fall of the twin towers, he said, had created 'the opportunity to rearrange things in the world in a way that would be beneficial to our country and to peace and to stability and to free systems', and that '[i]f the war does not significantly change the world's political map, the U.S. will not achieve its aim'.[24]

The content of the war on terror thus envisioned a wide-ranging policy of regime change from the outset. While the obvious and immediate focus of this would fall on Afghanistan for harbouring and protecting the al-Qaeda network, a series of other countries, including Iran, Syria and Iraq, were also highlighted as potential targets for military action.[25] A central feature of US strategic thinking on all of this was the need to establish and maintain credibility. As Dick Cheney, now the Vice President, put it, making an 'example' out of the Taliban would increase the leverage of the US with other states and build public confidence for other campaigns, and as Paul Wolfowitz, now the Deputy Secretary of Defense, noted, limiting military attacks to al-Qaeda and the Taliban risked producing 'meager' results and could, as a result, 'embolden' enemies of the US.[26] Similarly, Rumsfeld claimed that anything less than a 'confidence inspiring' military response by the United States could undermine the war on terror by questioning US resolve, and that 'impressive' results (involving at least one non al-Qaeda target) would therefore be required.[27] A prescient concern, he observed, was the need to consider: 'what signal did this send to the rest of the world?'[28] Indeed, according to the Defense Secretary, many of the problems currently faced by the US were directly related to an erosion of its credibility in the eyes of its opponents. As he explained:

> The capability of the US and the will of the US helped discipline the world in the sense that it contributed to stability and peace and order by virtue of the fact that people recognized that we had capabilities and we were willing to use them. And to the extent that we were not willing to use them, we had a reflexive pull-back. It encouraged people to do things that were against our interest.[29]

Of all the countries highlighted for potential regime change, however, the prime target in line for action after Afghanistan was Iraq. Indeed, although Bush may have fought the Presidential election on a non-interventionist foreign policy platform, and although the initial foreign policy concerns of the new administration lay with the issues of Russia and missile defence, the question of Iraq was also on the agenda from the outset. According to Paul O'Neill, the US Secretary of the Treasury, the removal of Saddam was 'topic "A"' at the inaugural meeting of the National Security Council at the end of January 2001,[30] and while Rumsfeld noted that discussions on Iraq during the summer had been 'inconclusive' (with the CIA tending to favour an internal coup rather than externally enforced regime change), it was also observed that '[a] major success with Iraq would enhance U.S. credibility and influence throughout the region'.[31] With the administration's initial policy of seeking an enhanced sanctions regime having fallen by the wayside during the summer, and with the influence of the Pentagon having been elevated by the turn to militarism, the events of 9/11 were thus seized on as a means of effecting a more robust approach. On the very day of the attacks, Rumsfeld's own notes infamously recorded his view that the aim of any response should be to 'hit SH [Saddam Hussein] at the same time. Not only UBL [Usama Bin Laden]. Go massive. Sweep it all up. Things related and not'.[32] And indeed, Bush too was anxious to take advantage of the opportunity, urging counter-terrorism officials to drag up 'any shred' of evidence that could be used to link Saddam to the attacks.[33]

That said, the majority view within the administration was to limit the initial military focus to the specific issue of al-Qaeda and the Taliban on the grounds that this would be an easier proposition around which to assemble the kind of international support and cooperation that would be needed if the US was to avoid having to shoulder the entire burden of operations.[34] As Wolfowitz put it, the discussions on Iraq were 'about not whether but when ... the disagreement was whether it should be in the immediate response or whether you should concentrate simply on Afghanistan first'. Bush, he explained, had opted to focus on Afghanistan as a matter of 'tactics and timing'.[35]

This conclusion was mirrored in the response of the British government. With Parliament in recess, this was determined by a small clique based in Downing Street, which, headed by Blair, offered unflinching support for Bush's Manichaean interpretation of events. Notwithstanding ministerial negativity about the phraseology of the 'war on terror', the Prime Minister denounced the attacks (the worst on British citizens since the Second World War) as an act of 'barbarism', and declared the country to be enjoined in a battle 'between the free and democratic world and terrorism' from which there could be no rest until the latter had been entirely eradicated.[36] As in the US, the qualitatively unique nature and severity of the attacks was also taken as an opportunity for refashioning the international order. As Blair put it, 9/11 was 'an event of such importance that suddenly everything was going to move around and take new shape', making a policy of active engagement 'the only serious foreign policy on offer'.[37] The civilised world, he said, was now engaged in 'the most fundamental struggle of our times', and the only place to be was 'in the thick of it'. Professing to have been imbued with 'a real sense of mission', the Prime Minister recalled that:

> the interventionism that I had promulgated as a policy around the time of Kosovo was going to have to be extended and used, but probably in very different circumstances, and in circumstances that would be profoundly disturbing to people.[38]

The necessity for such activism was also made clear by the new Foreign Secretary, Jack Straw. After 9/11, he explained, it was 'no longer possible to ignore distant and misgoverned parts of a world without borders', and that what was now required was a more activist and engaged foreign policy, with 'a diplomacy of foresight ... to have the vision to act before threats arise'. This, he maintained, was not merely a matter of moral responsibility, but a matter of 'profound national interest', in short: 'a survival mechanism for all our societies'.[39] Running alongside this, the response of the British government was also couched in humanitarian rhetoric. In Blair's words, the fight was nothing less than a global struggle for social justice, a campaign to promote 'the values of liberty, the rule of law, human rights and a pluralist society', and to bring the 'values of democracy and freedom to people around the world'.[40]

Only one outcome

Having pledged Britain's wholehearted support for the US, the aftermath of the 9/11 attacks saw Blair pitched as a central figure on the world stage, avidly engaged in intensive shuttle diplomacy in an attempt to build an international coalition for the war on terror. In this, despite concerns from the government's Director of Communications, Alastair Campbell, that the Prime Minister was in danger of 'getting hooked on the international stuff',[41] it remained clear that the strategic approach of limiting the initial focus to Afghanistan would be the mere opening phase in a far wider project. In Blair's words, Britain needed to be prepared 'for the long haul', since '[e]ven when al-Qaeda is dealt with, the job is not over'.[42]

Indeed, the approach taken towards the Taliban saw diplomacy usurped by invective. Offers to extradite bin Laden for trial in a third country on receipt of evidence supporting his involvement in 9/11 were rejected out-of-hand, regardless of how genuine they may have been, and instead the responsibility for war was pinned solely on the intransigence of the Afghan government.[43] As Blair put it, there was 'no doubt' that al-Qaeda were responsible for 9/11, and there could be 'no diplomacy with Bin Laden or the Taliban regime'. 'This', he said, 'is a battle with only one outcome: our victory not theirs'.[44] Bluntly echoing the point, the White House spokesman, Ari Fleischer, railed that there could be 'no discussions' with the Taliban, and that the time had come 'for actions not negotiations'.[45]

In early October the British government sought to further impress the necessity for war with the production of a dossier on al-Qaeda's responsibility for the 9/11 attacks. Yet the details it contained, and hence the justification for military action, remained circumstantial. The case it made amounted to nothing more than a catalogue of bin Laden's anti-Western diatribes, the notable similarities between 9/11 and previous al-Qaeda attacks, and the assertion that '[n]o other organisation has both the motivation and the capability to carry out attacks like those'. Moreover, while the absence of 'a prosecutable case' against bin Laden was explained away on the grounds that more detailed evidence (described by Blair as 'overwhelming') was simply 'too sensitive to release',[46] by the middle of 2009, despite the fact that the war against the Taliban was now heading towards its eighth year, this material remained highly classified, with the government refusing to allow its release on the grounds of national security.[47]

A similar situation was evident in the US. In mid-December a videotaped 'confession' from bin Laden was described by Bush as 'a devastating declaration' of guilt, a view mirroring the opinion of Rumsfeld, who maintained that there could be 'no doubt of bin Laden's responsibility'.[48] Once again, however, the passage of time failed to illuminate matters further. By the start of 2010, more than eight years after the 9/11 atrocities, bin Laden's website entry on the FBI's 'Most Wanted' list continued to make no reference whatsoever to the attacks, stating merely that he remained wanted for his involvement in the 1998 US embassy bombings and was a 'suspect' in other terrorist incidents around the world.[49] According to the FBI's Chief of Investigative Publicity, Rex Tomb, this omission was due to the fact that the Bureau had 'no hard evidence' linking him to the attacks that could be used to formally levy an indictment.[50]

While none of this is to doubt al-Qaeda's culpability for the events of 9/11, the discourse of 'no diplomacy' clearly illustrates the enthusiasm and determination with which the idea of a militaristic response was approached by both the US and Britain. Indeed, the actual strategy deployed for dealing with the Taliban, a three-stage process leading from an ultimatum for the extradition of bin Laden and covert support for anti-regime groups to overt military force, was essentially that which had been drawn up prior to the onset of the war on terror. On 7 October, the strategy reached its denouement as a US-led coalition of 16 nations launched military action against Afghanistan, codenamed Operation Enduring Freedom.[51] Principally centred on air strikes in support of the Northern Alliance, a loose collection of tribal warlords opposed to the Taliban regime, and with limited involvement from ground forces, the assault envisioned an intervention that was swift and limited, and that could be achieved at safe distance. This, according to Rumsfeld, reflected the broader 'strategic theme' of the war on terror, which would be to assist local people 'to free themselves of regimes that support terrorism',[52] and would provide decisive proof that the shift to a new imperialist 'military lite' approach, and with it the obsolescence of the Powell Doctrine, was now complete. As Richard Clarke, the National Security Council's chief anti-terror adviser, explained, the Defense Secretary regarded Afghanistan as the perfect 'laboratory' in which 'to prove his theory about the ability of small numbers of ground troops, coupled with airpower, to win decisive battles'.[53]

The official objectives of the war, as set out by Tony Blair, were far more limited; namely, to 'bring Bin Laden and other Al Qaida leaders to justice', to 'eliminate the terrorist threat they pose', and to change the Taliban regime should it refuse to cleanse Afghanistan of its terrorist infection.[54] By November, however, political tensions over the campaign were rising. According to the Home Secretary, David Blunkett, it had already become clear that 'there was no co-ordinated strategy between the US and Britain', while Britain's own military chiefs were purportedly 'less than convinced' about the government's strategy for managing the war.[55] With public opinion also turning in favour of a pause in the bombing in order to allow relief efforts to alleviate the humanitarian impact, the Prime Minister launched a renewed effort to legitimise the conflict, presenting it as being both just and unavoidable, and insisting that a refusal to act militarily would be inexcusable when faced with 'the sworn enemies of everything the civilised world stands for'. Describing al-Qaeda and the Taliban as being 'virtually a merged organisation', and reiterating that '[t]hey can't be negotiated with', Blair now confirmed that the removal of the Taliban had become a formal objective of the military campaign given that they had 'chosen to side with Al Qaida'.[56] Fortunately for the Prime Minister the risk of political crisis was soon forestalled by the rapid collapse of the Taliban regime and by the ostensible success of the military operation. By the end of the year a new provisional Afghan government had been established, and a United Nations security force, albeit of limited proportions and powers, was in place on the ground.[57]

Very, very unusual

While the attack on Afghanistan provided a visible manifestation of the new imperialist drive to global re-ordering, the war on terror also had an appreciable impact on the domestic sphere. In this, however, mundane considerations of party political advantage as well as national security issues were evident. Despite Blair's insistence that the government would not deliver 'a knee-jerk reaction' to 9/11, but would put together 'a carefully-appraised set of measures: tough, but balanced and proportionate to the risk we face',[58] its actual response, in the form of the Anti-Terrorism, Crime and Security Act (2001), was rather different. The initial proposals for this, coming just fifteen months after New Labour's first anti-terror legislation (the Terrorism Act (2000)), introduced a raft of wide-ranging measures; including increased security arrangements (such as making it an offence to aid the overseas development or use of WMD technology, or to publicly reveal details about the movements of nuclear waste), greater powers for intelligence-gathering and surveillance (covering airlines, ferry services, and internet and mobile phone providers) and extra powers for seizing the assets of individuals charged with terrorism offences. Contentiously, the proposals also included mechanisms for allowing confidential information held by any government department or local authority to be disclosed to the police and intelligence agencies for the purposes of non-terrorist criminal investigations. Most controversial of all, though, were measures permitting the Home Secretary to detain, without trial, and for an indefinite period, foreign nationals who it was claimed were 'reasonably suspected' of being involved in terrorist activity, but who could not be deported where there was a risk of torture in the destination state; this being prohibited by the European Convention on Human Rights. To compound matters, the new detention powers also required that the government derogate from Article 5 of the Convention, a move which, in turn, required that the terror situation be officially declared a 'state of emergency', an invocation that found Britain alone in the EU as being prepared to make.[59]

As well as marking a substantial shift in state–citizen relations, imposing restrictions on civil liberties and introducing new powers that were entirely unrelated to terrorism, the measures were also hastily conceived and were rushed through Parliament with a minimal amount of scrutiny. The contents of the Bill, amounting to 124 clauses, received a mere 16 hours of debate in the House of Commons and gave the Lords just nine days for reflection.[60] Not surprisingly, the proposals also met strong opposition. Amnesty International condemned the new detention powers as draconian, the director of the human rights group, Liberty, John Wadham, called the plans a 'fundamental violation of the rule of law, our rights and traditional British values', Muslim organisations claimed that there was a 'substantial risk' that the powers would be used 'in a discriminatory manner', and the Home Affairs Committee warned that the proposals had 'major implications for civil liberties' and declared that the Bill should not be passed 'in such a short period and with so little time for detailed examination'.[61]

The government's reaction to this was wholly diametric; insisting that the measures were nothing less than an entirely proper, sensible and defensive move. According to Blair, the proposals had been designed 'to deal with the threat against the liberty of our own citizens', while David Blunkett described them as a 'rational, reasonable and proportionate response to the threat',[62] and claimed that the government were seeking to protect, rather than erode, civil liberties. '[N]o one is going macho', he exclaimed, 'no one is trying to do this to promote a vitriolic or anti-human rights agenda'.[63] This particular assertion, though, rang somewhat hollow in the light of Blunkett's simultaneous attack on those opposed to the measures, who were derided for their preoccupation with what the Home Secretary described as 'airy-fairy' civil liberties.[64]

Nevertheless, faced with concerted opposition, most notably from the House of Lords, the government was forced to make a series of concessions in order to ensure that the proposals passed into law within the desired timescale. As a result, several aspects of the Bill were either watered-down or withdrawn. Powers for data retention and disclosure were scaled back, and a proposal to create a new offence of incitement to religious hatred was dropped (being revisited in the Racial and Religious Hatred Act (2006)). Provisions for greater oversight were also introduced, with the measures being made subject to an annual review by Parliament and to a review by the Privy Council in two years' time, and with the regime of detention without charge being subject to a 'sunset clause', under which its powers would expire if not renewed within five years. Thus set, the Bill cleared Parliament on 13 December and received Royal Assent the following day.[65]

In all this, the government's approach again reflected developments in the US. In October 2001 the passing of the Patriot Act bestowed extensive surveillance powers upon the federal government, authorised military tribunals with the power to hold secret trials, and approved indefinite imprisonment without charge for foreign terror suspects. Alongside this there also emerged one of the war on terror's most notorious icons with the establishment of Camp X-Ray, a secret detention and interrogation centre at a US naval base in Guantánamo Bay, Cuba, which began receiving detainees from January 2002. Those captured (initially in Afghanistan, but soon including other countries beyond the primary theatre of military operations) were categorised as 'unlawful combatants', being denied the entitlements of prisoners of war under the Geneva Conventions, and many were subjected to harsh methods of interrogation, including sleep and sensory deprivation, long periods in enforced stress positions, imprisonment in open air cages and, possibly the most extreme, if rarely used practise of all, waterboarding.[66] The establishment of Guantánamo Bay was accompanied by the formation of a secret network of global detention sites and a covert programme of 'extraordinary rendition'; the extra-judicial transfer of individuals for detention and interrogation, with those involved being taken either to Camp X-Ray or to a third-party state. While the use of such methods was clearly outside the scope of international law, their adoption was justified by the Bush administration's legal team on the grounds that the President possessed unlimited authority during wartime.[67] Indeed, in Rumsfeld's view, no interrogation practices could be considered illegal unless they produced a degree of pain equivalent to organ failure or 'even death'. As Cofer Black, a former CIA Chief of the Counterterrorist Center, put it: 'After 9/11 the gloves came off'.[68]

The reaction of the British government to all this was characterised by an overweening desire to avoid any overt criticism of Washington. Ministerial expressions of discontent and calls for assurances of humane treatment in respect of Guantánamo Bay, being prompted largely by concerns that images of detainees would have a negative impact on public opinion, were offset by their being couched in an exculpatory rhetoric that eschewed reference to specific points of international law in favour of vague notions of principles and norms. Jack Straw, for instance, maintained that British detainees should be treated in accordance with 'customary international law';[69] Ben Bradshaw, the Under Secretary of State at the Foreign Office, asserted that detainees were being treated 'in line with international humanitarian norms' (adding that the process of defining a prisoner of war was 'an extremely complicated matter'),[70] and the Defence Secretary, Geoff Hoon, while maintaining that detainees had to be treated 'with proper respect for international law', nonetheless insisted that there was 'little doubt that al-Qaeda terrorists do not, under any definition, qualify to be prisoners of war', and that there could be 'no doubting the legality in the way in which these combatants have been imprisoned'.[71] For Blair, despite an initial statement that detainees 'should be treated in accordance with the Geneva Convention and proper international norms',[72] the main theme was one of tacit approval for what was considered to be a short- to medium-term expedient. As the Prime Minister explained, Guantánamo was a 'very, very unusual situation', but a measure that was nevertheless required to gain information and deal with the threat of international terrorism. 'It would be irresponsible', he said, 'for us not to take every step we possibly can to make sure we have investigated every lead'.[73]

Conclusion

The advent of the war on terror was conditioned by both long-term as well as historically contingent factors. In the former of these, changing global conditions in the latter decades of the twentieth century, principally rooted in the dynamics of the Cold War, the shift to a new imperialist trajectory by the US and the emergence of a globally oriented form of radical Islamic terrorism, set the overarching framework for later developments. Accompanying this, the particular course of events was set by the internal dynamics of the Bush administration, avowedly pursuing a strategy of global re-ordering following the al-Qaeda terrorist attacks of 9/11, and was eagerly supported by a New Labour government keen to elevate the influence of the British state on the world stage. The immediate impact of the war on terror was readily apparent in several ways. In military terms the first phase of the campaign involved an invasion of Afghanistan, ostensibly designed to depose the ruling Taliban regime and to eliminate the threat posed by al-Qaeda. Going beyond this, a series of extra-legal measures were also put in place, involving a programme of extraordinary rendition and indefinite detentions at Guantánamo Bay for terrorist suspects. Strongly supporting the US response, the approach taken by the British government also involved an increase in the powers of the state, with the politically charged Anti-Terrorism, Crime and Security Act heralding an erosion of civil liberties in the supposed interests of national security. The form and direction of subsequent events in the course of the war on terror were shaped by the unfolding of these various dynamics.

Notes

1   Ahmed (2003); Burke (2004); Roy (2008).
2   National Security Strategy of the United States, August 1991.
3   The draft documentation is available at www.gwu.edu/~nsarchiv/nukevault/ebb245/index.htm, accessed 9 November 2010.
4   See Kettell (2006), Chapter 3.
5   Boot (2003), Chapter 14; Foster (2006).
6   Remarks during debate in the House of Commons, 17 December 1998.
7   Joint memo, May 1999, cited in Butler (2004), pp. 54–5.
8   Frontline interview with Tony Blair, 2000, www.pbs.org/wgbh/pages/frontline/shows/kosovo/interviews/blair.html, accessed 9 November 2010; also see Bello (2006); Kettell (2006), pp. 37–43; Chomsky (2008).
9   Tony Blair, speech at the Economic Club, Chicago, 24 April 1999.
10   Biddle (2002).
11   On these events see Kettell (2006), pp. 43–6.
12   Project for the New American Century (2000), www.newamericancentury.org/publicationsreports.htm, accessed 9 November 2010.
13   On these events see for example Youngs, Bowers and Oakes (2001); Rogers and Elworthy (2002); Burke (2004); Sageman (2004), Chapter 1; Kepel (2009). Also see 'Final Report of the National Commission on Terrorist Attacks Upon the United States' (hereafter, '9/11 Commission Report') (National Commission on Terrorist Attacks Upon the United States 2004), paras 2.3–2.5.
14   See for example: B. Gellman, 'U.S. was foiled multiple times in efforts to capture Bin Laden or have him killed', *Washington Post*, 3 October 2001; A. Gillan, 'Pakistani hit squad was trained by CIA to kill Bin Laden', *Guardian*, 4 October 2001; R. McFarlane, 'The tragedy of Abdul Haq', *Wall St. Journal*, 2 November 2001; 9/11 Commission Report, paras 4.2, 4.4, 11.2.
15   Evidence to the 9/11 Commission from Donald Rumsfeld, and from Colin Powell, both 23 March 2004.
16   9/11 Commission Report, paras 6.4–6.5.
17   G. Arney, 'US "planned attack on Taleban"', BBC News, 18 September 2001; J. Steele, E. MacAskill, R. Norton-Taylor and E. Harriman, 'Threat of US strikes passed to Taliban weeks before NY attack', *Guardian*, 22 September 2001; D. Cave, 'The conspiracy theory that wouldn't die', 15 August 2002, http://dir.salon.com, accessed 9 November 2010.
18   D. Cave, 'The conspiracy theory that wouldn't die', 15 August 2002, http://dir.salon.com, accessed 9 November 2010.
19   J-C. Brisard and D. Corn, 'Debating September 11', *The Nation*, 12 July 2002; D. Cave, 'The conspiracy theory that wouldn't die', 15 August 2002, http://dir.salon.com, accessed 9 November 2010.
20   This position was also confirmed by Lee Coldren, another US diplomat present at the meeting. See J. Steele, E. MacAskill, R. Norton-Taylor and E. Harriman, 'Threat of US strikes passed to Taliban weeks before NY Attack', *Guardian*, 22 September 2001.
21   9/11 Commission Report, paras 6.4–6.5; also see A. Johnson and J. Miklaszewski, 'White House given plan days before Sept. 11', MSNBC and NBC News, 16 May 2002; D. Rennie, 'US planned to hit bin Laden ahead of September 11', *Daily Telegraph*, 4 August 2002.
22   Address to Joint Session of Congress, 20 September 2001.

23 Written evidence to the 9/11 Commission from Colin Powell, 23 March 2004.

24 US Department of Defense, news transcript, 9 January 2002; Feith (2008), pp. 81–2.

25 Feith (2008); 9/11 Commission Report, para 10.3; Frontline interview with Paul Wolfowitz, 22 April 2002.

26 Feith (2008), pp. 49, 105.

27 *Ibid.* pp. 65–6, 95–6.

28 US Department of Defense, news transcript, 9 January 2002.

29 *Ibid.*

30 R. Leung, 'Bush sought "way" to invade Iraq?', CBS News, 11 January 2004; also see Frontline interview with Richard Clarke, 23 January 2006, www.pbs.org/wgbh/pages/frontline/shows/knew/interviews/clarke.html, accessed 9 November 2010.

31 Feith (2008), p. 200; Rumsfeld memo to Rice, 27 July 2001, reprinted in Feith (2008), pp. 535–8.

32 Kettell (2006), p. 50.

33 Clarke (2004), pp. 30–2; also see Frontline interview with Richard Clarke, 23 January 2006.

34 Feith (2008), p. 105.

35 Deputy Secretary Wolfowitz interview with Sam Tannenhaus, *Vanity Fair*, May 2003.

36 Statement to the Nation, 11 September 2001.

37 Speech at the Labour Party conference, 2 October 2001; 'Grasping the opportunities of an open world', speech at the Lord Mayor's Banquet, 12 November 2001; Frontline interview, 8 May 2002, www.pbs.org/wgbh/pages/frontline/shows/campaign/interviews/blair.html, accessed 9 November 2010.

38 *The Blair Years*, BBC1, 25 November 2007.

39 'Re-ordering the world', speech to the Foreign Policy Centre, 25 March 2002; Straw (2002), cols 98–9.

40 Speech at the Labour Party Conference, 2 October 2001; Blair (2002), cols 119–24.

41 Campbell (2007), p. 585.

42 Statement to the House of Commons, 8 October 2001; on this issue also see Campbell (2007), pp. 566–74.

43 See CBS News, 'Taliban won't turn over Bin Laden', 21 September 2001; P. Bishop, 'Pakistan blocks bin Laden trial', *Daily Telegraph*, 3 October 2001; Justice Not Vengeance, anti-war briefings, 02–06, starting www.j-n-v.org/AW_briefings/ARROW_briefing002.htm, accessed 9 November 2010.

44 Speech to Labour Party conference, 2 October 2001.

45 Justice Not Vengeance, 'The propaganda war: the Taliban did not refuse', anti-war briefing No.2, 24 September 2001, www.j-n-v.org/AW_briefings/ARROW_briefing002.htm, accessed 9 November 2010.

46 'Responsibility for the terrorist atrocities in the United States, 11 September 2001', October 2001, Prime Minister's Office; Tony Blair statement to the House of Commons, 4 October 2001.

47 A request for this information was made by the author under the terms of the 2000 Freedom of Information Act on 28 May 2009. The reply, received on 25 June 2009, stated that the information was covered by an 'absolute exemption' from the Act by virtue of the fact that its contents related to issues of national security.

48 www.CNN.com, 'Bush: Tape "a devastating declaration of guilt"', 14 December 2001; Department of Defense, press release, 13 December 2001.

49 FBI Most Wanted Terrorists: www.fbi.gov/wanted/terrorists/terbinladen.htm, accessed 14 January 2010.

50 Muckraker Report, 'FBI says, "no hard evidence connecting Bin Laden to 9/11"', Global Research, 10 June 2006, www.globalresearch.ca/index.php?context=va&aid=2623, accessed 9 November 2010; D. Eggen, 'Bin Laden, most wanted for embassy bombings?', *Washington Post*, 28 August 2006.

51 The British component of the invasion was known as Operation Veritas.

52 Feith (2008), pp. 75–82.

53 S. M. Hersh, 'The other war: why Bush's Afghanistan problem won't go away', *New Yorker*, 12 April 2004; also see Bello (2006).

54 Statement to the House of Commons, 4 October 2001.

55 Blunkett (2006), pp. 310–11.

56 Speech to the Welsh Assembly, 30 October 2001.

57 Youngs, Bowers and Oakes (2001).

58 Statement to the House of Commons, 4 October 2001.

59 Elliott (2006); also see A. Travis, 'Anti-terror bill damned for catch-all powers', *Guardian*, 14 November 2001.

60 Haubrich (2003).

61 'Detentions "won't abuse human rights"', *Daily Telegraph*, 12 November 2001; 'Blunkett bid to detain terror suspects without trial', *Daily Mail*, 14 November 2001; A. Travis, 'Blunkett to face rough ride over terror law', *Guardian*, 19 November 2001; The Muslim submission on the Anti-Terrorism, Crime and Security Bill 2001, November 2001, para. 10.

62 M. Tempest, 'Blunkett plays down fears over anti-terror bill', *Guardian*, 13 November 2001; M. Tempest, 'No-nonsense Blunkett defends "proportionate" anti-terror bill', *Guardian*, 19 November 2001.

63 S. Womack, 'My head's on the block over this, says Blunkett', *Daily Telegraph*, 19 November 2001.

64 'Mr Blunkett has quickly emerged as an intolerant, illiberal Home Secretary', *Independent*, 10 December 2001.

65 For a discussion see Elliott (2006).

66 Smith (2007).

67 House Committee on the Judiciary (2009).

68 J. Barry, M. Hirsh and M. Isikoff, 'The roots of torture', *Newsweek*, 24 May 2004; S. Shane, D. Johnston and J. Risen, 'Secret U.S. endorsement of severe interrogation', *New York Times*, 4 October 2007.

69 BBC News, 'Treat Cuba captives humanely', 20 January 2002.

70 Remarks in the House of Commons, 21 February 2002, *Hansard* cols 623 and 626.

71 Remarks in the House of Commons, 14 February 2002. *Hansard* col. 333; also see R. Norton-Taylor and M. White, 'Two more Britons flown to Cuba', *Guardian*, 15 January 2002.

72 A. McSmith, 'Blair wants detainees held in line with PoW convention', *Daily Telegraph*, 17 January 2002.

73 Press conference, 11 April 2002.

4

Chaos

Following the overthrow of the Taliban, the war on terror moved rapidly towards its second phase. The principal theme in this was the pursuit of regime change in Iraq, ostensibly as a means of defusing the threat posed by its illegal weapons of mass destruction, but in reality a policy designed to enhance the global influence of the US, not least by promoting the spread of free market democracy in the Middle East and by establishing its credible willingness to use force. For the New Labour leadership, the focus on WMD was adopted as a strategic means of overcoming the political and legal obstacles to British participation in military action. Efforts to galvanise international support against Iraq through the United Nations, however, failed to produce the desired result, and raised question marks over the legitimacy of the subsequent invasion as well as the viability of the government's transatlantic bridge approach. The consequences of the attack were also highly detrimental. While the initial invasion was completed relatively quickly, the new imperialist desire for a swift and limited intervention backfired in spectacular fashion. Anticipating a rapid transition to democratic governance, US plans for the post-war situation proved to be dangerously inadequate, leading to an outbreak of chaos, disorder and insurgency. Compounding this, political pressures over the war also mounted as the hunt for weapons of mass destruction drew a blank, and as the diversion of resources from Afghanistan allowed the Taliban and al-Qaeda to regenerate their capabilities.

The scope of the mission

By the spring of 2002, signs that not all was well in Britain's war on terror were starting to appear. The principal sense of unease at this point centred on Afghanistan, with questions starting to be raised about the precise boundaries of the dual peacekeeping and combat role being played by British troops, as well as the uncertain nature of the mission more generally. In the words of Lord Inge, the Chief of Defence Staff from 1994–97, the British army had become 'dangerously overcommitted' and the campaign had 'mission creep written all over it'.[1] Tensions were also rising over the nature and extent of the US commitment to the post-war effort, with Blunkett observing that differences between the US and British approaches were now showing up 'quite starkly', and claiming, erroneously as it transpired, that while London wanted to focus on issues of aid and development, officials in Washington were 'only interested in going after the Al Qaeda group and Bin Laden'.[2] Concerns about the mission were scarcely alleviated by remarks from the iteratively circumspect Geoff Hoon. 'Our exit strategy', he explained, 'is that we will leave when the task is completed', although the task itself, namely that of removing the terrorist threat, was one that remained enigmatically 'open-ended'.[3]

To compound matters, the central thrust of US attention was by this time starting to turn away from Afghanistan and towards the question of Iraq. This was presaged by a downplaying of US efforts to find bin Laden, who was now believed to have fled to Pakistan following a failed attempt to capture him at the Tora Bora mountain complex in December 2001.[4] Commenting on his fate, Bush remarked that it was now an open question as to whether bin Laden was 'in control of some network',[5] and claimed that the al-Qaeda leader had, in any case, been effectively 'marginalised' by the US operation. '[T]he idea of focusing on one person', he declared, 'really indicates to me [that] people don't understand the scope of the mission'.[6] But the main rhetorical thrust, however, centred on claims about Iraq's links to al-Qaeda and its possession of weapons of mass destruction. In January, the President's State of the Union Address denounced Iraq, along with Iran and North Korea, as constituting part of an 'axis of evil' that was determined to acquire WMD with which to 'threaten the peace of the world', and warned that the US would act pre-emptively, and unilaterally if necessary, to ensure that such threats did not come to fruition.[7]

The direct impetus for pursuing regime change in Iraq was an untidy, and frequently incoherent and contradictory mix of new imperialist as well as more individualist drivers and motivations, on the relative importance of which no consensus existed within the Bush administration. Alongside the removal of any perceived threat from illicit WMD, the numerous impulses here included a desire to expand the global reach of the US and enhance its geo-strategic leverage within the Middle East, to promote democratic political reform within the region (this being thought to provide security benefits and a greater integration into the world economy), to secure increased influence over international oil markets (with

Iraq possessing the second largest proven reserves in the world), and to conclude the sense of unfinished business hanging over from the first Gulf war. Crucially, too, a key ambition was to assert US credibility in the war on terror.[8] For this, Iraq offered a particularly enticing prospect; being simultaneously weak enough for military victory to be guaranteed, but sufficiently strong for this to enhance the credibility of the Washingtonian threat. As Rumsfeld put it, invading Iraq would overcome one of the chief limitations of the Afghan theatre; namely, that its lack of valuable infrastructure targets failed to provide a visible demonstration of US military prowess.[9] Or as Wolfowitz observed, a key allure of Iraq was precisely that it was 'do-able'.[10] In this context, the theme of weapons of mass destruction was therefore less of a principal concern as a coherent issue around which justifications for war could be erected. As Wolfowitz again revealed, the question of WMD was settled on '[f]or bureaucratic reasons … because it was the one reason everyone could agree on'.[11]

On the question of WMD, Blair too proved to be decidedly ambivalent. Despite claiming that the path to war was laid by the changed 'calculus of risk' concerning weapons of mass destruction in the wake of 9/11, the Prime Minister later conceded that he would have opted to join the US-led mission regardless of the weapons issue, and that one of the core drivers behind British participation was a desire to promote geo-political change in the Middle East. Insisting that '[t]here is no reason why the Arab and Muslim world can't have the same rights of freedom and democracy that everyone else has',[12] Blair argued that the necessity for regime change in Iraq was bound up with the broader fact 'of how that region was going to change'. While Saddam Hussein remained in place, he explained, 'it would have been very difficult to have changed it in the right way'. However, while proclaiming that 'I would still have thought it right to remove him' in spite of Iraq's possession of WMD, the Prime Minister pointed out that the discursive justifications for war would, in the absence of such weapons, naturally have had to be configured differently. '[O]bviously', he averred, 'you would have had to use and deploy different arguments, about the nature of the threat'.[13]

In this, the Prime Minister's views reflected the government's strategic approach towards Iraq in the months prior to the 9/11 attacks. In a new policy framework set out during the spring of 2001 it was decided that Britain and the US 'would re-make the case against Saddam Hussein' through a 'Contract with the Iraqi People', with the aim of achieving 'a peaceful, law-abiding Iraq, fully integrated into the international community … based on the rule of law, respect for human rights and economic freedom'. Noting, at the same time, that 'fundamental change' would be required for this to occur, the settled position was that 'when the circumstances were right, we would take practical steps to restore Iraq to its proper place in the region', and that 'pending such change, military measures ... would have to be at least tolerated'.[14]

The formal view of the British government post-9/11 was set out in a top secret Options Paper in March 2002. This reiterated New Labour's long-standing policy of reintegrating a territorially intact Iraq into the international community, noting that the only certain way of achieving this would be 'to invade and impose a new government', but also made clear that military action would need the express authorisation of the UN Security Council. Obtaining this, it observed, would require an Iraqi refusal to comply with UN weapons inspections, or 'incontrovertible' proof of 'large-scale' WMD activity.[15] While Blair insisted that no decisions on Iraq had yet been taken, and that it was 'complete rubbish' to suggest otherwise,[16] secret memos detailing top-level discussions between British and US officials during the spring point towards a rather different interpretation of events. Among their most prominent disclosures, Sir David Manning (Blair's main foreign policy adviser) recalled informing Condoleeza Rice (Bush's National Security Adviser) that the Prime Minister 'would not budge' in his support for regime change,[17] and Sir Christopher Meyer (the British ambassador to the US) detailed a meeting with Wolfowitz in which the Deputy Defense Secretary was informed that: 'We backed regime change, but the plan had to be clever and failure was not an option'.[18] The inference is also clear from notes of a meeting between Blair and Bush held in early April at the President's ranch at Crawford. Here it is recorded that the Prime Minister agreed to 'support military action to bring about regime change' on condition that efforts were made to revive the Arab–Israeli peace process and to pursue the issue of Iraqi WMD through the United Nations, a course of action that was deemed necessary to provide legal cover and build international support for the mission.[19] As Blair himself later concurred, '[t]he Americans are for regime change, we are for dealing with WMD. It is more a different way of expressing the same proposition'. The line taken at the Crawford meeting, then, was that while the UN process remained a political necessity, the Prime Minister would not be restricted by what, in the event, the United Nations would or would not decide. Thus, as Blair explained: 'If we tried the UN route and it failed, then my view was it had to be dealt with'. Or, as Manning put it:

> the Prime Minister was very clearly urging the President to adopt the UN route and a coalition strategy, but was absolutely prepared to say that, at the same time, he was willing to contemplate regime change if this didn't work.[20]

While the first of the 'Crawford Conditions' was soon undermined by Bush's support for a new wave of Israeli intervention in Palestine, and by the absence of any firm commitment to push through on the so-called 'roadmap' for peace in the Middle East, the British government continued to press ahead with plans to participate in an invasion of Iraq.[21] The political strategy for facilitating this was formalised at a top secret meeting at Downing Street in July and was made up of three components. The first of these was to focus attention on the issue of weapons of mass destruction, which was thought to be the most legally robust method of justifying regime change. While Foreign Office officials, along with the Attorney General, Lord Goldsmith, were keen to focus Blair's attention on the illegality of pursuing regime change per se (an opinion that Goldsmith noted was 'not terribly welcome'), the view recorded in the accompanying briefing paper was that if deposing Saddam could be presented as 'a necessary condition for controlling Iraqi WMD', then this would be a different matter altogether. Second, officials also highlighted the need for renewed UN weapons inspections as a means of providing legal cover and for springing a political trap, the hope being that 'an ultimatum could be cast in terms which Saddam would reject', thus providing a justification for military action. The third and final pillar of the government's strategy was the need for a concerted 'information campaign' in order to persuade public and international opinion as to the nature of the Iraqi threat, and hence of the need for stronger measures than those currently in place.[22]

But the nature of the Iraqi threat was far from clear-cut. According to the government's chief cipher of intelligence, the Joint Intelligence Committee, the available material on Iraqi WMD was 'patchy' and 'unclear', and contained 'very little evidence' of any unconventional weapons programmes. The general consensus, moreover, was that Saddam would only use WMD 'if his regime were threatened'.[23] Despite this, the main feature of the government's information campaign consisted of the publication, in September, of a now infamous dossier on Iraq's weapons of mass destruction that emphasised the danger in no uncertain terms.[24] Declaring that Iraq's possession of WMD had been 'established beyond doubt', and, most notably, that it could fire such weapons within 45 minutes, the dossier claimed that Iraq had 'existing and active military plans' for their use, and warned that the threat was 'serious and current'.[25]

We do not need a plan

While the political strategy for an invasion was proceeding apace, the issue of post-war planning remained an indeterminably grey area. For their part, at least, senior British officials had made no secret of the problem in their discussions with the Prime Minister. In the spring memos, Manning warned that Washington was giving insufficient consideration to the 'big questions' facing a post-war Iraq (such as 'what happens on the morning after?'), and Meyer pointed out that there was 'a black hole in American planning for the aftermath'.[26] The briefing paper for the Downing Street meeting in July also noted that 'little thought' had been given to 'the aftermath and how to shape it'.[27]

The reasons for this logistical deficit were not straightforward, and, like the drivers behind the invasion itself, were shaped by both new imperialist forces as well as more contingent factors. In the US a central feature of the post-war planning environment was that it was largely defined by intra-institutional and bureaucratic in-fighting between the Pentagon and the State Department. From October 2001, the latter had been engaged with a series of working groups in a comprehensive study and consultation exercise called the Future of Iraq Project. Although this never materialised into a practically implementable plan, the resulting documentation highlighted a range of expected difficulties and issues, and envisioned that a long occupation would be needed in order to construct and develop the kind of institutions required for a properly functioning democracy.[28] In the wake of 9/11, though, the institutional upper hand belonged to the Defense Department, where Rumsfeld and Wolfowitz (supported by Cheney) held rather different views. With the structural dynamics towards a quick, limited and high-tech intervention having been buoyed by its apparent successes in Kosovo and Afghanistan, the operating assumption here was that US troops would be welcomed as liberators, that the war would be over in a matter of months, and that a successful invasion would require no more than a middling quarter-of-a-million troops, a large proportion of which, it was thought, could be rapidly withdrawn once the conflict was over.[29] Also influential were concerns that the deployment of a larger force and the sustaining of a prolonged occupation would create an overtly imperial appearance and thereby exacerbate the dangers faced during the course of the invasion, resulting in higher costs, a loss of international support, greater anti-American sentiment and a dilution of focus and resources. Averse to any notion of becoming embroiled in a lengthy process of nation-building, the preferred choice of the Pentagon was to install a new Iraqi government comprised of high-profile exiles and to fund post-war stability measures out of Iraq's own oil revenues.[30]

The minimalist nature of post-war planning was exemplified by the establishment of the Office of Reconstruction and Humanitarian Assistance (ORHA), tasked with coordinating the rebuilding of Iraq's infrastructure and delivering humanitarian aid, a mere eight weeks before the invasion. Headed by the retired US General, Jay Garner, ORHA's ability to perform its designated function with any degree of effectiveness was hampered from the outset by political constraints, being placed under the tutelage of the Department of Defense and having limited access to resources and staff.[31] Here too, the overriding concern for a light military footprint was evident. A draft Mission Plan setting out the parameters for ORHA's field of work warned that a 'longer term occupation or heavy-handed post conflict activities would exacerbate anti-US feelings', and that '[t]his may in turn erode support for the global war on terrorism'. As such, what was needed, it maintained, was a rapid operation based on 'removing/reducing the levels of the US-led coalition "invading forces" as quickly as possible', and for coalition troops to 'be seen as a liberating force … whose prime purpose is to empower the Iraqi people to shape their own future'.[32]

Against this backdrop, in the autumn of 2002 General Sir Mike Jackson, Commander-in-Chief of the British army, dispatched Major General Tim Cross to the US to establish a clearer picture of the situation on post-war planning. What he found was deeply alarming. While military operations were now looking increasingly likely, the answers to basic questions, such as the means of reconstructing the Iraqi economy, and the form and goal of future political and legal structures, remained unanswered. With dissenting voices having been 'frozen out' by the Pentagon, the guiding assumption, as Cross recalled, was that 'everything would be fine once Saddam Hussein was toppled'; that 'following the invasion Iraq would emerge reasonably quickly as a stable democracy', allowing for the military commitment to be downsized in around six months. In short, he explained, 'there was no need for a long-term plan for reconstruction because the Iraqi people would reconstruct the nation'. In essence: '[t]he plan was, we do not need a plan'.[33]

The blasé and perfunctory optimism of the US, however, was not widely shared by British officials. According to Sir David Manning, the Pentagon view that a brief period of US military government would be automatically followed by 'a flowering … of democratic freedom' was no more than a 'neocon wishful thinking thesis', Peter Ricketts, the Director-General Political at the Foreign Office, similarly maintained that officials were 'very doubtful indeed about the neo con assumption that international forces would be welcomed as liberators', and Sir Michael Boyce, the Chief of the Defence Staff, warned that the US assumption that 'suddenly the following day [Iraq] would be a lovely democracy and everybody would be happy' was fatally flawed, and that troops would 'be lucky to get six hours worth of flowers and roses'.[34] Edward Chaplin, head of the Middle East department within the Foreign Office, summarised the situation thus. Pentagon officials, he said:

> had a touching faith that, once Iraq had been liberated from the terrible tyranny of Saddam Hussein, everyone would be grateful and dancing in the streets

and there would really be no further difficulty and the Iraqis would somehow magically take over and restore their state to the democratic state that it should be in. We tried to point out that that was extremely optimistic.[35]

By the same token, the Prime Minister was also purported to be anxious about the situation. Sally Morgan, Blair's former political secretary, maintained that the Prime Minister was 'tearing his hair out' over the issue, while Manning described him as having been 'very exercised' about his inability to influence the Pentagon.[36] Belying such apparent concerns, however, Whitehall itself performed no better than the US in devising effective reconstruction arrangements. While Chaplin subsequently described the British planning effort as having been 'pretty intense', and while Ricketts insisted that officials 'had been doing a lot of detailed planning' from Autumn 2002,[37] the principal organisation tasked with providing policy guidance on the practicalities of the post-war situation, the Iraq Planning Unit (later becoming the Iraq Policy Unit) was set up just eight weeks before the invasion. In similar fashion to ORHA, the Unit was also hampered by resourcing constraints, possessing no budget of its own and comprising just six members of staff at its inception.[38] The institutional wiring for the planning process more broadly was a source of some difficulty as well, with a lack of ministerial oversight and no routinised engagement from Cabinet level adding to the overall sense of discordancy. As Cross put it, there was 'no evidence of any particular planning for post-war operations', and no sense 'of who actually was overall leading us'. The whole effort, he remarked, 'wasn't being taken sufficiently seriously'.[39] In a similar fashion, preparations on the military side, too, were constrained by political factors. As Boyce attested, with ministers fearful that being seen to have given the green light for military operations would cause considerable political problems while the legal and diplomatic situations remained uncertain and ongoing, the need for secrecy concerning the plans meant that procurement and deployment processes were delayed. The specific details of the planning, he explained, were restricted 'to a very small group' of officials 'in order not to give any signals … that we were doing overt military planning while the UN negotiations were going on'.[40] Purporting to have been 'anxious to make sure people did not think there was an inevitability about this', Blair himself concurred that senior political officials did not want to make the planning process visible 'for fear of triggering an assumption that we were actually going to do military action irrespective of what was going to be happening at the United Nations'.[41]

In sum, preparations for the war and its aftermath were noticeably and disturbingly thin on every level. Admonishing those responsible, Cross lamented that there had been no clearly accepted 'end state' in Whitehall concerning post-war Iraq, and no coherence or consensus on what the government wanted to achieve. Blair, he said, had bluntly failed to 'understand the scope and complexity of what was going to be needed in the aftermath of an invasion', as well as 'what the possible consequences could be'.[42] Sir Christopher Meyer was harshly critical too. A main source of the problem, he averred, was not just that Number 10 had failed to challenge the US on the issue, but that it had allowed itself to be consumed by 'an intoxicating brew' of its own perceived geopolitical influence. Government officials, he chided, became 'so carried away by the mission' that they failed to scrutinise the 'hard details of postwar planning'.[43] But in this, domestic pressures were also crucial. With political attentions during this period being dominated by concerns about the management of public and parliamentary opinion involving the war, any anxieties about the state of US planning remained distinctly second in order of priority. According to Peter Mandelson, one of the architects of New Labour and one of Blair's closest political confidants, the Prime Minister had been fully aware of the inadequacy of the post-war arrangements but had taken the view that the issue was 'chiefly America's responsibility, not ours'.[44] Or, as Dominick Chilcott, the head of the Iraq Policy Unit, put it, the situation was that 'we had much bigger things to worry about'.[45]

The government's defence of its post-war arrangements, amidst sustained criticism in the wake of the conflict, was based on a mixture of denial and attempts to shift the responsibility onto the idiosyncrasies of the Bush administration. According to Manning the US had simply kept ministers in the dark 'about the way post-war Iraq was going to be run', while Geoff Hoon claimed that the government had been thrown off-balance by the interpersonal relationships and internal politicking within Washington, the key feature of which was that Cheney had turned out to have been the most important actor in the decision-making process, and that this fact had simply been missed by British officials.[46] Blair's own view, however, was unequivocal in its lack of remorse. As he maintained, 'I was not concerned about the lack of preparation' for post-war affairs, and on the basis of what was known at the time the state of the government's post-war planning was 'perfectly sensible', and its institutional machinery 'perfectly adequate'.[47]

A new type of war

Following the publication of the September dossier, which failed singularly in its attempt to persuade public opinion of the need for military action, officials began pressing ahead with the remaining elements of the strategy

53

determined at July's Downing Street meeting. In November a new round of United Nations weapons inspections was initiated under the terms of UN resolution 1441. The provisions of this, requiring a diplomatic fudge in the face of Security Council divisions between the adventurist US/British pairing and a more cautious French, German and Russian alliance, stated that Iraqi non-compliance would result in the Council being called on to 'consider' (rather than 'decide') what further action to take, a consciously vague form of words that led to divergent interpretations about the extent to which the resolution provided the necessary legal authority to use military force.[48] The government's argument of choice on the matter, namely that the use of force would be justified by pre-existing UN resolutions (the so-called 'revival argument'), was also problematic. In the opinion of the Attorney General, this position would only stand up to scrutiny if there was demonstrable hard evidence of Iraqi non-compliance and non-cooperation with the inspections, and that, as such, a second UN resolution providing explicit and unambiguous authority for military action would be 'the safest legal course'.[49]

At the end of January 2003, with the inspections process failing to make any significant headway, Bush and Blair convened for a summit at the White House to discuss the situation. With Blair emphasising the necessity for having 'international cover' in the event of war, the decision was formally taken to pursue a second UN resolution, though on this the President's acquiescence remained heavily caveated, leaving the Prime Minister under no illusion that military action would ensue whether a further resolution was secured or not. The expectations of the two leaders about the results of the forthcoming invasion were also highly sanguine. The prevailing belief was that the war would be over in a matter of days, that the transition to a new regime would be achieved within a short period, and that all this would take place amidst a propitious post-war environment in which there was 'unlikely to be any internecine warfare between the different religious and ethnic groups'. In this light, discussions on post-war planning remained brief. Any concerns that Blair may have been harbouring were effectively assuaged by Condoleeza Rice, who informed him that the Defense Department 'was looking at all aspects' of the situation, and that it 'would deploy to Iraq to direct operations as soon as the military action was over'.[50]

But the attempt to secure a second resolution faltered in the face of concerted opposition within the Security Council to terminating the inspections before they had been given sufficient time to yield results. With the UN process crumbling, in February the government pushed out a further dossier, seeking this time to bolster public opinion in favour of tougher measures by outlining Iraq's human rights abuses as well as its record of obfuscation and concealment in respect of the weapons issue. The move backfired in spectacular fashion, however, when it was discovered that extensive parts of the dossier had been blatantly plagiarised from an academic article based on a 12-year-old Ph.D. thesis, leaving the government's position perspicuously weakened.[51] Nevertheless, Blair remained undeterred in his use of humanitarian and moral assertions as a means of justifying what had, by now, become a virtually inevitable course of action. Denying that efforts to promote the global spread of freedom and democracy were an attempt to construct a world order based around 'Western values',[52] the Prime Minister proclaimed that while the moral imperative 'was not the reason we act … it is the reason, frankly, why if we do have to act, we should do so with a clear conscience'.[53] Accompanying this were assertions designed to legitimise the invasion by embedding the issue of Iraq within the broader framework of the war on terror. Warning that the future convergence of WMD, international terrorism and rogue states presaged the emergence of a unique and unparalleled threat, Blair insisted that Britain was now involved in 'a new type of war, fought in a different way by different means', and that, as such, a new and novel response was required. '[T]hese are new times', he implored: 'New threats need new measures'.[54] Flowing from this, invariably, were also warnings about the need for credibility. Alleging that any refusal to take action, having now set the stakes at the highest possible level, would serve to strengthen Saddam and embolden other potentially deviant regimes, the Prime Minister declared that Iraq was 'the test of whether we treat the threat seriously', that 'it was dangerous if such regimes disbelieve us', and that the issue was about 'sending a signal to the whole of the world'.[55]

Providing a backdrop to this discursive framing was a series of high-profile events that formed an ongoing reminder of the realities of the terror threat. Amongst these, the bombing of a nightclub in Bali in October 2002 may have been the most destructive, killing more than two hundred people, but a variety of other incidents all, in various ways, underscored the danger. These included actual threats, such as an al-Qaeda attack on a hotel and aircraft in Kenya in November 2002; potential threats, graphically illustrated by the conviction of the attempted 'shoe bomber', Richard Reid, in January 2003; and illusory threats, a category which itself varied from the precautionary stop and search of a cargo ship in the English Channel in December 2002 (the 'deadly' contents of which turned out to be sugar), to the politically suspect, such as the deployment of tanks and troops at Heathrow airport in February 2003, and, most notably, the wrongly proclaimed discovery of ricin at a North London flat the month before. Regardless of its veracity, the latter episode was nonetheless seized on by Blair as a clear illustration of the apparent dangers posed by Saddam Hussein. In a discussion of the incident on the BBC's *Newsnight* programme, and contrary to the views of the intelligence agencies, the Prime Minister declared that 'it would not be correct to say there is no evidence linking Al Qaeda and Iraq'.[56]

For all this, the principal justification for going to war remained centred on the issue of WMD. As was noted in the July strategy meeting, this offered the safest legal route to securing regime change, since the removal of Saddam Hussein could be presented as a necessary measure to secure the goal of disarmament. As Blair explained: 'If the only means of achieving the disarmament of Iraq of weapons of mass destruction is the removal of the regime, then the removal of the regime has to be our objective'.[57] But political and legal tensions on the matter remained fraught. For one, with the attempt to gain a second UN resolution facing certain defeat, the legal basis for any invasion was by no means secure. Moreover, with senior military figures threatening to disobey an order to attack without unequivocal legal clearance, the need for clarity was now imperative.[58] At the midnight hour, just three days before the commencement of military action, the Attorney General brought deliverance. Having since taken advice on the content and merits of his earlier opinion that a second resolution would probably be required, Lord Goldsmith now presented a new and more assertive view in which it was stated that the provisions of resolution 1441 were a sufficient legal basis on which to mount military action after all.[59] With the legal ballast in place, the Prime Minister, now blaming French intransigence for the failure to secure a second resolution, moved to face his final political hurdle in the form of a parliamentary vote on committing troops to action. Having been forced to concede this under intense pressure from the Labour backbenches, the full might of the party machine, along with the support of Conservative MPs, proved vital to securing a successful outcome. Prefaced by the resignation of the ex-Foreign Secretary, Robin Cook, and provoking a huge backbench rebellion involving around one-third of all Labour MPs (139 in total), the vote may have bestowed a legitimacy of sorts upon military action, but it remained clear that the roots of political support for war were far from deep.[60]

Strategic failure

Within hours of the Parliamentary vote, on 19 March 2003, the invasion of Iraq began. Presented by Blair as a war of 'liberation not conquest',[61] the initial conflict, led overwhelmingly by the US but also involving troops from Australia, Poland and Britain (with a contingent of some

46,000 personnel) was rapidly over. Within a month Iraq's governing regime had collapsed, an outcome achieved with fewer casualties and with less regional disturbance than many had predicted.[62] For the most part, domestic political turbulence was also avoided. Notwithstanding the belated resignation in May of the International Development Secretary, Clare Short, the majority of parliamentary and public opinion now fell in behind the war effort. After less than six weeks of fighting, on 1 May, Bush announced the official end to 'major combat operations'. On the same day Rumsfeld declared that the US had reached a similar point in Afghanistan, announcing a move 'from major combat activity to a period of stability and stabilization and reconstruction activities'.[63] But such optimism proved to be fatally premature and events in both theatres soon took a decidedly sharp turn for the worse. In Iraq, the demise of Saddam's regime was followed by a swift descent into chaos and anarchy, replete with widespread looting, crime and the disintegration of government structures. To this, though, the official reaction was one of complacency and nonchalance. Rumsfeld's proclamation that freedom was a messy business in which 'stuff happens',[64] was mirrored by the response from Geoff Hoon, who claimed that the looting was merely a case of citizens 'liberating items from the regime' and 'redistributing that wealth among the Iraqi people'.[65]

These incipient tensions were merely a foretaste of what was to come. While the rapid success of the initial invasion was seen to further vindicate the new imperialist approach to warfare, the scale of troops on the ground proved to be pitiably insufficient for providing any form of meaningful security for the post-war reconstruction and humanitarian effort.[66] Furthermore, the heavy-handed and distant approach taken by US forces served to antagonise and alienate many Iraqis from the outset, as did the distorted and contradictory priorities of the post-conflict arrangements. In one symbolic instance, US troops were tasked to defend the oil ministry in Baghdad while allowing the nearby Iraqi national museum, an internationally renowned repository of ancient Mesopotamian artefacts, to be casually ransacked. The British position in all of this was scarcely any better. Indeed, even the logistics for supplying appropriate war materiel were proving to be deeply flawed, with only 10% of decontamination systems for use in the event of a chemical or biological weapons attack having arrived by the start of hostilities.[67] As the absence of firm planning and adequate security led to deteriorating conditions on the ground, tensions between government officials and the armed forces also began to emerge. As Blunkett observed: 'The military ... were insisting that their job was to fight the war, and not to police the area and protect the citizens or vital equipment'.[68]

To make matters worse, for bureaucratic and security reasons the main agency responsible for the humanitarian and reconstruction effort, ORHA, was itself unable to enter Iraq until 12 days after the collapse of the Iraqi regime, by which time the process of disintegration was already well under way. Along with this, within a matter of days Jay Garner had been unceremoniously dumped as head of the Organisation, being replaced on Presidential fiat by Paul Bremer, who rapidly assumed a position in charge of the newly established Coalition Provisional Authority (CPA), which superseded ORHA in April. Bremer's first actions as the effective viceroy in Iraq were also instructive. At Washington's behest (and as Rumsfeld put it, regardless of any 'administrative inconvenience' that it might cause),[69] CPA Order #1, issued on 16 May, initiated a process of de-Ba'athification designed to purge Iraqi society of the remaining elements of Saddam's regime. CPA Order #2, issued a week later, announced the formal disbanding of the 400,000-strong Iraqi army, many of whom subsequently re-emerged to confront the coalition presence as part of a growing insurgency.[70] While Bremer himself remained critical of the postwar situation, contending that the number of troops on the ground would need to be doubled in order to provide the necessary level of security, the justification for the disbanding was that the Iraqi army had by now effectively ceased to exist, and that it was, in any event, irredeemably corrupt and institutionally dysfunctional.[71] Bremer's approach to the economic and political restructuring of Iraq also caused controversy. The introduction of liberalisation measures from June triggered the onset of an enforced and destabilising wave of privatisation in an attempt to rapidly convert the command mechanisms of the Saddam era into a flourishing free market economy. While this provided lucrative opportunities for Western (and primarily US) corporations, the results, a further morass of bedlam, corruption and incompetence, brought little if any benefit to the domestic population. At the same time, while plans devised by Garner for the holding of rapid elections were now deemed to be practically impossible given the lack of an electoral register, clearly defined voting rules and properly constituted political parties, the Pentagon's preference for appointing exiles to key governing positions was also rejected by Bremer on the grounds that the legitimacy of any new regime would depend on its leaders being properly representative.[72] That said, the remaining alternative; namely, the adoption of longer-term and more substantive measures, was also wholly unattractive. Not only did this run contrary to the new imperialist tenets of a rapid and limited incursion, but it also required a commodity that was now in increasingly short supply: time.

Demonstrating this, civil discontent grew steadily throughout the summer, being fuelled by the slow pace of post-war reconstruction, an absence of basic amenities and rising levels of crime and unemployment.

Accompanying this, the deteriorating security situation was marked by a series of high-profile and highly violent incidents, including a truck bomb attack on the UN headquarters in Baghdad that prompted the agency to withdraw from Iraq altogether. By October, less than six months after major combat operations had been officially declared over, two-thirds of the population of the Iraqi capital had settled on a view of US troops as occupiers rather than liberators (up from 46% in April), and figures from other parts of the country were even higher. The same problem was also affecting British operations. In Basra, Iraq's second city and the key point for Britain's involvement, no fewer than three-quarters of local residents regarded troops as an occupying force, up from 52% in the immediate aftermath of the invasion.[73]

The unfolding sense of disaster was captured in a series of warnings sent to the Prime Minister by senior diplomatic and military officials. In a damning report from the Prime Minister's special representative to Iraq, John Sawers, ORHA was described as nothing less than a complete disaster. It was, he said, 'an unbelievable mess': 'No leadership. No strategy. No co-ordination. No structure'. In similarly prescient warnings, General Sir Mike Jackson (now Chief of the General Staff) cautioned that coalition forces had around one hundred days in which to win or lose the peace, and Major General Albert Whitley, Britain's most senior officer with US forces in Iraq, denounced the post-war arrangements as having been based on 'the supposition that just because this was a liberation then all was going to be fine', and predicted that there was now a very real risk of 'strategic failure'.[74] Sir Jeremy Greenstock (Britain's envoy to the post-war administration in Baghdad) was also sharply critical. Describing the post-war plans as 'woefully inadequate', Greenstock later maintained that there was no evidence to suggest that the coalition 'ever analysed correctly the resources that needed to be put into security and the primary importance that there was in securing the territory of Iraq after the invasion was over'.[75] Outlining the situation in Basra, Sir Hilary Synnott, the head of the CPA in Southern Iraq from July 2003 to January 2004, was equally scathing. 'There was a complete absence of any plan', he lambasted, and 'everything had to be created from nothing but against a background where it was not clear what the task was'.[76]

The wrong sort of aftermath

The official response to the unfolding disaster was marked by a blunt refusal to accept any responsibility for the course of events, and by an inability even to face up to the reality of what was happening. Instead, the formally stated line was that the ongoing violence was being driven not by disaffected members of the Iraqi populace but by an amalgam of Saddamists and Islamic radicals from outside the country, and that the current difficulties were due not to any lack of forethought and preparation on the part of the coalition, but to the fact that the post-war situation had developed in a wholly unexpected and unpredictable way. Paul Bremer, for instance, maintained that the problem was that the US had 'planned for the wrong contingency', and Rumsfeld insisted that there had been 'extensive' planning for a humanitarian emergency, but that 'because the war was so fast, it didn't happen'. At the same time, the Defense Secretary also rejected growing calls for a greater military presence to deal with the security situation, claiming that commanders on the ground did not believe that extra troops were needed, and, perversely, that sending extra troops would only make matters worse by antagonising the local population.[77] While Bremer accused policy-makers in Washington of indulging in 'wishful thinking' about the situation, Rumsfeld insisted that '[o]ur goal should be to ... find ways to put less stress on our forces, enabling us to reduce the US role', and that the US should not be involved in the provision of security and reconstruction. It was, he said, 'the responsibility of the Iraqi people to take control of their country and to provide the kind of security and stability and an environment that's hospitable to economic recovery and political recovery'.[78]

The same approach was evident on the British side. Here, Jack Straw claimed that the problems in Iraq had been due to the unexpectedly rapid collapse of Saddam's regime, which, simply put, had occurred 'more quickly than was anticipated'. The working assumption, he explained, had been that 'there would be quite a long, protracted military phase', and that Iraqi forces 'would be better organised, have better command and control and put up much more of a fight than they did'.[79] Similar points were made by Sir Kevin Tebbit, Permanent Secretary at the Ministry of Defence, who claimed that the emergence of post-war turmoil was simply unexpected and had 'surprised everybody', and by Blair's Chief of Staff, Jonathan Powell, who later claimed that Britain had prepared 'for the wrong sort of aftermath', having focused on the provision of humanitarian relief rather than counter-insurrection measures.[80] Geoff Hoon, too, indulged the confessional mood. Claiming that the sheer speed of the military advance had allowed insurgents and al-Qaeda to link-up behind coalition lines, the Defence Secretary explained that the main problem was that 'we didn't plan for the right sort of aftermath' and conceded, in retrospect, that: 'Maybe we were too optimistic about the idea of the streets being lined with cheering people'.[81] Ploughing the same furrow, Sir David Manning admitted that the immediate post-war situation had been

'a failure' and conceded that the government had been 'over-optimistic …
about the powers of this place to regenerate itself'.[82] The image presented
by Blair, on the other hand, was one of calm omnipotence. Proclaiming
that some degree of disorder was 'inevitable', the Prime Minister benignly
explained that: 'Just as we had a strategy for war, so we have a strategy
for peace'.[83] Thus:

> This was never going to be a situation where you could just go in, invade a
> country, topple the Government and walk away afterwards. And, therefore, I
> don't think it is the least surprising that the withdrawal will take some time.[84]

Such claims, of course, were less than ingenuous. Firstly, and as has been
well documented, the entirety of US and British war planning had been
based on assumptions of a swift military campaign and a quick withdrawal
of military force.[85] In addition, the increasing scale of the insurgency was
at this point being fuelled not by external elements but by a rising sense
of alienation and disquiet amongst Iraqis themselves, and the government
had hardly suffered from a shortage of advice on the likely difficulties
that would be faced during the post-war period. Indeed, while Tim Cross
purported to have been 'struck by the years of neglect' and by the fact
that Iraq was in 'a lot worse condition than I had anticipated' (being
'held together by chicken wire and chewing gum)',[86] the poor state of the
Iraqi infrastructure should not have come as that much of a surprise. As
Hilary Synnott pointed out, '[s]ince we had done much to weaken Iraq's
infrastructure and institutions as a result of twelve years of sanctions, we
should have expected the unexpected'.[87] Belying Blair's claims that everything was proceeding exactly as planned, then, a closer approximation
to the real state of affairs was that recounted by Greenstock. As he put
it, 'I don't think he [Blair] wanted to analyse fully in his own mind the
consequences' of what had been done, and his response to the post-war
disorder had been that of a political ostrich: to stick his head in the sand
and hope that 'surely this has got to go right at some point'.[88]

Alongside the onset of an increasingly vicious insurgency, a second key
theme of the initial post-war period was the growing political controversy
over the absence of WMD. Central to this in Britain were media allegations, arising principally from the BBC, about the government's misuse
of intelligence material in the run-up to the invasion, chiefly focusing on
the construction of the 2002 September dossier, which prompted both
the Foreign Affairs Committee (FAC) and the Intelligence and Security
Committee (ISC) to launch inquiries into the issue.[89] The government's
response to this turn of events was twofold. The first, moving to restrict
the capacities of the FAC inquiry by denying it access to documents and
senior officials, proved to be partially successful. Although public opinion remained deeply sceptical about the government's actions preceding

the war, and while both inquiries strongly criticised its use of intelligence material, both nonetheless cleared it of engaging in the wilful misuse of intelligence for political gain.[90]

The second strand of the government's post-war management strategy was to counter the allegations by deliberately misrepresenting them. While the real gap between the actual intelligence and that presented to the public had emerged through the judicious removal of its accompanying caveats and qualifications, the government sought to frame the allegations as constituting a claim that officials (particularly Alastair Campbell and Tony Blair) had deliberately 'inserted' false intelligence into the dossier. With the BBC duly refusing to yield to government demands for it to apologise, and with a public refutation of the charge unable to be secured, officials were forced to adopt a different approach. At the end of June, Dr David Kelly, a government expert on WMD who had discussed Iraq with the main BBC journalist responsible for the story, confessed to the Ministry of Defence that he may well have been the source for the allegations, but denied having made any claims about the misuse of intelligence. Believing that the BBC had therefore misrepresented Kelly, officials in Downing Street began to try and discredit the story by finding a way in which this information could be made publicly available. This was achieved when journalists, following a series of broad hints from government figures, accurately identified Kelly as being the BBC's source. The scientist's outing, though, produced anything but the desired effect. Under intense pressure, in mid-July Kelly committed suicide, leading to the establishment of a high-profile inquiry into his death, conducted by Lord Hutton, which ran throughout the rest of the year. The eventual publication of the Hutton report in January 2004 cleared the government of improper conduct in the affair, but the widespread perception was that its utterly one-sided conclusions were nothing short of a whitewash. With the political air having thus yet to be cleared, and with the government coming under fresh pressure following a US decision to hold an inquiry into the state of the pre-war intelligence, ministers found themselves compelled to initiate a similar review, being headed by Lord Butler, in an attempt to regain some element of control over the political agenda.[91]

Running parallel to these events, both US and British officials also sought to dull the increasingly sharp barbs of criticism surrounding the Iraq war by discursively framing it as a fight for democratic freedom, and by embedding it within the broader justificatory framework of the war on terror. As Bush put it, the creation of an Iraqi democracy would be 'a watershed event in the global democratic revolution', that would set an example to the entire region and serve to 'undermine the ideologies of terror and hatred'. The US, he declared, had a 'mission to promote liberty around the world', and Iraq was now 'a central front, a new front in the war on terror'.[92] For Blair, the historical epic was cut from the same quixotic cloth. Asserting that Iraq was 'another act' in the global drama triggered by 9/11 and that 'many further struggles will be set upon this stage before it's over', the Prime Minister sought to legitimise the war by reasserting the uniqueness of the present situation. As he exclaimed, the threat from international terrorism was 'sometimes hard for people to understand, because it's of such a different nature than the threats we have faced before'. On this platform was also mounted a strident defence of the special relationship between Britain and the US, and hence of the more unipolar direction that New Labour's foreign policy had now taken. Proclaiming that Iraq had become 'the battleground on which this battle, in respect of terrorism, is being fought out', Blair declared that it was the 'destiny' of the US to ensure the spread of freedom, and that it was Britain's 'job' to support them in this endeavour.[93]

A long, hard slog

The momentum behind the insurgency in Iraq, which had been building progressively since the summer of 2003, sharpened dramatically during the spring and summer of 2004. To this, government officials once more displayed a marked refusal to acknowledge the reality of the situation, and remained adamant that the uprising remained the preserve of Saddamists and external terrorist elements, even though the dynamics of the insurgency had failed to improve following the capture of Saddam Hussein in December. As David Blunkett insisted, the insurgency was a 'loose, franchise network that constitutes al Qaeda', the composition of which was 'very substantially not Iraqis but people from outside the country'.[94] According to Jack Straw, the insurgency was made up of extremists from outside Iraq, along with 'former regime elements and some fanatics'.[95] Moreover, while the Foreign Secretary later acknowledged that 'the greater part of the insurgency stems from Iraqi groups and individuals', he continued to maintain that 'evidence does not suggest a popular insurgency across the country', insisting that 'most attacks in Iraq are still the work of elements of the former regime'.[96]

Alongside this, Blair also sought to step up the discursive positioning of Iraq as part of the broader war on terror. Seeking to draw a line under the controversy surrounding the invasion by rebranding the current turmoil as a 'new Iraqi conflict', he endeavoured to frame the war as a fight for democratic values, proclaiming, following a handover of formal (although not de facto) sovereignty to a new Iraqi government in June, that the only side to be on was 'the side of liberty and democracy'. Iraq, he said, had now become 'the crucible in which the future of this global terrorism will be determined'.[97] The government's commitment to Iraq's newly established democracy, though, was not unconditional, and remained tempered by geopolitical concerns. In particular, the need to uphold a unified Iraq and to avoid any potentially destabilising form of secessionism remained paramount. As Peter Ricketts explained, '[w]e were clear about the importance of territorial integrity for Iraq, that we did not want to see Iraq come apart with an independent Kurdish state being formed'.[98] Or, as Jack Straw put it, while the transplanting of democracy may have been the desired end, 'there are some outcomes – outcomes that would lead to a change in the territorial integrity of Iraq – that would be unacceptable'.[99]

Two other main themes permeated the question of Iraq during the summer of 2004. One of these was a progressive backsliding from Bush and Blair on the issue of weapons of mass destruction. In contrast to the certainty with which the existence of Iraqi WMD was initially asserted, both leaders now began to move into ever more tangential fields of reasoning, their justifications for the invasion centring instead on claims about Saddam's involvement in WMD-related programmes, and, following publication of the final report of the Iraq Survey Group in September (which definitively concluded that Iraq had possessed no WMD prior to the start of the war), Saddam's intentions regarding Iraq's future accumulation of such weapons once sanctions had been lifted.[100] The second motif of the period reprised the issue of the government's pre-war use of intelligence. In July both Washington and London were cleared of misusing intelligence material by their respective inquiries into the matter, although the report of the Butler review, while claiming to have found 'no evidence of deliberate distortion or of culpable negligence' on the part of the British government, remained highly critical not only of the intelligence, but of the processes that had been used for its assessment and presentation as well as the style of New Labour policy-making more generally.[101] True to the point, Blair's peroration on the report reasserted the government's misrepresentation of the initial allegations. Claiming that Lord Butler had shown that '[n]o-one inserted things into the dossier against the advice of the intelligence services', the Prime Minister insisted that everyone involved had 'genuinely tried to do their best in good faith'. The mantra that was subsequently adopted was that officials had now been cleared of any wrongdoing by no fewer than four independent inquiries.[102]

As conditions in Iraq were deteriorating, so too were matters in Afghanistan. By this time the arm's-length approach taken to the deposing of the Taliban regime was also proving to have been wholly incompatible with the establishment of post-war stability. With per capita levels of reconstruction funding remaining lower than those for comparable post-conflict situations, and with the structure of aid and reconstruction programmes recycling the majority of these funds to UN agencies, international financial institutions and non-government organisations, the position of the central Afghan government *vis-a-vis* local power-holders throughout the rest of the country (and hence its ability to command authority on a nationwide scale), remained weak.[103] Although full control of the peacekeeping force had by August been passed over to NATO (now acting in its first 'out of area' operation), prospects for an improvement in the security and humanitarian situation were also undermined by the new imperialist approach of outsourcing the provision of law and order. Designed to avoid a deeper, longer and more costly commitment from the US, the strategy merely served to entrench the power of militias and regional warlords, many, if not all of whom, were wholly antithetical to notions of human rights and democratic governance.[104]

Belying public statements of progress in the broader war on terror, with Bush claiming that the US was progressively 'dismantling the al Qaeda network', and with the FBI Director, Robert Mueller, asserting that the war had reached a 'turning of the tide', actual indicators of success were proving difficult to find here as well.[105] By the end of 2004 the costs of the Afghan and Iraq wars themselves were already telling. In addition to the 1,335 US military personnel and the 75 British troops to have lost their lives, the number of civilian deaths was currently estimated to be higher than this by several orders of magnitude, while the financial cost, now standing at £5.5 billion for Britain and around $209 billion for the US, was also rising far beyond expected limits.[106] Anxieties about the current status of the campaign within Washington, too, were increasing. In a leaked memo from Rumsfeld, the Defense Secretary confided that 'we lack metrics to know if we are winning or losing the global war on terror', that the results by any measure were 'mixed', and that the US was facing 'a long, hard slog' in Afghanistan and Iraq.[107]

Worse still, while much of this had been due to the switching of attention and resources away from Afghanistan in the pursuit of regime change in Iraq, the strategic diversion was now also bearing a bitter fruit, with the invasion of Iraq having given the Taliban and al-Qaeda the breathing space needed to regroup and reorganise. Some three years after being removed from power, the Taliban were now mounting an escalating series of attacks on coalition and government forces in Afghanistan, while al-Qaeda had taken advantage of the opportunity to leach out into the porous border region with Pakistan, morphing from a loosely hierarchical organisation with a well-defined structure into a decentralised and deterritorialised franchise model. Indeed, the ideology and style of al-Qaeda, its global 'terror brand', were now inspiring a variety of replicant groups and plots around the world, notable instances of which included the Bali bomb of October 2002 and the Madrid bombings of March 2004.[108] According to the International Institute of Strategic Studies, while the al-Qaeda of mid-2004 remained 'just as dangerous' as its pre-9/11 incarnation, the network had now become 'even more difficult to combat', an analysis similar to that produced by the Oxford Research Group, which claimed that al-Qaeda remained 'active and effective, drawing on a stronger support base and mounting a higher intensity of attacks than before 11th September'.[109] While the official view of the government was, as Jack Straw insisted, that the impact of the Iraq war on the terrorist threat had been 'completely benign', the FAC also concluded that 'the war against terrorism is far from being won', and warned that al-Qaeda remained 'a serious threat' that 'may have grown more difficult to tackle in the years since 11 September 2001 owing to the fragmentation of groups and individuals' associated with it.[110] On this point, the statistical evidence was also impossible to ignore. A comparative analysis from the World Markets Research Centre showed that Britain now stood joint tenth in a global index of terrorist attacks, notably far ahead of its erstwhile opponents to the war in Iraq, France and Germany, which were ranked 23rd and 41st respectively.[111]

Conclusion

As the new imperialist strategy of the US reached its apogee in the invasion of Iraq, so the conditions for a light and limited intervention to which it gave rise lit the touchpaper for its eventual unravelling. With expectations of a pain-free and rapid transition to free market democracy having produced little in the way of post-war planning, and with security arrangements proving to be wholly ineffectual, the collapse of the Iraqi regime was followed by an outbreak of chaos and discontent, leading to the emergence of an increasingly violent insurgency. At the same time, while intra-European splits over the invasion had undermined the precepts of the transatlantic bridge strategy, growing political controversy over the war, due not least to the absence of WMD, also fuelled domestic political disquiet, prompting efforts to bolster support for the conflict by discursively embedding it within the broader thematic framework of the war on terror. But signs of success in this were also proving hard to find. To a significant degree, this was a direct result of the Iraq war itself. Having diverted attention and resources away from Afghanistan, the pursuit of regime change in Iraq had now provided the Taliban and al-Qaeda with the breathing space needed to reorganise and regroup. The consequences would prove to be catastrophic.

Notes

1 P. Wintour, 'Defence chiefs warn Blair over Afghan mission', *Guardian*, 18 December 2001.
2 Blunkett (2006), p. 341.
3 'Commitment to Afghanistan "open-ended"', *Daily Telegraph*, 19 March 2002; N. Watt, '"No exit" fear for troops in Afghanistan', Guardian, 21 March 2002.
4 www.CNN.com, 'Report: "Bin Laden was within our grasp"', 29 November 2001.
5 Press conference with Tommy Franks, 28/12/01.
6 White House press conference, 13 March 2002.
7 State of the Union Address, 29 January 2002.
8 On the foreign policy approach of the Bush administration, see McCrisken (2009, 2010). On these issues also see George Bush, speech to the UN General Assembly, 12 September 2002; and at the Hilton Hotel, Washington, 26 February 2003; Interview with Wolfowitz, *Vanity Fair*, 9 May 2003; BBC News, 'Rice calls for Mid-East democracy', 20 June 05; Wishnick (2002); Feith (2008).
9 Feith (2008), p. 15.
10 Woodward (2002), p. 83.
11 Interview with *Vanity Fair*, 9 May 2003.
12 Downing Street monthly news conference, 16 March 2006.
13 *Fern Britton meets* ..., BBC1, 12 December 2009.
14 'Iraq: New Policy Framework', Memo. John Sawers to Sherard Cowpers-Coles, 7 March 2001.
15 'Iraq: Options Paper', Overseas and Defence Secretariat, Cabinet Office, 8 March 2002.
16 *The Blair Years*, BBC1, 25 November 2007.
17 Memo. from Manning to Blair, 14 March 2002.
18 Memo. from Meyer to Manning, 18 March 2002.
19 'Iraq: Conditions for Military Action', Cabinet Office briefing paper (July 2002), reproduced in the *Sunday Times*, 12 June 2005.
20 Evidence to the Chilcot inquiry from Tony Blair, 29 January 2010, and David Manning, 30 November 2009. The same point was also made during the evidence from Sir Christopher Meyer, 26 November 2009.
21 Meyer (2005), pp. 244–5.
22 'Iraq: Conditions for Military Action'; also see evidence from Lord Goldsmith to the Chilcot inquiry, 27 January 2010.
23 See Butler (2004), paras.5.2–5.4 and Annex B; also see Intelligence and Security Committee (2003), paras 58–63. Similar views were held by intelligence agencies in the US. See Senate Committee on Intelligence (2004).
24 On this see Kettell (2006), pp. 71–9; also see Kettell (2008).
25 See HMG (2002).
26 Memo. Manning to Blair, 14 March 2002; *No Plan No Peace*, BBC1, 7 October 2007.
27 'Iraq: Conditions for Military Action'.
28 See Bremer (2006), p. 25; Feith (2008), pp. 375–8; Synnott (2008), Chapter 10.

29 Bowman (2003); Bello (2005), p. 62; Feith (2008), p. 218; T. Reid, 'War on Saddam will be over fast, says Rumsfeld', *The Times*, 16 November 2002; also see 'Bush's War', Frontline, www.pbs.org/wgbh/pages/frontline/bushswar/, accessed 9 November 2010.

30 See D. Reiff. 'Blueprint for a mess', *New York Times*, 2 November 2003; Feith (2008), Chapters 9–12 and passim.

31 *No Plan No Peace*, BBC1, 7 October 2007; also see Bremer (2006), p. 24.

32 Draft Unified Mission Plan, April 2003.

33 *No Plan No Peace*, BBC1, 7 October 2007; Evidence to the Chilcot inquiry, 7 December 2009.

34 *No Plan No Peace*, BBC1, 7 October 2007; Evidence to the Chilcot inquiry from Sir David Manning, 30 November 2009; from Sir Michael Boyce, 3 December 2009; and from Peter Ricketts, 1 December 2009.

35 Evidence to the Chilcot inquiry, 1 December 2009.

36 N. Watt, 'Blair knew US had no post-war plan for Iraq', *Observer*, 17 June 2007; J. Ware, 'Blair was warned of looming disaster in Iraq', *Daily Telegraph*, 28 October 2007.

37 Evidence to the Chilcot inquiry from Edward Chaplin, 1 December 2009, and from Peter Ricketts, 1 December 2009.

38 Jack Straw, answer to Parliamentary question, *Hansard*, 10 June 2003, col. 795.

39 Evidence to the Chilcot inquiry, 7 December 2009.

40 Evidence to the Chilcot inquiry, 3 December 2009.

41 Evidence to the Chilcot inquiry from Tony Blair, 29 January 2010,

42 H. Kingstone, 'Toppled in Baghdad, clueless in Whitehall', *Sunday Times*, 21 October 2007.

43 Interview for Frontline, 20 December 2007, www.pbs.org/wgbh/pages/frontline/shows/blair/interviews/meyer.html.

44 N. Watt, 'Blair knew US had no post-war plan for Iraq', *Observer*, 17 June 2007.

45 Evidence to the Chilcot inquiry, 8 December 2009.

46 P. Wintour, 'Hoon admits fatal errors in planning for post-war Iraq', *Guardian*, 2 May 2007; G. Hurst, 'Washington "misled" Blair over plans for post-war Iraq', *The Times*, 13 September 2007.

47 Evidence to the Liaison Committee, 18/6/07, Q. 177; Evidence to the Chilcot inquiry, 29 January 2010.

48 See Kettell (2006), pp. 101–4.

49 Memo, Attorney General to the Prime Minister, 7 March 2003.

50 R. Norton-Taylor, 'Blair-Bush deal before Iraq war revealed in secret memo', *Guardian*, 3 February 2006; D. Van Natta Jr, 'Bush was set on path to war, memo by British adviser says', *New York Times*, 27 March 2006; also see Meyer (2005), pp. 261–2.

51 See HMSO (2003).

52 Speech at the Foreign Office conference, 7 January 2003.

53 Speech to the Scottish Labour Party Conference, 14 February 2003.

54 Speech to the Lord Mayor's Banquet, 11 November 2002.

55 Speech at the Foreign Office conference, 7 January 2003; Press conference, 13 January 2003; Speech to the House of Commons, 18 March 2003.

56 Interview on BBC *Newsnight*, 6 February 2003. On the ricin case also see Oborne (2006).

57 B. Russell, 'PM admits removing Saddam from power is campaign's aim', *Independent*, 20 March 2003.

58 Kettell (2006), p. 100.
59 Memo, Attorney General to the Prime Minister, 17 March 2003.
60 On these events see Kettell (2006), Chapter 5.
61 Statement to the House of Commons, 14 April 2003.
62 The adoption of UN resolution 1483 in May gave the US and Britain legal status as occupying powers.
63 Speech by George Bush on USS *Abraham Lincoln*, 1 May 2003; Joint press conference with Donald Rumsfeld and Hamid Karzai, 1 May 2003.
64 Speech in New York, 28 May 2003.
65 *No Plan No Peace*, BBC1, 7 October 2007.
66 Diamond (2004).
67 A. Gilligan, 'Iraq report: troops "rushed" into battle without armour or training', *Daily Telegraph*, 21 November 2009.
68 Blunkett (2006), p. 480.
69 Bremer (2006), p. 39.
70 *No Plan No Peace*, BBC1, 7 October 2007.
71 Bremer (2006), pp. 53, 105–6. For a contrasting view see Frontline interview with Jay Garner, 11 August 2006, www.pbs.org/wgbh/pages/frontline/shows/truth/interviews/garner.html, accessed 9 November 2010.
72 On these issues see Chatterjee (2004); Diamond (2004); Bremer (2006), pp. 42–4, 89.
73 Steele (2008), pp. 26–7, 178–9.
74 Memo, Sawyers to Blair, 11 May 2003; *No Plan No Peace*, BBC1, 7 October 2007; E. MacAskill, 'US post-war Iraq strategy a mess, Blair was told', *Guardian*, 14 March 2006.
75 R. Norton-Taylor, 'Diplomat attacks war planning', *Guardian*, 9 April 2008; Oral evidence to the Iraq Commission, 8 June 2007, Channel 4.
76 C. Lamb, 'Tales of chaos, by our man in Basra', *Sunday Times*, 2/3/08.
77 Bremer (2006), pp. 26, 162.
78 Bremer (2006), p. 117; Rumsfeld. Press conference, 25 August 2003; also see Feith (2008), Chapter 15.
79 Evidence to the Foreign Affairs Committee, 29 April 2003, Q. 227; and to the Chilcot inquiry, 21 January 2010.
80 Evidence to the Chilcot inquiry from Sir Kevin Tebbitt, 3 December 2009; A. Grice and N. Morris, 'There WILL be a public inquiry into Iraq, says Brown', *Independent*, 17 March 2008.
81 P. Wintour, 'Hoon admits fatal errors in planning for post-war Iraq', Guardian, 2 May 2007.
82 J. Kampfner, interview with Sir David Manning, *New Statesman*, 12 September 2007.
83 Statement to the House of Commons, 14 April 2003.
84 K. Ahmed, 'Blair "expected war to last four months"', *Observer*, 6 July 2003.
85 This point was also noted by John Scarlett, the then head of the Joint Intelligence Committee. As he put it during his evidence to the Chilcot inquiry (8 December 2009), the view of British intelligence had been that in the event of war the Iraqi military 'would probably splinter very quickly and collapse very quickly'.
86 Evidence to the Chilcot inquiry, 7 December 2009.
87 R. Norton-Taylor, 'Iraq: the legacy – ill equipped, poorly trained, and mired in a "bloody mess"', *Guardian*, 17 April 2009.
88 *No Plan No Peace*, BBC1, 7 October 2007.

89 The Foreign Affairs Committee is the main parliamentary committee charged with the oversight of foreign policy issues. The Intelligence and Security Committee is the primary body charged with overseeing the work of the intelligence and security agencies.

90 FAC (2003); ISC (2003).

91 On these events see Kettell (2006), Chapter 6.

92 Keynote address to the twentieth anniversary of the National Endowment for Democracy, 6 November 2003; remarks at a joint press conference with Tony Blair, 17 July 2003; and during a White House press conference, 28 October 2003.

93 Speech to the US Congress, 17 July 2003; Joint press conference with George Bush, 17 July 2003.

94 Evidence to the Home Affairs Committee, 2 November 2004, Qs 40–1.

95 *Talking Point*, BBC, 15 May 2004.

96 HMG (2005), para. 15.

97 Joint press conference with Ayad Illawi, 19 September 2004.

98 Evidence to the Chilcot inquiry, 1 December 2009.

99 Remarks in the House of Commons, *Hansard*, 28/4/03, col. 126.

100 Comprehensive Report of the Special Advisor to the DCI on Iraqi WMD, 30 September 2004.

101 Butler (2004).

102 Statement to the House of Commons, 14 July 2004.

103 J. Sifton, 'We're losing the war in Afghanistan, too', 21 August 2003, http://dir.salon.com/news/feature/2003/08/21/afghanwar/index.html, accessed 9 November 2010; J. Pilger, 'Bush's "war on terror" is a cruel hoax', *Green Left Weekly*, 1 October 2003; L. Kleveman, 'How America makes terrorists of its allies', *New Statesman*, 13 October 2003; also see Marsden (2003).

104 B. Maddox, 'Afghan security taking Nato to brink of failure', *The Times*, 25 June 2004.

105 George Bush, joint press conference with Tony Blair, 17 July 2003; Fox News, 'Officials confident US is winning war on terror', 9 May 2003.

106 G. Jones, 'Britain spends £5.5bn in war on terrorism', *Daily Telegraph*, 12 May 2003. In September 2002 the expectation within Whitehall was that an invasion of Iraq would last for six months and cost around £2.5 billion. The predicted worst case scenario on the eve of the war was for an outlay of £5.5 billion. See J. Packard and J. Blitz, 'High cost of Iraq war surprised Whitehall', *Financial Times*, 21 August 2009. US figures are calculated from Belasco (2009), Table 1.

107 Memo, Rumsfeld to General Dick Meyers and Paul Wolfowitz, 16 October 2003.

108 See Burke (2004), pp. 166–72.

109 Rogers (2005); also see S. Jenkins, 'Case proven – war does not eradicate terrorism', *The Times*, 14 May 2003.

110 BBC News, 'War helped terror fight says Straw', 29 April 2003; FAC (2005), paras 16, 25, 27; also see HMG (2005).

111 'World terrorism index: Key findings', *Guardian*, 18 August 2003.

5

Above the law

Along with military interventions in Iraq and Afghanistan, one of the central features of the war on terror was the use of extra-legal measures by the Bush administration. These involved indefinite detentions at Guantánamo Bay and so-called 'black site' facilities at secret locations around the world, the use of extraordinary renditions and the deployment of 'controversial' interrogation techniques, amounting, in some cases, to the use of torture. As details about these practices emerged, New Labour officials came under increasing pressure over their tacit support for, as well as their complicity in such activities. At the same time, developments in the government's own anti-terror strategy also proved to be contentious. Involving a further recalibration of the balance between civil liberties and the security provisions of the state, this included the introduction of a regime of control orders and an extension of the period for which terrorist suspects could be held without charge. Accompanying this, terrorist attacks in Madrid and London placed the issue of domestic radicalisation, and questions about a blowback effect from the invasion of Iraq squarely on the political agenda. The government's response, in denying any possibility of a link to foreign policy, gave its strategy towards the war on terror a new, contradictory and dangerous dynamic.

The new reality

The launching of a war on terror, and in particular the invasion of Iraq, dovetailed perfectly with al-Qaeda's broad objective of provoking a 'clash of civilisations'-style conflagration between the West and the 'Muslim world'. Fuelling suspicions that the real goal of the Bush administration was to extend the global dominance of the US and gain control of Middle East oil, and having served to elevate the status and legitimacy of Islamic terrorism in many Muslim countries, the militarism of the US was also undermining any moral authority being claimed on its behalf. Offering no means of addressing the underlying causes of terrorist violence, containing no measures (or even any evident concern) for alleviating far greater causes of human misery such as global inequality, poverty and disease, and bringing scant pressure to bear on geo-strategic allies such as Pakistan, Saudi Arabia and Egypt over their decrepit records on human rights and democratic governance, the idea that the US-led campaign marked a fight for humanitarian ideals was one that was looking increasingly untenable.[1] Conversely, these sins of omission were compounded by the multiple acts of commission being perpetuated in the name of combating international terrorism. This was clearly evident in the ongoing tensions over Guantánamo Bay, where the vast majority of detainees had yet to be charged with any offence,[2] and was brutally tangible in the rising number of cases to have emerged concerning the abuse of prisoners (leading in some cases to death) at the hands of US and British forces. Of these, the breaking scandal at Abu Ghraib in May 2004 was merely the most notorious. Alongside this, details about the US programme of extraordinary rendition and the use of illegal interrogation techniques by US officials were also now emerging, providing a stark contrast to public statements from Bush that the use of torture was 'never acceptable'.[3]

With details about the darker side of the war on terror coming to light, the British government found itself under pressure over the anaemic nature of its response to the more nefarious activities being carried out by the US, not to mention its tacit support for, and alleged complicity in these operations. Criticisms from Amnesty, which declared that 'the drive to counter-terrorism at home and abroad' was 'eroding and, in some cases removing, the human rights of individuals', were roundly echoed.[4] Steve Crawshaw, the UN advocacy director of Human Rights Watch, maintained that the abuses carried out at Abu Ghraib were not simply the work of a few 'bad apples', but were 'part of a pattern of wishing to push boundaries, of thinking of torture as being a useful tool to apply in the war on terror', and the Foreign Affairs Committee called on the government to 'make strong public representations to the US administration about the lack of due process and oppressive conditions', both at Guantánamo Bay and other US-controlled detention facilities around the world. The FAC also claimed that Britain had made facilities available to US aircraft conducting extraordinary rendition operations, and that ministers had deployed a 'policy of obfuscation' in an attempt to conceal the facts of the matter.[5] Illustrative too was the case of Craig Murray, the British Ambassador to Uzbekistan, who was removed from his post in October 2004 after criticising the government's approach to the use of torture. Protesting that intelligence being received from Uzbekistan via the US had been extracted from '[t]ortured dupes', and that the Uzbek government, then a key Eurasian base for the US, was simply telling the Americans what they wanted to hear, Murray claimed that the information being gleaned from using such methods was nothing short of 'useless', and that, in short, the British services were 'selling our souls for dross'.[6]

The response from the British government combined staunch denials with ardently repeated claims about its opposition to the use of torture. Bill Rammell, under-secretary of state at the Foreign Office, told the Intelligence and Security Committee that ministers were 'emphatically and vehemently oppose[d] to torture as a matter of fundamental principle', and both Jack Straw and Tony Blair maintained that the government would 'always seek assurances on issues such as the treatment of detainees' at Guantánamo and elsewhere.[7] Further still, in May 2004 the Prime Minister informed the ISC that the terms under which members of the intelligence and security services could participate in the questioning of detainees had now been altered so as to require officers to report any suspicion that the people they were questioning were being subjected to inhumane or degrading treatment.[8] Equally, the official line on Britain's involvement in extraordinary rendition was that this was prohibited by the European Convention on Human Rights, as well as by the Geneva Conventions and the United Nations Convention Against Torture, and that once agents had become aware of the programme, and of cases of detainee abuse from early 2002, instructions had been issued informing them that 'we cannot be party to such ill treatment nor can we be seen to condone it'.[9] Allegations that British bases on the Indian Ocean island of Diego Garcia had been used by the US during the process of extraordinary rendition were also flatly denied. As Jack Straw put it, the US government had 'explicitly assured us that there have never been any prisoners in detention on any US vessels moored in Diego Garcia waters', and that ministers were 'satisfied that this is correct'.[10]

But the official view on these issues also contained another, more permissive side. This was manifest as sympathy for the actions taken by the US, combined with assertions about the need for more activist measures. The new guidelines on the questioning of detainees, for instance, may well have required agents to report any suspicions of abuse, but they also highlighted the fact that there was no legal obligation to intervene '[g]iven that they are not within our custody or control'. Indeed, Blair insisted that the participation of British officials in the interrogation of Guantánamo detainees was essential 'to gather information that might prove valuable to the protection of the UK and its citizens from terrorism'.[11] Moreover, the Director-General of the British security services (MI5), Eliza Manningham-Buller, pointed out that it was simply impossible for British agencies to know if information being supplied to them by foreign security services had been obtained by dubious methods, and warned that attempting to uncover the provenance of such information would 'be likely to damage cooperation and the future flow of intelligence'.[12] The head of the intelligence agencies (MI6), John Scarlett, held a similarly equivocal position. Despite revelations about the extra-legal and abusive practices of the Bush administration, despite noting a distinct unwillingness on the part of the US to share information with British agencies (with extraordinary rendition, in particular, being described as 'an impenetrable subject'), and despite the fact that British concerns about intelligence-sharing had been ignored by US agencies on at least one occasion (with assurances about the non-rendition of two individuals on whom British officials had provided information having been disregarded), Scarlett nonetheless maintained that 'it never crossed my mind' that any of the intelligence being provided by the US 'was coming from torture', because: 'We are talking about the Americans, our closest ally'.[13]

A belligerently defensive position was also adopted by Jack Straw. According to the Foreign Secretary, the debate about conditions and events at Guantánamo needed 'to take account of the context in which the detentions took place', and, given this, the approach that had been taken by the Americans was 'understandable'. 'The international conventions on the treatment of prisoners of war, the Geneva conventions', he maintained, 'were designed before we faced the threat of international terrorism and failing states, so the instruments have not quite caught up with the new reality'.[14] Furthermore, Straw also maintained, similarly to Blair, that on certain occasions opposition to the use of torture could be overshadowed by the necessity of obtaining information. As he explained, there were instances in which the government would get intelligence from a partner 'where we know ... that their practices are well below the line', but that such cases posed an intractable 'moral hazard' given that 'it does not follow that if it is extracted under torture, it is automatically untrue'. The 'moral calculus', then, required that the entire panoply of factors be considered, with the abstract principles of opposition to torture being juxtaposed to the possible benefits of being able to prevent another attack on the scale of 9/11. '[T]orture is completely unacceptable', he adjured, 'but you cannot ignore it if the price of ignoring it is 3,000 people dead'.[15]

Worse than ever

The unfolding dynamics of the war on terror also impacted further on the balance between the security of the state and the civil liberties of its citizens. By the end of 2003, the measures that had been ushered in by the Anti-Terror, Crime and Security Act in the wake of the 9/11 attacks were coming under increasing pressure. Indeed, difficulties had begun to emerge within months of its provisions reaching the statute book. In July 2002, a ruling from the Special Immigration Appeals Commission, part of the Act's oversight mechanics, declared that the regime of detention without trial was discriminatory, given that it applied only to foreign nationals, and that, as such, it was in breach of the European Convention on Human Rights. Although the decision was overturned by the Appeal Court in October, in December 2003 the Newton Committee, set up by David Blunkett to examine the workings of the Act, also issued a scathing indictment of its contents.[16] Noting, amongst other things, that the government's inclusion of non-terrorist measures in the initial Bill had been a crude attempt 'to take advantage of its accelerated passage and limited scrutiny, in order to avoid the difficulties which had previously been experienced in securing Parliamentary approval' for such proposals, this warned that the Act had elevated the danger of miscarriages of justice due to the lower standard of proof it required, with this turning on 'reasonable belief and suspicion' rather than on 'a balance of probabilities' or on the establishing of terrorist involvement 'beyond all reasonable doubt'. The Committee also called for the regime of detention without trial to be 'replaced as a matter of urgency', given that it applied only to foreign nationals while almost half of those suspected by the authorities of being involved in international terrorism were British.[17] Such criticisms, though, were brushed aside by the government. As far as Blunkett was concerned, the Act offered essential protection from terrorism, and that, since the threat of prosecution was an insufficient deterrent for suicide bombers, the ability to intervene before a crime was committed remained crucial. 'This is a whole different ball game to anything that we have ever known before', he countered, and it was 'nigh on impossible' to square the circle between curtailing individual human rights and protecting democracy.[18]

The practical consequences of this were made clear in early 2004, when the Home Secretary announced a further step-up in New Labour's anti-terror drive. Under the auspices of the government's 'Contest' strategy, set up the year before on the principles of 'Prevent', 'Pursue', 'Protect' and 'Prepare', the justifications for this were both shaped and facilitated by the war on terror. Again warning that the global terror threat 'was different to anything we had experienced before', and that it therefore required 'a different response', Blunkett declared that trials of British-born terrorist suspects should be held in secret before non-jury courts, and that it was now also necessary to lower the burden of proof to a 'balance of probabilities' beyond detention without trial in order to make it easier to secure actual convictions. Added to this, proposals for the introduction of identity (ID) cards were also now being sold on the need to combat the 'substantial and continuing threat' from international terrorism.[19] In contrast to the Home Secretary's previously stated view that the issues of citizenship and entitlement to public services were 'far more important' than national security considerations in government plans for ID cards, Blunkett's new position was that it was 'obvious that terrorist networks would target the countries that had made the least progress in developing the capacity to provide this protection'.[20]

The draft bill for establishing a system of identity cards was introduced in April 2004 and was the subject of much criticism. Among the most prominent themes to be raised in objection concerned their ineffectiveness as a means of dealing with terrorism, with opponents pointing out that their use would not have stopped the 9/11 atrocities and that the large majority of those countries currently worst affected by terrorism had systems of ID cards in place. The Home Affairs Committee, despite noting a high level of public support for the proposal, and despite claiming that the government had made a 'convincing case', also expressed concerns about the changing rationale for the scheme as well as a 'lack of clarity and openness' in the development of the policy, and warned that the scope of the proposals went beyond that which was 'justified by the fight against organised crime and terrorism'.[21]

But while the threat of terrorism was being played for political advantage, providing officials with a useful means of appearing tough and decisive (a point also alluded to in the alarmist reactions to the non-existent 'ricin' and 'Old Trafford' plots), the danger itself was nevertheless very real.[22] In March 2004 this reality was underscored as an al-Qaeda inspired bombing attack ripped through the Madrid rail system, killing almost two hundred people and injuring almost two thousand others. The political impact of the bombings was also huge. Raising questions about the blow-back effects of the wars in Afghanistan and Iraq, the attacks forced the issue of radicalisation to the centre of domestic and international spheres of concern. The government's views on this were set out in April in a joint Home and Foreign Office paper, entitled 'Young Muslims and Extremism'. This highlighted a range of factors involved in the radicalisation process, including problems of identity conflict between Islam and secularism, perceptions of bias in the application of anti-terrorism powers, social exclusion, alienation from mainstream politics and Islamophobia. However, while observing that British foreign policy was 'a particularly strong cause of disillusionment amongst Muslims', and that 'the war on terror, and in Iraq and Afghanistan are all seen by a section of British Muslims as having been acts against Islam', the paper refused to accept any responsibility for this on the part of the British government, and instead centred on a 'perception of "double standards"', such as the view that Western states sought to preach the language of democracy while oppressing Muslims in places such as Palestine, Iraq, Afghanistan and Chechnya. The paper also claimed that a substantial portion of Muslims in Britain held opinions that were likely to adversely constrain the effectiveness of counter-terror measures, recording that up to 13% defended terrorist actions and that up to 26% did not feel loyal to Britain.[23] These points were also emphasised in a subsequent memo to the Cabinet Secretary, Sir Andrew Turnbull, from the Foreign Office permanent under-secretary, Michael Jay. In this, Jay observed that British foreign policy, and especially its involvement in the Iraq war, was a 'recurring theme' in the Muslim community and 'a key driver behind recruitment by extremist organisations'. In an accompanying strategy document, entitled 'Building Bridges with Mainstream Islam', ministers were also warned that Britain was increasingly viewed as a 'crusader state', and that it was now on a par with the US as a potential terrorist target. As Jay put it, 'Muslim resentment towards the West' was 'worse than ever'.[24]

The government's practical reaction to this was shaped by its refusal to accept any causal role for British foreign policy in having helped to make and exacerbate the threat from radical Islamic terrorism. With the focus on 'perceptions' about Western foreign policy, rather than foreign policy itself, the need for any policy change was thereby foreclosed. As such, the key aims of counter terrorism strategy centred instead on the politicisation of British Muslims. Emphasising the need to secure 'the active cooperation' of Britain's Muslim communities, and (in contrast to the discourse of civilisational peril being perpetuated by the Prime Minister) stating that the term 'Islamic fundamentalism' was 'unhelpful and should be avoided', the declared objective was to prevent radicalisation by promoting moderate Muslim opinion to the detriment of extremist ideas. The projected means of achieving this was through addressing relevant social, cultural and economic issues, and by involving a broader range of groups and agencies (such as community groups, local authorities and faith leaders) in the policy-making process.[25]

The real threat

By the end of the year the government's anti-terror plans were in turmoil. In mid-December a ruling by the Law Lords threw the future of the detention without trial regime for foreign nationals into doubt by declaring it to be incompatible with the European Convention on Human Rights.[26] Accompanying the judgement, Lord Hoffmann, one of the senior judges involved in the decision, sternly rebuked the government for its cavalier approach to civil liberties, declaring that: 'The real threat to the life of the nation, in the sense of a people living in accordance with its traditional laws and political values, comes not from terrorism but from laws such as these'.[27] The ruling also signified a truculent baptism for Charles Clarke, the new Home Secretary following David Blunkett's resignation amidst allegations that he had sought to fast-track a visa for his child's nanny. The government's reaction to the ruling, though, was robust. Refusing to yield, Clarke announced that all those currently being held under the regime would continue to be detained on the grounds that they remained 'a significant threat to our security'.[28]

Although the Law Lords possessed no power to strike down the detention provisions, the ruling nonetheless ensured that Part IV of the Anti-Terror, Crime and Security Act, which was now poised to expire under its original terms (meaning that the detainees would either have to be charged or released), would not be reconstituted in its current form. In February 2005 the government revealed a new set of anti-terror measures in the Prevention of Terrorism Bill, one of the chief aims of which was to replace the existing detention regime with a system based on curfews, electronic tagging, internet and telephone monitoring, restrictions on contacts and the use of control orders. All of this, it was also proposed, could be put in place 'on the balance of probabilities' that an individual was involved in 'terrorism-related activity', and could be imposed without suspects either being charged with, or put on trial for an alleged offence.[29] The unveiling of the new measures was also accompanied by a spate of official exhortations designed to reiterate the nature of the terrorist threat and to legitimise and build support for the proposals. Sir John Stevens, the Metropolitan Police Commissioner at the time of the 9/11 attacks, claimed that the new plans would be 'vital' in the fight against terror, and asserted that there were at least one hundred al-Qaeda trained fighters in Britain, with the real figure likely to be double this amount.[30] In equivalent fashion, Tony Blair warned that it was 'very easy to become complacent' about the terrorist threat, and maintained that there were 'several hundred' people in Britain who were believed to be 'engaged in plotting or trying to commit terrorist acts'.[31] According to Charles Clarke, who described al-Qaeda as a threat to 'the very fundamentals of our democracy', there were now 'a significant number of individuals and organisations' seeking to commit terrorist attacks against Britain, and the new measures, by necessity, would 'represent a significant increase in the powers of the state in relation to UK citizens'.[32]

With time running out for the old regime, and with the current session of Parliament rapidly coming to an end, the Prevention of Terrorism Bill was rushed through the Commons and the Lords in just six days. In this, the government once again faced its strongest opposition in the Upper Chamber, as concerns about the standard of proof required for the use of control orders, as well as about the extent and form of judicial involvement in the new arrangements, forced it to make a series of concessions, principally rendering control orders dependent on judicial approval and introducing a review of the provisions after twelve months. The Bill was eventually passed on 11 March after an intense all-night session of political ping-pong, in which its contents were passed back and forth between the Lords and an increasingly fraught Commons, and received Royal Assent hours later.[33]

The combination of increased state powers and measures to deal with the dangers of radicalisation may have had the appearance of an activist and comprehensive counter-terror package, but the content of the government's approach remained substantially flawed. With officials admitting that '[o]ur understanding of the radicalisation process … is still developing',[34] the anti-terror strategy remained chiefly focused on dealing with its symptoms rather than its underlying causes. While studies show there to be no single or definitive pathway to radicalism, nor any single profile fitting all Islamic extremists, a common theme concerning the process of radicalisation in Western societies is that of its intimate connection to the impact of modernity and globalisation on socially isolated, alienated and disenchanted young Muslim males, usually second- or third-generation migrants experiencing some form of personal identity crisis resulting from an inability to forge a meaningful life amidst contrasting cultural pressures. Often religiously ignorant, such individuals are thus susceptible to an extreme, though historically specific and Westernised form of Islamic doctrine that places a premium on satisfying personal needs and desires, and which, shorn of any community obligations and constraints, promotes an individualistic form of jihad against Western oppression that provides meaning for their lives.[35]

Given this, while focusing on socio-economic factors was thus a necessary part of the policy mix, especially given their contributory impact to grievances surrounding social exclusion and the prevalence of such issues among British Muslims, the majority of adherents to radical Islamic dogma in the West betrayed no obvious background of social and economic disadvantage, but, on the contrary, were often, to all appearances, well-educated, well-balanced and well-integrated members of their communities.[36] Moreover, the aim of promoting inclusiveness and moderacy was itself undermined by the effects of other government policies. Among the most obvious of these was the impact of anti-terror legislation. Based on a flawed zero-sum conception of security and civil liberties, in which the former was to be secured only by a diminution of the latter, the negative effects of this, being felt predominantly by Muslims, did little to ease feelings of social alienation and thus undermined the networks of social trust upon which an effective and successful strategy for countering terrorism would ultimately have to rest. So too, moving beyond this, did New Labour's overarching policy of promoting diversity within a multicultural social agenda. Though also at odds with other aspects of government policy, such as its general approach towards the war on terror, not to mention its celebratory regard for Britain's imperial past and occasional forays into assimilationist rhetoric, this sought to reconcile growing social tensions over issues such as race, ethnicity and immigration by fostering increased sensitivity towards different forms of ethno-cultural and religious identity as a means of inspiring 'community cohesion'.[37] While laudable in its aim of promoting mutual respect and tolerance, the consequences in practice proved to be rather more fractious. Helping to augment and sustain a prevailing sense of 'otherness' between differing social groups, the result, in part, was to entrench segregational, inward-looking practices, to strengthen reactionary and 'conservative' forces in immigrant communities (being typically presented as the most legitimate cultural representatives), and to thereby sharpen and enhance social divisions.[38]

Another core problem with the government's anti-radicalisation approach remained its steadfast refusal to accept any role for foreign policy as a key causal and compounding factor. Indeed, while foreign policy itself may not have been a sufficient variable for the radicalisation process, its interactive effect (not to mention its international impact) often served to reinforce domestic social, cultural and economic sources of marginalisation and discontent.[39] To this extent, New Labour's counter-terrorism strategy not only foreclosed an effective response to the threat from radical Islam, but exacerbated the dynamics of the war on terror by maintaining a geo-strategically driven foreign policy approach that had helped to foster and sustain numerous sources of global grievance. With the prosecution of the war on terror, both internally and externally, doing much to erode the liberal values and freedoms that it purported to be defending, all of this also served to highlight the glaring contradiction in the government's ethical claims to be fighting for democracy, civil liberties and human rights.[40]

For all this, questions about the war on terror, and especially the controversies surrounding the invasion of Iraq, remained largely peripheral to the 2005 General Election campaign until relatively late in the day. Furthermore, even as the issue rose up the political agenda as polling day approached, Blair maintained a defiant stance. Insisting that the government had been vindicated over any questions of deceit and wrongdoing by 'four separate inquiries', he also remained adamant that the invasion had been 'the right thing to do' on the grounds that a course of inactivity would have undermined the credibility of the 'international community' and made the world a more dangerous place.[41] The election itself, which saw New Labour winning another (albeit much reduced) Parliamentary majority, was also accompanied by a new attempt to close down the issue, with Blair now claiming that the poll had drawn a line under the conflict and that it was time for the British people 'to move on'.[42]

A life or death battle

But the effects of the war on terror continued to be vividly felt. On 7 July 2005, concerns about domestic radicalisation were brought home in shocking fashion as four suicide bombers attacked the London transport network, killing 52 innocent people and wounding more than 700 others. The attacks were followed a fortnight later by a failed copycat strike, and by the shooting of an unarmed Brazilian, Jean Charles de Menezes, by the London Metropolitan police, who ostensibly mistook him for a suicide bomber. The '7/7' attacks also threw an uncomfortable spotlight on the intelligence agencies, whose failure to uncover the plot was compounded by a downgrading of the risk assessment less than a month earlier, and thrust the issue of 'home-grown' radicalism onto the agenda for the first time.[43] Until this point, the attention of the agencies had been centred on members of external terror organisations, the aims of which lay in conducting terrorist operations overseas.[44] As the ISC later recorded, prior to the 7 July bombings 'the development of the home-grown threat and the radicalization of British citizens were not fully understood or applied to strategic thinking'.[45]

The attacks also forced the issue of Iraq back to the top of the political agenda. For many commentators, the link between British foreign policy and the London bombings was one that was simply too strong to ignore. While much of the criticism on this issue came from stalwart opponents of the war, such as Clare Short and Robin Cook, more mainstream and less combative organisations also emphasised the deleterious impact of the invasion. According to Chatham House (formerly the Royal Institute of International Affairs), there could be 'no doubt that the situation over Iraq' had 'imposed particular difficulties for the UK', while the government's own Joint Terrorism Analysis Centre stated that events in Iraq were 'continuing to act as motivation and a focus of a range of terrorist related activity in the U.K'.[46] As Sir Christopher Meyer put it: there was 'plenty of evidence ... that home-grown terrorism was partly radicalised and fuelled by what is going on in Iraq'.[47]

Sensitive to the political dangers of any link between the bombings and its participation in the war, the government's response was shaped by an overarching desire to avoid any sense of culpability, with ministers vehemently denying that the bombings had any connection to Iraq whatsoever. Charles Clarke, for example, decried claims of a link as suffering from 'serious intellectual flabbiness' given that al-Qaeda had been attacking the West prior to the invasion, Jack Straw emphasised the fact that terrorists had 'struck across the world' and in countries unrelated to the Iraq conflict, and Blair insisted that the causal mechanics involved in the process of radicalisation were 'very deep' and could not be reduced to a simple lineage from Iraq.[48] In common with previous assertions, this official response not merely precluded any form of self-reflection in terms of the causal role of British foreign policy, but, moreover, presented any such reflexivity as ultimately self-defeating and positively dangerous. Thus, Blair's claim that terrorists 'want us to believe that terrorism is somehow our responsibility' yielded the logical corollary that the only viable response was one of unflinching resolve and the expunging of any scintilla of self-doubt. From this, it was but a short step to the Prime Minister's subsequent assertion that the 'root cause' of radical Islamic terrorism was 'not a decision on foreign policy, however contentious', but that it was simply the result of 'a doctrine of fanaticism'.[49]

The themes of this 'Doctrine of No Responsibility' marked a significant shift in the discursive framing (although not, it would transpire, the actual content) of the government's approach to the war on terror, and were set out more fully by Blair in a trio of major set-piece speeches on foreign policy delivered to the Foreign Policy Centre, the Australian Parliament and Georgetown University.[50] One of the central features of this was an attempt to frame the government's policy aims in the war on terror as progressive, and to pose the available policy choices in terms of a false dichotomy between vigorous action or passivity. Declaring himself to be 'ardently in favour of spreading democracy round the world', the Prime Minister asserted that '[t]he true division in foreign policy today' was between 'those who believe that the long-term interests of a country lie in it being out there, engaged, interactive, and those who think the short-term pain of such a policy and its decisions, too great'. In this formulation, critics of New Labour's foreign policy were thus pigeon-holed as adherents to 'a doctrine of benign inactivity', in which US foreign policy since 9/11 was regarded as 'a gross overreaction', and in which the chaos in Iraq, Afghanistan and throughout the Middle East was 'an entirely understandable consequence of US/UK imperialism or worse, of just plain stupidity'. Once erected, this critical straw man was duly denounced by Blair as 'a posture of weakness', as an attitude which '[i]nstead of challenging the extremism ... panders to it and therefore instead of choking it, feeds its growth'. Not surprisingly, this interpretation of the causes of terrorism was distinctly void of any culpability on the part of the West. On offer instead was a singularly one-dimensional narrative in which the roots of global terrorism were to be found in 'decades of alienation, victimhood and political oppression in the Arab and Muslim world', a tale of events containing no reference to the long history of Western imperialism and its support for backward and repressive regimes in the Middle East, but one that instead portrayed the West as a passive, progressive and wholly benign entity, before transforming it into a victim of the irrationality and insecurities of the Islamic world. According to Blair, the renaissance, reformation and enlightenment on which the rise of the West had been based had left the Muslim and Arab world feeling 'uncertain, insecure and on the defensive', and had led many there to the conclusion that the poor state of Muslim countries was reflective of the poor state of Islam.

This conceptual map, such as it was, contained a further logical inversion; namely, that any further deterioration of the situation in Iraq would become a reason not for withdrawal, but for a greater intensity of action; a sign, not of failure, but 'a reason for persevering and succeeding'. As the Prime Minister explained: 'we must reject the thought that somehow we are the authors of our own distress; that if only we altered this decision or that, the extremism would fade away'. With the idea of any change in foreign policy therefore being equated with nothing short of appeasement, the route to victory was consequently to be found in confronting the ideas of terrorism 'head-on, in their essence, at their core'. The present situation, then, was framed in typically dichotomous terms. It was, Blair explained, 'the age-old battle between progress and reaction, between those who embrace and see opportunity in the modern world and those who reject its existence; between optimism and hope on the one hand; and pessimism and fear on the other'. In short, the single, inescapable conclusion was that the civilised world was engaged in a struggle 'between extremism and progress' that was 'utterly determinative of our future here in Britain'.

At the centre of this Manichaean epic stood the ongoing war on terror, the core of which revolved around the military theatres in Iraq and Afghanistan. Presenting these as a struggle between violence and democracy 'in its most pure form', as 'a life or death battle for freedom ... ultimately, a battle about modernity', the Prime Minister sought once more to make a clean break from the past and to draw a line under the controversies surrounding the invasion of Iraq by reaffirming a view of the war on terror itself as being embedded within a progressive agenda of 'justice and opportunity for all', combining action on world poverty, third world debt, disease, governance, conflict resolution, climate change, the Middle East peace process, reform of international institutions and so on. As Blair maintained, establishing a successful democracy in Iraq would be 'the most effective message possible against their wretched propaganda about America, the West, the rest of the world'. In sum, the terrorist threat could 'only be defeated through pulling it up by its roots', by dealing with 'its presumed and false sense of grievance against the West, its attempt to persuade us that it is we and not they who are responsible for its violence'. The values of democracy and human rights, he said, were 'not western still less American or Anglo-Saxon values but values in the common ownership of humanity, universal values'.

Deeply irresponsible

The government's response to the 7/7 bombings also involved a further battery of anti-terror measures. Among the main proposals to be put forward, which included an ad hoc series of measures announced by the Prime Minister at his monthly press conference in August, were a tightening-up of the rules for asylum and deportation, a clampdown on extremist websites and bookshops, the closure of mosques used to foment extremism, an extension of control orders, and the creation of several new offences, including inciting terrorism, the glorification of terrorism, giving or receiving training in terrorist techniques, and committing 'acts preparatory to terrorism'. 'Let no-one be in any doubt', Blair exclaimed, 'the rules of the game are changing'.[51] The most controversial of the government's new proposals, however, involved extending the period for which terrorist suspects could be held without charge beyond the current limit of 14 days, with the preferred option from senior officials being for a new maximum period of three months. Alongside reassertions about the scale and dynamics of the dangers currently faced from international terrorism, the argument for this centred on the growing complexity of terrorist cases and on the sheer mass of physical and computer-based evidence that experts were required to analyse. The Deputy Assistant Commissioner of the Metropolitan Police, Peter Clarke, insisted, for instance, that 'the changed nature of the threat' meant that 'on any calculation we need more than 14 days to be in a position to have sensible constructive interviews, to fully understand the nature of the conspiracies that we are looking at, which are global and complex'.[52] The Chief Commissioner himself, Ian Blair, warned that the security services were monitoring up to 250 British Muslims trained in al-Qaeda terrorist camps, and claimed that two weeks was 'not a very long period of time' for the kind of investigation that was now needed.[53] At the ministerial level, Charles Clarke also stated that the agencies were keeping an extremely close watch on 'hundreds of individuals' whom they considered to be a security threat, and the Prime Minister warned that the world faced the threat of 'terrorism without limit', and declared that extending the detention period was 'the right thing for this country's security'.[54]

As with the previous round of anti-terror measures, the government's plans were met with stern criticism, the primary themes of which once more centred on the lack of consultation, on the ineffectiveness and impracticality of the proposals, and on the disproportionate and unwarranted impact that they would have on civil liberties. Denying that the current limit of 14 days was inadequate, the human rights group, JUSTICE, pointed out that there had been no cases of a terrorist suspect being detained for the maximum period before having to be released without charge, and claimed that that the proposals were thus unnecessary and would merely encourage the use of 'fishing expeditions' for information by the police.[55] Shami Chakrabarti, the Director of Liberty, warned that continuing to allow New Labour's authoritarian tendencies to reign unchecked would undermine British democracy 'in ways that the suicide bombers could only have dreamed of', and John Denham, the Labour chairman of the Home Affairs Committee, later described the proposals set out by the Prime Minister as having been 'half-baked', and 'driven by public and media pressure in this area, rather than a concern for what is most effective'.[56] The government's anti-terror approach as a whole was also subjected to criticism from within Whitehall itself. According to a leaked paper from the Prime Minister's delivery unit, the government's entire handling of the issue had been 'immature' and 'disjointed', the levels of accountability for delivery remained 'weak', and, in sum, it was 'very difficult to demonstrate that progress has been made'.[57]

In the event, the scale and vehemence of the opposition blew a significant hole in the government's plans. While the subsequent Terrorism Act successfully cleared Parliament in January 2006 (gaining Royal Assent in March), ministers were forced to make numerous concessions in order to secure its passage, and incurred a spectacular reverse on the issue of 90 days detention in the process. Presenting Blair with his first Prime Ministerial defeat in the Commons, in November MPs voted by 322 to 291 (with 49 Labour rebels joining the dissenters) to reject the proposal, preferring instead an alternative proposition for a doubling of the detention period to 28 days. To this, however, the Prime Minister remained unyielding. Describing the Parliamentary rejection as having been a 'deeply irresponsible' move, Blair lambasted that: '[s]ometimes it is better to lose and do the right thing than to win and do the wrong thing'.[58]

Another key feature of the government's reaction to the London bomb-ings centred on the assertion that the emergence of home-grown terrorism had been due primarily to the inadequate integration of the Muslim com-munity into the British way of life. This was manifest in the introduction of a series of Home Office measures designed to improve integration un-der the rubric of the Preventing Extremism Together project. Consisting of a number of working groups set up to address a variety of concerns around the issue of radicalisation, including Muslim youth and women's issues, education, the training of imams and the role of mosques, this led to a series of reports, which produced 64 recommendations for actions to be undertaken by Muslim community groups and officials (although many of these were subsequently ignored or altered by the government).[59] In July 2006 this was followed by the publication of a new and over-arching anti-terror strategy, entitled 'Countering International Terrorism'. Warning that the threat from radical Islamic terrorism was 'serious and sustained', and that the danger was 'not likely to diminish significantly for some years', the main thrust of this was to promote and strengthen moderate Muslim opinion, and to help Muslim communities themselves deal with the problem of radicalisation via measures designed to address issues of socio-economic disadvantage, inequality and discrimination. The stated objective, it claimed, was to secure international human rights, equality, social inclusion, community cohesion and an actively engaged citizenry.[60] Part of this, too, involved a displacement of responsibility for radicalism away from officials and onto the Muslim community itself, which was presented as having been too complacent about weeding out the extremists in its midst. As Blair put it, the problem of radicalisation had not been the result of any inaction on the part of the government, but was principally due to the fact that the Muslim community was 'not having a debate of a fundamental enough nature ... where the moderate majority go and stand up against the ideas of these people'. '[I]n the end', he maintained, 'Government itself cannot go and root out the extremism in these communities ... It is better that you mobilise the Islamic commu-nity itself to do this'.[61]

A similar theme was also emphasised by the new Defence Secretary, John Reid (having replaced Geoff Hoon in May 2005), who sought to displace public cynicism about government assessments of the terror threat onto the Western media. Describing this as 'a borderless virtual battleground' in which 'swaying public opinion away from support for necessary cam-paigns might be ... a quick way of undermining our public morale and endurance', Reid maintained that success in the war on terror required 'a comprehensive strategy' based on promoting alternative and more attrac-tive values and ideas; for 'encouraging democracy and political change as widely as possible', and for providing 'generous and farseeing assistance around the globe' in terms of aid and development.[62] But as with the government's refusal to accept any responsibility for the radicalising effect of its foreign policy, this emphasis on promoting moderate ideas and values, especially within the Muslim community, was also problematic given the obvious and growing social tensions around the issue. In an apt demonstration of the point, the Danish 'Cartoons Crisis' of early 2006 underlined the fragility of Islamic relations right across Western Europe, as high-profile protests and demonstrations around the issue of free speech threw questions about the values underpinning Western society into sharp focus. Reflecting this, surveys conducted by Pew showed a notable fall in positive attitudes towards Muslims in Britain over the previous year, from 72% to 63%, and a corresponding rise in anxieties about Islamic extremism, with concerns about this now being expressed by more than three-quarters (77%) of the British public. Moreover, while 69% of British Muslims themselves professed to be worried about the spread of radical Islam, some 15% claimed that the use of violence against civilians to defend Islam was sometimes or often justified, 14% expressed confidence in Osama bin Laden to 'do the right thing' in world affairs (the second highest proportion in Europe, behind Spain with 16%), almost two-thirds (64%) claimed that Muslims did not want to integrate into British society, and more than three-quarters (77%) noted the emergence of a strong sense of Islamic identity in Britain, up from 63% in 2005.[63]

An extraordinary operation

The government's response to the 7/7 attacks also took place against a backdrop of renewed pressure over the subject of extra-legal practices in the war on terror. By the end of 2005 an increasing number of stories were now starting to emerge about the CIA's use of a global network of secret prisons, or 'black sites' (thought to be located in a range of countries including Thailand, Afghanistan, Poland and Romania) for the interrogation of terrorist suspects.[64] Provoking widespread consternation, and generating calls for an EU inquiry into the acquiescence of its member states in the American transportation of detainees, the diplomatic response from the US combined assertions of innocence and necessity, insisting that no prisoners had been taken to a country where it was 'believed' that they would be tortured, but maintaining the need for pre-emptive action in the war on terror on security grounds. As Condoleeza Rice (by now the US Secretary of State) put it, extraordinary rendition was 'a vital tool in combating transnational terrorism', and '[o]ne of the difficult issues in this new kind of conflict is what to do with captured individuals who we know or believe to be terrorists'.[65]

With analyses of flight records showing that CIA rendition aircraft had used a range of British airports at least 210 times since 9/11 (including Biggin Hill, Birmingham, Glasgow, Brize Norton, Farnborough, Gatwick, Heathrow, Northolt and Stansted), the revelations also posed difficulties for the New Labour government.[66] However, while prompting an outcry about ministerial complicity in such activities, with the Foreign Affairs Committee later stating that the use of British airports was 'facilitating rendition' even if the stops had been purely logistical and if the planes had contained no actual detainees at the time,[67] government officials re-asserted their previous denials of any British involvement, and repeated their claim that no rules had been broken. According to Kim Howells, the Secretary of State for Foreign and Commonwealth Affairs, the government's policy was that it 'would not facilitate the transfer of an individual from or through the UK to another State where there were grounds to believe that the person would face a real risk of torture',[68] while Jack Straw insisted that, after a 'very thorough' examination of government files, officials were certain that there was 'no record whatsoever' of any rendition request from the US. Thus:

> Unless we all start to believe in conspiracy theories and that the officials are lying ... that behind this there is some kind of secret state which is in league with some dark forces in the United States ... there simply is no truth in the claims that the United Kingdom has been involved in rendition.[69]

These dismissals were accompanied by official efforts to frustrate any investigations into the flights and to deflect attention away from the issue and onto the broader, legitimising theme of the war on terror. On 7 December, following a request from Number 10 for advice on the 'substance and handling' of the matter, Irfan Siddiq, a private secretary at the Foreign Office, replied with a memo warning that any British involvement in extraordinary rendition would be 'almost certainly illegal', but pointed out that officials had no idea if any prisoners captured by British forces in Iraq and Afghanistan had been sent on to US interrogation centres, since there was 'no mechanism' for establishing if this had taken place or not. As such, the government were advised 'to avoid getting drawn on detail' about 'the specifics of rendition, extraordinary or otherwise', and to be as proactive as possible in trying to 'move the debate on', 'underlining all the time the strong counter-terrorist rationale for close cooperation with the US', and to 'bring out the other side of the balance, in terms of the huge challenge which the threat of terrorism poses to all countries'.[70]

Not for the last time, though, the official position on British involvement in extraordinary rendition soon changed. Contrary to previous assertions, in January 2006 Straw disclosed that an internal search of government records had uncovered that the US had, in fact, made four rendition requests, but noted that these had occurred in 1998 under the Clinton administration (of which two had been approved). However, while the Foreign Secretary also disclosed that the US had ongoing permission to overfly British airspace and use airfields without seeking prior approval, and that British airfields were under no legal obligation to record passenger details of the flights, Straw rejected calls for an investigation into the matter, stating that the government had received 'clear assurances' that British airspace would not be used for rendition operations, and that, in any case, an inquiry would simply be too impractical. As the Parliamentary Under-Secretary at the Foreign Office, Lord Triesman, put it:

> there are 3.5 million takeoffs and landings in the United Kingdom and 1.1 million of them are non-commercial flights ... the provision of passenger lists on that kind of basis, without grounds for believing that something is actually happening other than unsubstantiated allegations, would be an extraordinary operation.[71]

Calls for an inquiry were similarly rebuffed by the Prime Minister. At his monthly Downing Street press conference, Blair declared that there was 'absolutely no evidence to suggest that anything illegal has been happening here at all', and stated 'I am not going to start ordering inquiries into this, that or the next thing when I have got no evidence to show whether this is right or not'. Asked if he approved of rendition, the Prime Minister's response was equally dismissive. Despite the fact that extraordinary rendition operations had no legitimacy whatsoever in international law, Blair's view was that: 'It all depends what you mean by rendition. If it is something that's illegal, I totally disapprove of it. If it is lawful, I don't disapprove of it'.[72]

But the government's response failed to calm the waters. In February a draft report by the European Parliament (being finalised by the end of the year) accused EU member states of having 'turned a blind eye' to extraordinary renditions across their territory and airspace, in May the Parliamentary Joint Committee on Human Rights accused the government of making insufficient efforts to investigate whether British airports were being used by secret CIA flights (adding that there was 'a reasonable suspicion that certain aircraft passing through the UK may have been carrying suspects where they may have faced torture'), and in June a report by the Council of Europe claimed that several European governments, including Britain, had collaborated with the US in extraordinary rendition operations.[73] Somewhat embarrassingly, the denials of the British government, along with those of other member states, were also repudiated by the now-ex US Secretary of State, Colin Powell. Maintaining that it was disingenuous for European governments to deny knowledge of renditions, Powell retorted that the practice was neither 'new or unknown' to Europe, and that 'most of our European friends cannot be shocked that this kind of thing takes place'.[74]

To enhance the government's discomfort, pressures over Guantánamo Bay also returned to the political agenda amidst growing evidence of detainee abuse, and with Washington now stepping up its efforts to repatriate prisoners, having found itself unable to bring more than a few of the remaining detainees before a military tribunal. The logistical quandary, or at least as it was explained by Bush, was that while the President was in favour of closing the camp, some of the people being held there were simply too 'darned dangerous' to release.[75] The attitude of the British government, though, was entirely predictable. Notwithstanding a heightened willingness to be seen to be critical on the part of some officials, with Lord Goldsmith declaring that the camp was 'unacceptable', and with the unelected Secretary of State for Constitutional Affairs, Lord Falconer, later describing it as a 'shocking affront to the principles of democracy', the official line maintained the nuanced and qualified position set out in the aftermath of 9/11, melding an ostensible dislike of the camp with an exonerating narrative rooted in the necessary logic of the war on terror.[76] As Jack Straw put it, while the US would prefer the situation at Guantánamo to be 'other than it is', it nevertheless remained 'important to recognise that there is another side to this, which is called September 11'. Making the same point, the Prime Minister offered an equally qualified assessment. Purporting to have 'always made it clear that I think Guantánamo should close', Blair implored people to 'look back and remember how all this arose', and bemoaned that 'one of the most difficult things is people forgetting September 11'.[77]

Conclusion

The domestic effects of the war on terror were significant in a number of ways. Controversies about New Labour's support for the extra-legal practices of the US were accompanied by political pressures and discontent over the civil liberties impact of further anti-terror legislation. Alongside this, questions about the radicalising impact of the Iraq war were also planted firmly on the domestic agenda following the Madrid bombings and the 7/7 attacks in London. Politically unable to countenance any causal role for foreign policy, the official response to this involved a notable shift in the discursive framing of the war on terror. Based on a 'Doctrine of No Responsibility', this sought to emphasise the importance of values and ideas as key weapons in the fight against terrorism, and aimed to promote moderate Islamic opinion as a means of countering the dogmas of violent extremism. Precluding any critical analysis of British foreign policy, this approach effectively locked government strategy into a self-reinforcing dynamic, in which the growth of terrorist violence merely served as the cue for pursuing a more intensely obdurate policy direction. This would prove to have negative consequences not only for the effectiveness of the government's anti-terror strategy, but for the political future of Tony Blair himself.

Notes

1. See for instance: J. Pilger, 'War on terror: false victory', *Daily Mirror*, 16 November 2001; J. Carroll, 'Religious comfort for bin Laden', *New York Times*, 15 September 2008; Pew (2008a).
2. All of the nine British detainees being held at the camp at the start of 2004 were eventually released without charge.
3. J. Mayer, 'Outsourcing torture', *The New Yorker*, 14 February 2005; S. Shane, D. Johnston and J. Risen, 'Secret US endorsement of severe interrogations', *New York Times*, 4 October 2007. In September 2006, Corporal Donald Payne became the first British soldier in history to admit to a war crime over his involvement in the death of an Iraqi hotel receptionist, Baha Mousa.
4. FAC (2005), para. 52.
5. *Ibid.*, paras 63–5, 98.
6. See C. Ruchala, 'Selling our souls for dross', Sobaka's Notebook, 15 November 2004, www.craigmurray.org.uk/archives/2004/11/selling_our_sou.html, accessed 9 November 2010.
7. ISC (2005), para.31; HMG (2005), paras 8–9.
8. I. Cobain, 'The truth about torture', *Guardian*, 8 July 2009.
9. ISC (2007), paras 51–60; FAC (2009).
10. Written answer to question in the House of Commons, *Hansard*, 11 September 2003, col. 440.
11. See ISC (2005), para. 65; Human Rights Watch (2009).
12. Statement to the Court of Appeal, 20 September 2005.
13. See ISC (2007), paras 65–74.
14. Remarks in House of Commons, *Hansard*, 24 February 2004, cols 145–50; and 11 January 2005, col.184.
15. ISC (2005), para.33; also see FAC (2007a).
16. Privy Councillor Review Committee (2003), paras 183–4. By April 2004, 16 foreign nationals had been detained under the Anti-Terror, Crime and Security Act. Of these, 2 had voluntarily left the UK, 1 had been freed, and the rest remained in detention.
17. *Ibid.*, paras 193, 203 and 333.
18. BBC News, 'Blunkett hails anti-terror laws', 30 January 2004.
19. See Evidence to the Home Affairs Committee, 2 March 2004, Qs 2, 57; Comments in the House of Commons, 26 February 2004, col. 298; also see Home Office (2003); D. Charter, 'Blunkett to spell out anti-terrorism plans', *The Times*, 23 February 2004; R. Ford, 'Terrorism trials plan "an affront to rule of law"', *The Times*, 3 February 2004.

20 See Home Office (2002); Statement on ID cards to the House of Commons, 11 November 2003.
21 See Home Affairs Committee (2004), paras 90–1 and *passim*.
22 See Oborne (2006).
23 'Draft Report on Young Muslims and Extremism', April 2004.
24 Michael Jay quoted in M. Bright, 'Leak shows Blair told of Iraq war terror link', *Observer*, 28/8/05. In April 2005 the Joint Intelligence Committee also stated that the Iraq war had 'exacerbated the threat from international terrorism', and that it was 'likely to be an important motivating factor for some time to come' in the radicalisation of British Muslims and other extremists. See D. Leppard, 'Iraq terror backlash in UK "for years"', *Sunday Times*, 2 April 2006.
25 'Draft Report on Young Muslims and Extremism', April 2004.
26 Walker (2006). The provisions had been applied to 17 people by January 2005.
27 'Opinions of the Lords of Appeal for Judgment in the Cause ...', 16 December 2004.
28 P. Naughton, 'Clarke stands firm over terror detainees after ruling', *The Times*, 16 December 2004; G. Jones and J. Rozenberg, 'Anti-terror laws rejected on Clarke's first day', *Daily Telegraph*, 17 December 2004.
29 Elliott (2006).
30 B. Bourne, 'Up to 200 Al-Qaeda terrorists in Britain', *The Times*, 6 March 2005.
31 J. Booth, 'Blair defends controversial anti-terror laws', *The Times*, 5 January 2005; R. Bennett, D. McGrory and S. Tendler, '"Several hundred" plotting terror acts, warns Blair', *The Times*, 1 March 2005.
32 Evidence to the Home Affairs Committee, 8 February 2005, Qs 2, 5, 36.
33 P. Webster, R. Ford and T. Baldwin, 'Belmarsh ten to be freed as Clarke faces terror law fight', *The Times*, 23 February 2005.
34 'Draft Report on Young Muslims and Extremism', April 2004.
35 See for example: Roy (2004); Sageman (2004); Abbas (2007, 2007a); Kepel (2009). For an overview of the literature in this area see Al-Lami (2009).
36 Hewitt (2008), pp. 74–5; Saggar (2009), Chapter 1.
37 See for example, Home Office (2004). On the Janus-faced nature of New Labour's approach to multiculturalism, see Back, Khan, Shukra *et al.*, (2002); Archer (2009).
38 See for example: Alleyne (2002); Kelly (2005). Also see T. Philips, 'Multiculturalism's legacy is "have a nice day" racism', *Guardian*, 28 May 2004. Similar findings were produced by the official Cantle Report into riots in several Northern towns during 2001. See Home Office (2001).
39 O'Duffy (2008).
40 On this point also see Buzan (2006), and O'Duffy (2008).
41 Tony Blair interview with Jeremy Paxman, *Newsnight*, BBC1, 20 April 2005.
42 Kettell (2006), pp. 167–70.
43 E. Sciolino and D. Van Natta Jr, 'June report led Britain to lower it's terror alert', *New York Times*, 19 July 2005.
44 Hewitt (2008), pp. 62–6; HMG (2009).
45 ISC (2006), para. 108.
46 Chatham House (2005), p. 3; E. Sciolino and D. Van Natta Jr, 'June report led Britain to lower it's terror alert', *New York Times*, 19 July 2005.
47 J. Glover and E. MacAskill, 'A political war that backfired', *Guardian*, 5 November 2005.
48 Comments in the House of Commons by Charles Clarke, *Hansard*, 20 July 2005, col. 1264; J. Sturke, 'Straw rejects war link to bombings', *Guardian*, 18 July 2005; P.

Bale, 'Blair vows attack on roots of terror', *The Times*, 9 July 2005.
49 Statement to the UN Security Council, 14 September 2005.
50 The following sections are compiled from: 'Clash about civilisations', Tony Blair speech to the Foreign Policy Centre, 21 March 2006; 'Global alliance for global values', speech to the Australian Parliament, 27 March 2006; and speech to Georgetown University, Washington DC, 26 May 2006.
51 Monthly press conference, 5 August 2005.
52 Home Affairs Committee (2006), para. 141.
53 P. Webster, '9/11 wake-up call ignored, Blair says in swipe at obstructive judges', *The Times*, 27 July 2005; J. Booth, 'Blears outlines tough new anti-terror laws', *The Times*, 15 July 2005.
54 Evidence to the Home Affairs Committee from Charles Clarke, 13 September 2005, Q. 5; Tony Blair, monthly press conference, 7 November 2005.
55 See Home Affairs Committee (2006), para. 136; Evidence to the Home Affairs Committee by Dr Eric Metcalfe, 11 October 2005.
56 S. Chakrabarti, 'The price of a chilling and counterproductive recipe', *Guardian*, 8 August 2005; Oborne (2006).
57 D. Leppard, 'Labour's war on terror is failing, says leaked report', *Sunday Times*, 23 October 2005.
58 M. Tempest, 'Blair defeated on terror bill', *Guardian*, 9 November 2005.
59 Home Office (2005); Oborne (2006).
60 Home Office (2006).
61 Evidence to the Liaison Committee, 4 July 2006, Qs 355, 357; Klausen (2007).
62 Speech to the Council on Foreign Relations, 5 April 2006; also see speech to Kings College, 20 February 2006.
63 Pew (2005, 2006a). Similar findings were reported by other surveys. See Saggar (2009).
64 See for example: D. Priest, 'CIA holds terror suspects in secret prisons', *Washington Post*, 2 November 2005; D. McGrory and T. Reid, 'CIA accused of running secret jails in Europe for terrorists', *The Times*, 3 November 2005.
65 BBC News, 'EU to look into "secret US jails"', 3 November 2005; A. Browne, 'Europe demands answers on CIA and the secret terror jails', *The Times*, 30 November 2005; 'America's dark secret', *Guardian*, 10 November 2005; B. Ross and R. Esposito, 'Sources tell ABC News top Al Qaeda figures held in secret CIA prisons', ABC News, 5 December 2005; S. Knight, 'Rice admits CIA transfers but denies torture', *The Times*, 5 December 2005.
66 I. Cobain, S. Grey and R. Norton-Taylor, 'Destination Cairo: human rights fears over CIA flights', *Guardian*, 12 September 2005; S. Freeman, 'UK airports "are stop-offs in torture flights"', *The Times*, 30 November 2005; also see I. Cobain, S. Grey and R. Norton-Taylor, 'Britain's role in war on terror revealed', *Guardian*, 6 December 2005.
67 FAC (2007a), paras 77–8.
68 Remarks in the House of Commons, 20 December 2005, col. 2840.
69 Evidence to the FAC, 13 December 2005, Qs 22–3.
70 Memo, Irfan Siddiq to Grace Cassy, December 2005; also see I. Evans, 'CIA torture flights "cover-up"', *The Times*, 19 January 2006; M. Bright, 'A secret memo reveals the truth', *New Statesman*, 23 January 2006.
71 Remarks in the House of Lords, *Hansard*, 18 July 2006, col. 1224; also see FAC (2007a).
72 Press Conference, 22 December 2005.

73 See Joint Committee on Human Rights (2006), para. 168; D. Dombey, J. Cienski and C. Condon, 'Europeans "aided US renditions"', 8 June 2007, www.ft.com/cms/s/496e8ca4-15f1-11dc-a7ce-000b5df10621.html, accessed 9 November 2010.

74 BBC News, 'Powell raps Europe on CIA flights', 17 December 2005, www.ft.com/cms/s/496e8ca4-15f1-11dc-a7ce-000b5df10621.html, accessed 9 November 2010.

75 S. Baxter, 'US set to close Guantánamo', *Sunday Times*, 14 May 2006; 'Bush: "I'd like to close Guantánamo Bay"', *The Times*, 14 June 2006. While the US Supreme Court ruled against the use of military commissions for Guantánamo detainees at the end of June, in October the Military Commissions Act stripped US courts of the jurisdiction to consider legal challenges from non-U.S citizens held as 'enemy combatants' in US custody.

76 Lord Goldsmith, speech to the Royal United Services Institute, 9 May 2006; D. Fickling, 'Falconer condemns "shocking" Guantánamo', *Guardian*, 13 September 2006.

77 P. Naughton, 'Straw says Guantánamo should not become America's gulag', *The Times*, 21 February 2006; Evidence to the Liaison Committee from Tony Blair, 4 July 2006, Q. 442.

6

A road well travelled

The context for Britain's role in the war on terror shifted significantly during the course of 2006. As conditions in Afghanistan and Iraq continued to deteriorate, the government's strategies in both theatres underwent considerable adjustment. While the military campaign in the former was dramatically expanded as part of an effort to combat the ongoing resurgence of the Taliban, in Iraq officials began to emphasise a tentative move towards withdrawal. This created tensions with Washington, whose strategic approach had now embraced a large-scale troop surge designed to quell the ever-rising violence of the insurgency. Events elsewhere in the region also had a dramatic impact. In particular, the outbreak of war between Israel and Lebanon led to a critical weakening of Tony Blair, with his unyielding support for the US position hastening his eventual departure from office. Although Blair's successor as Prime Minister, Gordon Brown, sought to emphasise the distinctive qualities of his incoming government, similarities with the previous regime remained clear. With the new administration refusing to accept any causal role for foreign policy in the threat from international terrorism, placing a premium on the role of values and ideas, hailing the importance of the special relationship and pressing ahead with further anti-terror legislation, the overall theme in terms of the war on terror was one of continuity rather than change.

A complete renaissance

In 2006 the political and discursive contexts surrounding Britain's war on terror took a decisive turn. One of the central drivers in this was the ongoing violence in Afghanistan and Iraq, where conditions continued to go from worse to worse-still. In the latter, John Reid's assessment at the end of 2005 that the Iraqi army should soon be in a position to start taking the lead on security issues, was looking ever more fanciful by the day.[1] By the spring, a stream of high-profile atrocities, including a massacre of civilians by US troops at Haditha the previous November, and a Sunni attack on the Shia Golden Mosque in Samarra in February, had led to an intensification of sectarian violence and had dragged the country to the brink of a precipice. Belying the Defence Secretary's description of the situation as 'serious but not terminal', the former Iraqi Prime Minister, Ayad Allawi, declared that 'if this is not civil war, then God knows what civil war is'.[2]

In Afghanistan the situation was also dire. With a Taliban resurgence now in full flow, in the spring British troops embarked on their first large-scale operation in the country, with more than three thousand military personnel being deployed to Helmand province as part of Operation Herrick. As with the initial small-scale mission of 2001, the aims of this were again couched in humanitarian as well as security terms. According to Blair, the purpose of the campaign was to prevent Afghanistan from relapsing into a base for terrorists and to establish a 'secular democracy'.[3] According to Reid, the goal was to provide the Afghan people with 'a seamless package of democratic, political, developmental and military assistance'.[4] But problems with the campaign soon emerged. Under pressure from the Afghan government to help extend the range of its authority beyond Kabul, British troops were rapidly sucked in to an escalation of fighting. As momentum gathered behind the Taliban, so a vicious circle now began to develop. With the extension of the military campaign leaving less time and resources for the work of reconstruction and the building of political stability, and with the absence of stability and development providing still more fuel for the Taliban, the pressure on the military operation steadily rose and the situation on the ground became progressively worse.[5]

As the ferocity of the Afghan theatre increased, so too did the casualty figures for British service personnel. By the end of the year the official death toll from the Ministry of Defence stood at 44, of which 37 had occurred from the middle of June, a fatality rate that now superseded that for Iraq over the previous twelve months.[6] Accompanying this, concerns about the objectives of the campaign and the condition of the armed forces were becoming increasingly notable. In the spring the House of Commons Defence Committee highlighted 'critical shortages' in personnel and called on the government to 'be more forthcoming' about how the success of the mission was to be adjudged; in November a damning report by the National Audit Office showed that the armed services had been operating beyond planned levels for the past five years in order to sustain troop levels in Iraq and Afghanistan; and a study conducted by the MoD during the last quarter of 2005 uncovered shortfalls in recruitment and retention, declining levels of morale across the armed services and a desire among one-quarter of its members to leave at the earliest possible opportunity.[7] In September, the new head of the British army, Sir Richard Dannatt, warned that the military was now 'meeting challenges on the hoof' and was 'running hot' with the demands being made on it.[8]

The government's response to these difficulties was typically repudiative. Once more seeking to frame events as 'a struggle for freedom, for moderation and for democracy', Blair insisted that troops in Afghanistan would have '[a]nything they need and ask for', and that talk of uncertainty over the mission was 'a lot of nonsense'.[9] On this, John Reid, too, was adamant. '[T]here is clarity about exactly what we are doing in Afghanistan', he said, and that was 'to help the democratically elected Government of Afghanistan extend their democratic authority and build their own security forces, and to assist them in their economic development'.[10] The official line was put with comparable rectitude by Des Browne, the new Defence Secretary following Reid's move to the Home Office in May. Admitting that the mission had 'been even harder than we expected', and that the scale of resistance from the Taliban had 'been a surprise', Browne asserted that the campaign was 'vital … not only for Afghanistan but also for the threat that a lawless Afghanistan poses to the region and to the world and also, now that NATO has taken it on, for NATO's own credibility'.[11]

Against this backdrop, the tectonic plates on which New Labour's support for the war on terror had been based shifted significantly during the summer. The trigger for this was an outbreak of hostilities between Israel and the Lebanese politico-paramilitary group, Hezbollah, the immediate cause of which was the killing, by the latter, of eight Israeli soldiers and the kidnapping of two others. The defining feature of the conflict, which lasted for 33 days, was the disproportionate nature of the Israeli response. While Hezbollah fired a constant, if largely ineffectual hail of rockets into Israeli territory, the Israeli military took full advantage of its superior capabilities to launch a full-scale assault on Lebanese towns, villages and infrastructure in a fashion that attracted widespread criticism for its indiscrimination and excess. Conversely, the initial reaction to the crisis from Britain and the US was defined by inaction in the form of a marked refusal to call for an immediate ceasefire; a move broadly interpreted as being designed to provide Israel with a free hand in its efforts to destroy Hezbollah and bring Lebanon to heel for having voted its militants into office. Indeed, the formal position was that the 'right' conditions, including a UN resolution and an avowed desire for peace from both parties, needed to be in place before any ceasefire could be effective. As the Prime Minister argued, it was pointless to 'talk about a meaningful cease-fire unless it was one that was agreed within a political framework that meant it stopped on both sides'.[12] This response, however, also betrayed the transpicuous motives of Bush and Blair, both of whom presented the crisis from within the prism of the war on terror as a prime opportunity for geopolitical reordering. For Bush, the war was seen as a chance to secure 'broader change in the region ... to build a stable and democratic Middle East', while for Blair, the crisis offered the prospect of securing 'a different strategic direction for the whole of that region'. '[T]he conflict in Lebanon', he augured, 'was just a proxy for another, deeper, conflict ... part of a strategy of outside powers in a bigger game'.[13]

The Prime Minister's unflinching support for the US line, coupled with revelations that British airports were being used as part of the US transportation route for delivering weapons to Israel, provoked an intense domestic backlash. Attracting vehement criticism from human rights groups, all sides of the media, public and parliamentary opinion, and not to mention backbench MPs and the Labour Party in general, the stance also led to open tensions within the Cabinet, including a widely reported split between the Prime Minister and the new Foreign Secretary, Margaret Beckett, and with Jack Straw (now leader of the House of Commons) publicly criticising the 'disproportionate' nature of the Israeli offensive.[14] With Blair looking increasingly isolated, and with his approval ratings falling to their lowest ever levels,[15] at the end of July the Prime Minister announced a sharp change in his position, now calling for 'an urgent cessation of hostilities' and declaring a need 'to change dramatically the focus of our policy' and to initiate 'a complete renaissance of our strategy'.[16]

But the shift was more rhetorical than real. Indeed, its defining features involved a fervent reassertion of the Doctrine of No Responsibility that had been set out by the Prime Minister during the spring, as well as a restatement of the core themes of the domestic anti-radicalisation agenda, with a prominent emphasis being placed on the role of values and ideas as the primary weapons in the fight against global terrorism. Reworking Bush's 'axis of evil' narrative, Blair now declared there to be 'an arc of extremism' stretching across the Middle East, the countering of which required the construction of 'an alliance of moderation' and a confrontation driven 'at the level of values as much as force'. Proclaiming that international terrorism was being fuelled by 'a completely false sense of grievance against the West', the Prime Minister asserted that it was 'almost incredible ... that so much of Western opinion appears to buy the idea that the emergence of this global terrorism is somehow our fault', and chided his opponents for being 'in a complete state of denial' about the nature and challenge of the threat faced. The key reason why the West was currently failing in the war on terror, he maintained, was because it was 'not being bold enough, consistent enough, thorough enough, in fighting for the values we believe in'. To further emphasise the point, Blair insisted that the wars in Iraq and Afghanistan were 'not just about changing regimes but changing the values systems governing the nations concerned', and that '[t]he banner was not actually "regime change" it was "values change"'. '[O]ne of the things we have got to stop doing', he said, 'is to stop apologising for our own positions'.[17] Thus:

> we will not win until we shake ourselves free of the wretched capitulation to the propaganda of the enemy, that somehow we are the ones responsible. This terrorism isn't our fault. We didn't cause it. It's not the consequence of foreign policy ... This is a war fought by extremists who pervert the true faith of Islam.[18]

Although the ability to pursue a dual-sided transatlantic bridge strategy had been undermined by the decision to invade Iraq, and despite public disapproval of New Labour's foreign policy approach (with 73% of respondents to a *Populus* poll claiming that this had 'significantly increased' Britain's exposure to a terrorist attack, and with 62% wanting a more distant relationship with the US),[19] Blair also mounted a staunch defence of the government's geopolitical positioning. Insisting on the need to maintain a strong relationship with the US, and for Britain to continue to play a leading role in world affairs, the Prime Minister warned that any attempt to retreat from such a position would be 'a craven act of surrender' that would 'put our future security in the deepest peril'. Whatever the benefits of a looser relationship with the US, he continued, 'the cost in terms of power, weight and influence for Britain would be infinitely greater'.[20] In short, the line was that the country would have 'no prospect' of pursuing its national interest in isolation, and that it would be literally 'insane' to give up either pole of the European or US relationship, since it was Britain's position at the intersection of these alliances that provided 'the vital life source of British power, influence and weight in the new global community taking shape around us'.[21]

When the job is done

The political impact of the Lebanon crisis was far-reaching and enduring. With the Prime Minister's position significantly weakened, and with anti-Blair passions in the Labour Party having been further inflamed during the course of the summer by his refusal to set a timetable for leaving office (having declared during the 2005 General Election that he would not serve beyond a third term), in November the Prime Minister's opponents sought to capitalise on events by mounting a campaign to drive him out. Although the attempted putsch failed in its immediate objectives, the result for the rebellious faction was favourable nonetheless. Acknowledging that his time at Number 10 was rapidly drawing to a close, and that attempting to stay on until the next general election would be prohibitively destabilising for the government, Blair now agreed to stand down as Prime Minister within the next twelve months, leaving the Chancellor, Gordon Brown, the clear favourite to succeed him.[22]

Having cut short the Prime Minister's tenure, problems over foreign policy continued to bedevil the government throughout the latter half of the year. A leading theme in this involved a recurrence of the increasingly visible tensions between the government and the armed forces. In October these were brought clearly into public view following highly critical remarks made by General Dannatt in an interview with the *Daily Mail*. Most prominently, the head of the army claimed that the presence of British troops in Iraq was exacerbating the security problems both there and around the world, attacked the post-war arrangements as having been 'based more on optimism than sound planning', and criticised the goals of the entire mission, describing as a 'naive hope' the notion of installing 'a liberal democracy that was an exemplar for the region, was pro West and might have a beneficial effect on the balance within the Middle East'. With the General adding that the government was at risk of breaking the covenant between the nation and the army, Dannatt's comments struck a chord amongst military figures, several of whom jumped on the opportunity to rail against the government.[23] Amongst them were the ex-Chiefs of General Staff, Field Marshal Lord Inge and General Lord Guthrie, the former of which claimed that ministers lacked 'a clear strategy in either Afghanistan or Iraq', while the latter described the recent deployment of British troops to Afghanistan at a time when the army was tied up in Iraq as 'cuckoo'.[24] Somewhat more diplomatically, Dannatt's predecessor, General Jackson observed that one of the problems with the government's Iraq policy was that 'Western liberal democracy may not of itself export that easily'.[25]

Increasingly under the kosh, and anxious to shift the terms of the debate, government ministers now began to highlight the potential for a withdrawal of troops from Iraq, and to focus the discussion on the conditions under which military personnel could be pulled out. So it was that the British campaign that had been initially justified on the basis of a threat from weapons of mass destruction, and that had since morphed into an effort of helping to support the birth of Iraqi democracy, entered a final phase of treading water until a politico-military solution that would allow troops to be withdrawn while Iraqi and US forces took up the remaining slack could be arranged.[26] While the Ministry of Defence upheld the official line that Britain had 'a clear strategy' in Iraq and that

Dannatt's comments were ill-measured, Des Browne let it be known that British troop numbers would now start to decline, and would be 'significantly lower' by the end of 2007. Blair himself, while maintaining that the strategy was to withdraw from Iraq only 'when the job is done', also declared that the policy now was for a 'progressive withdrawal', during which Iraqi security forces would step up and assume a greater share of the responsibilities.[27]

The government's domestic difficulties over Iraq heightened further at the end of October as ministers were forced to fend off parliamentary pressures for a full inquiry into the war during a House of Commons debate, only the second to have been held on the issue since the start of the invasion. The official line in this, as put by Margaret Beckett (with Blair refusing to attend on the grounds that he did not participate in debates initiated by backbenchers), was that it would be 'perfectly sensible and legitimate' for the government to hold an inquiry into all the events surrounding the war at some future point, but that doing so at the present time would be counterproductive and would exacerbate the situation in Iraq by providing a sign of weakness that would embolden the forces of the insurgency. To hold an inquiry while troops were still in action, she declared, would send out 'the wrong signals' and would risk 'appearing to set a deadline for our operations in Iraq which would be politically and militarily damaging'.[28] The paradox of the government refusing to permit an inquiry on one of the most pressing issues for the country on the grounds that it would be damaging to a war effort being waged in the name of democracy was only exacerbated by its imposition of a three-line whip to ensure that the motion for an inquiry was defeated. But even here, the government's authority on the matter remained notably diminished. The margin of victory, at 298 votes to 273, was anything but convincing.[29]

The political context surrounding the issue of Iraq was by this time also being shaped by electoral dynamics in the US, where, as in Britain, public discontent with the war was creating pressure for a change in strategy. With the Democrats successfully portraying Iraq as having been a diversion from the real fight against terrorism, and managing to catch the public mood with calls for a timetable for withdrawal, the line from Washington, too, became ever more centred on the need for the Iraqi government to increase its own security provisions. On this, Rumsfeld in particular was in the vanguard, calling for a reassertion of the original military lite approach to the invasion, and claiming that the situation required a 'major adjustment'. Urging that the aim should now be to 'go minimalist', the Defense Secretary pressed for a programme of troop withdrawals and for 'an accelerated drawdown of US bases' in order to make it clear to the Iraqi government that 'they have to pull up their socks, step up and take responsibility for their country'.[30] The clarion call, however, would go unheeded. In November a series of disastrous mid-term election results for the Republicans left the Democrats in control of both Houses of Congress, an outcome that prompted Rumsfeld's resignation and left Bush visibly eviscerated as a world leader.[31]

By the end of the year, the new imperialist strategy that had been unleashed by the US in the guise of a 'war on terror', and which had been supported by New Labour as a means of elevating Britain's global influence, was crumbling into the Potomac. In both Afghanistan and Iraq the cornerstone of an arm's-length, swift and limited military intervention had palpably failed, with operations in the former having been exacerbated by the diversion of resources and energies to the latter, and with the absence of any substantive post-war planning for Iraq having created the conditions for a vicious insurgency and having provided both the Taliban and al-Qaeda with the space to recover and regenerate. Moreover, while the scale and intensity of the violence had become progressively worse, with the Taliban now resurgent in Afghanistan, and with the insurgency in Iraq proving unsatiated by the trial and subsequent execution of Saddam Hussein, the terror threat from al-Qaeda, the excising of which provided the purported *raison d'etre* of the entire war on terror, also remained undimmed. Conversely, the notion that military action could provide the precursor for embedding free market democracy in the Middle East was now looking increasingly forlorn, with democratic politics struggling in Afghanistan and Iraq, and with little sign of reforms elsewhere in the region. Added to this, the legitimacy of the humanitarian discourse within which the content of the war on terror had been embedded was also in crisis, with human rights still lacking in the two active theatres of war, with the rule of law and due process having been undermined by Guantánamo Bay and the programme of extraordinary rendition, and with domestic civil liberties in both the US and Britain having been progressively eroded by a series of legislative measures justified with recourse to an unparalleled terrorist threat.

Completing the roll-call of failure, the US invasions, conducted in part as a means of establishing US credibility and of easing its maintenance of global order, had only served to make the international sphere less certain and more unstable. Having divided and undermined the United Nations, and having led to political ruptures both within and beyond the Middle East, the collapse of the new imperialist strategy had also emboldened anti-Western regimes, most obviously in North Korea and Iran, the latter of which had now been transformed into the leading power in the Middle East by the elimination of its main competitors, and was re-engaging in its development of a nuclear programme, a move justified by Tehran on the grounds of energy production but one that many regarded as a cover for the pursuit of weapons technology.[32] In the spring of 2007 this loss of credibility was starkly exposed when the Iranian navy kidnapped 15 British marines on the Shatt-al-Arab waterway, holding them for twelve days prior to their eventual release and publicly highlighting the impotency of both the US and Britain in the process. The event also underscored the extent to which Britain's influence and standing in world affairs had been damaged by its close proximity to the Bush administration, with ministerial calls for a ban on EU exports to Iran attracting no support from member states, and with an appeal to the United Nations eliciting nothing more than a weak statement of disapproval from the Security Council.[33]

Core British values

In early 2007, and contrary to the recommendations of the Iraq Study Group set up to examine the available options for US strategy (and which had just concluded in favour of a military withdrawal), Bush announced a policy shift in favour of a 'surge', involving more than 20,000 extra troops in an attempt to allay the rising tide of violence and to enforce US control of the situation.[34] The following month the scale of the divergence that had now emerged between British and US policy on Iraq was clearly exposed as Blair announced that British troops would now start to be withdrawn over the course of the year, and that their role would increasingly shift to one of providing support for Iraqi forces.[35] However, while this raised questions about strains in the transatlantic relationship, the official line was that the bifurcation was not evidence of a policy split, but was rather the result of a commonly agreed position; namely, the need to focus more intently on building up Iraq's own security capability. Declaring that the British drawdown was being driven precisely by success in this area, Blair maintained that Iraqi forces now had 'the primary role for security' in most parts of Basra, though at the same time, ever keen to uphold a tough stance on the war on terror, insisted that troops would remain in Iraq 'for as long as we are wanted and have a job to do'.[36] In the same vein, in February the Prime Minister announced that British troop levels in Afghanistan would now start to rise, with extra deployments bringing the total number to around 7,700, and again insisted that they would stay 'until the job is done'.[37]

Such assertions, though, were now also at odds with the state of public opinion, as domestic support for the Iraq war fell to an all time low.

According to a BBC/ICM survey, less than one-third (29%) of British people now believed the war to be justified (down from 46% in 2004), around half (51%) stated that they would not trust the government if it claimed that military action was needed to deal with a threat to national security in the future, and just 5% considered that Britain was now a safer place in the wake of the invasion. In Iraq, too, the mood was increasingly pessimistic. According to the BBC, fewer than two-fifths of Iraqis now claimed that life in the country was good (compared to 71% in 2005). According to a poll conducted for several major media outlets, more than four-fifths of Iraqis (82%) expressed little or no confidence in the ongoing occupation.[38]

These events were accompanied by further domestic measures designed to deal with the threat from international terrorism. The most notable of these centred on a reorganisation of the Home Office, with its national security and justice functions being split off to a newly created Justice Department in order to allow the Home Secretary to focus more specifically on terrorism, and on declarations of intent concerning a further round of anti-terror legislation, the main feature of which consisted of renewed assertions about the need to extend the period for which terror suspects could be detained without trial. Along with this, official warnings about the nature of the terror threat were *de rigueur* once more. John Reid, for example (by now Home Secretary, having taken over from Charles Clarke in May 2006), warned that the scale of the danger was at a 'very high level',[39] while Eliza Manningham-Buller warned that there had been 'a steady increase' in the terrorist threat, and that the problem was likely to 'last a generation'. On the specific details of this, MI5's Director General stated that five major conspiracies had been thwarted since 7/7, and that the security services were currently tracking around 30 further plots and were dealing with around 200 groupings or networks, containing more than 1,600 individuals who were believed to be 'actively engaged' in terrorist activities.[40]

Notice as to the government's intentions for a new phase of anti-terror laws, and that this would involve a further recalibration of the 'balance' between civil liberties and the security apparatus of the state, had been served during the latter months of 2006. At his final speech to the Labour Party conference in September, Blair set down a marker by insisting that currently held conceptions of liberty were outdated and were 'not keeping pace with change in reality'. Once more applying the argument that unique dangers required unique actions, the Prime Minister's line of thought conveyed an ominous tone. 'We can only protect liberty', he said, 'by making it relevant to the modern world'.[41] On this, John Reid, too, was in full agreement. Warning that the rights and freedoms of Britain's free society were being abused by 'fascist individuals', the Home Secretary declared that actions to close this loophole of opportunity were now necessary. That selling such measures to the British public required them to be presented as a temporary expedient, and that this appeared to be somewhat incongruent with the long-term and existentially challenging nature of the threat that such measures were precisely supposed to address, did not, apparently, seem to matter. As he put it:

> Sometimes we may have to modify some of our own freedoms in the short term in order to prevent their misuse and abuse by those who oppose our fundamental values and would destroy all of our freedoms in the long term.[42]

By this point, however, the phraseology of the 'war on terror' itself, the legitimising basis of New Labour's foreign and domestic policy approach for more than half a decade, was increasingly under question. In January 2007 the Director of Public Prosecutions, Sir Ken Macdonald, launched a high-profile attack on the use of the term, stating that there was 'no such thing' as a 'war' on terror, and that those responsible for atrocities such as the 7/7 bombings were not 'soldiers', but 'deluded, narcissistic inadequates', 'criminals' and 'fantasists' who should be dealt with by the criminal justice system. The government's anti-terror measures also came under fire, with Macdonald claiming that a 'fear-driven and inappropriate' response to terrorism risked sacrificing 'fundamental values critical to the maintenance of the rule of law'. 'We must protect ourselves from these atrocious crimes', he said, 'without abandoning our traditions of freedom'.[43] Claims about the severity of the terrorist threat, too, clashed with a notable absence of cogency at the international level. As Margaret Beckett revealed, on whether there was a coherent, long-term global plan for dealing with international terrorism: 'The answer to that question will certainly be no'.[44]

By the spring, the government's discursive framing of the war on terror was again being subtly but significantly altered. While senior officials had spent the best part of the previous twelve months attempting to justify and legitimise their actions by redefining the 'war' in terms of a humanitarian, values-based discourse, this new rhetorical content was now used as the basis for dissolving the use of the term 'war on terror' itself, which was now presented as being incompatible with its very essence. In short, since the war on terror was a fight about values and ideas, then, by definition, there was no 'war' on terror. Outlining the new approach, in April the International Development Secretary, Hilary Benn, declared that there was no global war in the sense of a fight against an organised enemy 'with a clear identity and a coherent set of objectives'. Rather, the situation was one of a struggle for the universal values of freedom and democracy in the face of a violent campaign being conducted by 'a small number of loose, shifting and disparate groups who have relatively little in common apart from their identification with others who share their distorted view of the world'. Continuing to describe the struggle in the militaristic terms of the war on terror, he said, was thus not only inaccurate but also counterproductive, giving succour to terrorists by encouraging them to feel 'part of something bigger'.[45]

The government's domestic plans for dealing with violent extremism were also cast in a similar light. In a document produced by the Department for Community and Local Government, entitled *Preventing Violent Extremism*, the fight against terrorism was explicitly framed not as a 'clash of civilisations or a struggle between Islam and "the West"', but as a clash between adherents to 'core British values' and 'a small fringe of terrorists and their extremist supporters'. The only way to effectively deal with this, it claimed, was to succeed in the battle for hearts and minds within the Muslim community in order to prevent individuals who may be vulnerable to violent extremism from becoming radicalised. Building on the recommendations of the *Preventing Extremism Together* project, the aim of government policy, it observed, should be to '[f]undamentally rebalance our engagement towards those organisations that uphold shared values and reject and condemn violent extremism'.[46]

Yet this discursive reformulation entailed no shift in the practical content of New Labour's overall strategic approach. On the contrary, the final stage of Blair's protracted departure from office was characterised by a staunchly vigorous defence of an interventionist foreign policy. Belying comments from Sir Jock Stirrup that there was 'not much more left in the locker' given the intensity and duration of the military deployments in the Middle East, and that the armed forces would not be able to engage in any new large-scale fighting 'for some years to come', the Prime Minister again warned that withdrawing from an active role in foreign affairs would qualitatively reduce Britain's 'reach, effect and influence' in the world.[47] Stated thus, Blair's wholesale commitment to the self-ratcheting dynamics of the Doctrine of No Responsibility was adroitly reaffirmed, with the Prime Minister now placing the blame for public antipathy towards the war on terror at the door of the media, which was lambasted for having constantly bombarded the public with the 'propaganda of the enemy'.[48] Once more insisting that any shift in foreign policy would be not only 'futile' but 'catastrophic' for the fight against global terrorism given that none of this had anything to do with the actions of the West, let alone the foreign policy of the New Labour government, Blair warned that the real risk to Britain's national interest was that future political leaders (a thinly coded reference to the incoming Brown administration) might now opt to sideline the use of 'hard' power and relegate the British military 'to an essentially peacekeeping role'. Adamantly maintaining that Britain needed 'to be warfighters as well as peacekeepers', and that the ability to intervene was 'the only way we are going to make this country count in the modern world', the necessity, he said, was to retain a foreign policy that 'keeps our American alliance strong and is prepared to project hard as well as soft power'.[49]

In like fashion, Blair's departure from the British political stage was accompanied by one last rhetorical flourish. In a final attempt to cast the terms of his legacy in a positive light, the Prime Minister implored, at his resignation speech in May, that '[h]and on heart ... I did what I thought was right for our country', and, in bidding farewell to the Commons the following month, insisted that he was 'truly sorry' for the dangers that Britain's armed forces now faced. Relinquishing power to a standing ovation from all sides of the House, Blair subsequently departed, in a display of bitterly exquisite irony, to take up a new post working for the Quartet of Russia, the US, the UN and the EU, as their envoy for peace in the Middle East.[50]

A great project

Having finally disposed of his principal antagonist for the throne, on 27 June 2007 Gordon Brown assumed the role of Prime Minister, proclaiming that his would be 'a new Government with new priorities'. In this, the new government's first and top priority was to put measurable distance between itself and the Blair regime in order to create the impression of a fresh administration. The key features of this consisted of a series of new appointments to the Cabinet, the hallmarks of which saw David Miliband taking over as Foreign Secretary (becoming the youngest holder of the office in three decades), Jacqui Smith, the former Chief Whip, replacing John Reid as Home Secretary, and the former navy chief, Admiral Sir Alan West, becoming Security Minister. Wide-ranging proposals for constitutional reform, including the removal of the Prime Minister's ability to declare war, also featured highly, as did noises about a reconfiguring of the transatlantic relationship, with the new International Development Secretary, Douglas Alexander, calling for 'a rules-based international system', and with Lord Malloch-Brown, the new minister for Africa, Asia and the UN, declaring that Britain and the US would no longer be 'joined at the hip'.[51]

Brown's line on the war on terror was also immediately tested. Coinciding with his ascension to the Premiership, a trio of failed car bomb attacks in London and Glasgow provided a pertinent, if ultimately impotent reminder of the terrorist threat. The attacks also presented Brown with an opportunity to further differentiate himself from his predecessor. In this, his decision to eschew Blair's eschatological demeanour in favour of a sombre, calm and low-key approach, and his treatment of the attacks as a criminal justice matter rather than an instance of existential struggle, drew wide admiration and popular support.[52] Differentiation, too, was evident in the government's broader approach to the fight against international terrorism. With Brown placing a greater emphasis on economic development and reconstruction, speaking of a need for investment in fragile countries 'so that people genuinely have a stake in the future', a dividing line was also drawn on the issue of Iraq. '[O]ne of the failures at the beginning' of the war, he said, 'was that we didn't put the resources and the help into the economic reconstruction that was necessary'.[53]

But the idea that a New Labour government under Brown would diverge significantly from that led by Blair was illusory. Beyond tactical differences and the new Prime Minister's desire to start life in the highest office with as clean a slate as possible, strong and substantial elements of continuity between the two eras remained. Belying appearances of a clean break from Blair, this too was immediately apparent in the distinctly Blairite way in which the new Prime Minister sought to discursively frame the attacks in London and Glasgow. Insisting that the attempted bombings had no connection whatsoever to New Labour's foreign policy, and that Britain would be at risk 'whatever was happening in Afghanistan or Iraq', Brown firmly emphasised the importance of ideas and values in the war on terror, presenting the target of the attacks as the 'values that we represent', and restating that the fight against terrorism needed to be conducted 'not just militarily' but on a 'cultural and ideological' level.[54] Moreover, contrary to initial intimations that the Brown government would pursue a looser relationship with the US than its predecessor, the underlying substance here was also familiar. Declaring that the United States remained Britain's 'single most important bilateral relationship', the Prime Minister warned that he had 'no truck with anti-Americanism' and insisted that the world was 'stronger' when the two countries worked together for a common goal. The Bush administration, he said, was owed a great debt for its 'leadership' in the ongoing fight against the threat of global terrorism, and foreign policy in the post-Blair era would continue to be based on making the most of 'our enduring values and our network of alliances'.[55]

These themes were further elucidated by David Miliband. In a series of set-piece speeches, designed as much to cauterise the political wounds inflicted by the Iraq war as to outline the new government's approach to international affairs, the Foreign Secretary declared that Britain was now entering 'the second wave of New Labour foreign policy' and stressed that the Brown government was determined to 'learn the right lessons' from the Blair era. Yet the policy formulation that emerged from this analysis bore close resemblance to that which had preceded it; namely, that the experience of the past few years had demonstrated the limitations of military measures, but that the promotion of humanitarian and democratic values abroad remained a valuable endeavour. Divisions over Iraq and Afghanistan, Miliband stated, should not 'obscure our national interest, never mind our moral impulse, in supporting movements for democracy', the spread of which was hailed as being 'the best long term defence against global terrorism and conflict'. While retaining the right to use military force in 'extreme cases' (such as genocide or ethnic cleansing) the central thrust of foreign policy under Brown, then, was to be a 'new diplomacy', designed to promote democratic values by using Britain's influence within global institutions such as the WTO and the EU, and by utilising the leverage of 'incentives and sanctions' afforded by virtue of Britain's economic and financial position. Also key, however, remained the ability to function as a strong transatlantic bridge between Europe and the US. Declaring that the government would actively strive to capitalise on 'Britain's ability to be a global hub' as a means of 'promoting our values and interests on the global stage', Miliband maintained that this would require upholding close links between London and Washington. Calling on Britain and the US to 'come together in a great project' of disseminating the universal values of democracy and human rights, the Foreign Secretary averred that in order to pursue 'an active foreign policy' it was essential to have 'a strong relationship with the leading global power'.[56]

But despite such reassertions, any hopes that the Brown administration may have harboured about reviving a Blairite transatlantic bridge approach were rapidly imperilled. Though signing up to the EU's Lisbon treaty in December, Brown's refusal to adhere to a long-standing Labour commitment to hold a referendum on the matter created an air of mistrust about the extent to which the new regime would engage seriously in European issues, and further inflamed the already predominant Eurosceptic tendency within the British electorate. On the other hand, the rhetoric of Atlanticism, too, proved to be far from trouble-free. While one of the first acts of the new government was to assent to a US request to use the RAF Menwith Hill monitoring station in North Yorkshire as part of its missile defence system (ostensibly as a means of protection against rogue states, although the prevailing suspicion was that Russia posed the most likely target),[57] transatlantic tensions soon emerged over the divergent strategies that were now being pursued in Iraq. At the same time as the US was stepping up its surge policy in an effort to address spiralling levels of violence in the country, the British approach was now shifting increasingly from engagement to withdrawal. In September, British troops in Basra pulled back from their main palatial base to the airport located on the outskirts of the city, as part of a tactical shift to an 'overwatch' role. In this, British forces were to assist the Iraqi authorities in the maintenance of order, if required, but would now focus their efforts on training the Iraqi services so as to facilitate the transfer of responsibility for security provision. Preparations for a formal handover of Basra province (the last remaining province under British control) to the Iraqi authorities were completed in mid-December, and plans for a reduction in troop levels to 2,500 by March 2008 were put in place.[58]

Yet while some form of endgame in Iraq was clearly approaching for the British government, officials were unbending in their refusal to set a fixed deadline for a complete withdrawal. Outlining the shift to an overwatch role, Gordon Brown stated that British troops still had 'clear obligations to discharge', and that setting a timetable for their exit, in strengthening the hand of the enemy, would merely be 'hindering the task of our armed forces and increasing the risks they face'. Sensitive to political perceptions that the delay was in response to US displeasure with the British military drawdown, officials also remained keen to avoid any sign of undue US influence. According to the Ministry of Defence, the city of Basra had been given over to the Iraqis 'only when the conditions were right', while according to Miliband the withdrawal process would be determined entirely by the British national interest, and would at all times 'reflect the situation on the ground'.[59] Denying that the drawdown had led to tensions with the US, Des Browne, too, asserted that the reduction of troop numbers was being driven by operational requirements, and insisted that it was 'not, by any stretch of the imagination, a political decision'.[60]

But the move also highlighted the scale of British impotence in Iraq. According to Rory Stewart, the deputy governor of two southern Iraqi provinces from 2003 to 2004, the pullback was a reflection of the fact that 'we simply do not have any control over southern Iraq', a state of affairs which, he concluded, had endured for the last two-and-a-half years.[61] A similar understanding of the situation was also evident from the House of Commons Defence Committee. As it noted, in the wake of the British pullback Basra remained dominated not by the Iraqi authorities, but by 'murderous, corrupt and militia-infiltrated elements', and that any 'relative security' owed more 'to the dominance of militias and criminal gangs … than to the success of the multinational and Iraqi security forces in tackling the root causes of the violence'.[62] This view was also reflected in Iraqi public opinion itself. According to a BBC survey, more than 85% of the residents of Basra considered British troops to have had a negative effect on the province since their arrival, more than half (56%) believed that their presence had led to an increase in the levels of militia violence, and two-thirds were of the opinion that the security situation would improve once British troops left.[63] Domestic polls in Britain made glum reading for the government as well. According to a survey for BBC *Newsnight*, more than two-thirds of the British public now considered British troops to be losing the war in Iraq, more than two-fifths (42%) wanted them to be withdrawn as soon as possible (with just 27% believing that they should remain for as long as the Iraqi authorities wanted), and only one-fifth considered British forces to be improving the security situation, while one-third thought them to be making matters worse.[64]

To compound matters further, the sustained pressures that had been placed on the British military by New Labour's foreign policy exertions, and the sense of overstretch that was now coming increasingly to the fore, were also becoming keen political issues. An attack on Brown from General Lord Guthrie, who pilloried the Prime Minister's 'most unsympathetic' attitude to defence when Chancellor, and who accused him of bearing 'much of the blame' for the current situation, was reflected in concerns from the Royal British Legion of a 'growing sense of disillusionment among service personnel', and in claims from the think-tank, Demos, that the armed forces were now 'running on empty' and could take up to a decade to recover.[65] Mirroring these anxieties, leaked comments from General Dannatt also caught the head of the armed forces bemoaning that troops were feeling 'devalued, angry and suffering from Iraq fatigue', and that years of government under-funding had left the British army with 'almost no capability to react to the unexpected'.[66]

Reconciliation

Bringing home the grim salience of this point, the Taliban resurgence and the increasingly tumultuous state of affairs in Afghanistan was now turning 2007 into the bloodiest year there since the war began. As the internal situation degenerated, the risk that disorder could now spill over and destabilise the wider region also became worryingly real. The immediate concern here centred on Afghanistan's porous and wholly ungovernable border region with Pakistan, where it was believed that both al-Qaeda and senior Taliban operatives were taking refuge, and from where operations against the coalition were being planned and conducted.[67] As tensions between Pakistan and the US increased, with the latter accusing the former of making insufficiently serious efforts to combat the threat of Islamic radicalism and to securitise the border areas, political conditions inside

Pakistan itself began to give cause for alarm.[68] In December, a declaration of martial law by the Pakistani President, Pervez Musharraf, following a series of deadly suicide bombings by Islamic extremists ahead of a forthcoming election (one of which had assassinated the leading opposition candidate, Benazir Bhutto), did little to assuage fears that the course of events was moving in an ever more perilous direction.[69]

Against this backdrop, throughout the latter half of the year the government's Afghan strategy began to shift. With the amount of British troops in the country now exceeding the levels deployed in Iraq, with the scale and intensity of military operations now among the most significant since the Second World War, and with all talk of setting a firm date for withdrawal having been abandoned, the political debate over the exact purpose of the mission, still loosely based around notions of reconstruction, democracy and the defeat of the Taliban, was again driven to the forefront of the domestic agenda.[70] As usual, much of the government's response was entirely expected, if not entirely coherent. While Lord Malloch-Brown assertively denied that the Taliban posed a credible threat to the Afghan government, the Prime Minister warned that defeat in Afghanistan would have adverse consequences for 'the whole of the civilised world', and Des Browne called for more NATO countries to help 'share the burden' of combat operations.[71] Beyond this, however, soundings about the need to develop a new and comprehensive approach could also be discerned. Calling for an 'overarching campaign' and a 'strategic plan' for Afghanistan, the Defence Secretary warned that the longer the tide of violence was allowed to run against the coalition, the more diminished the prospects for success would become. 'In the long term', he said, 'the risk is that the politicisation of the coverage of operations will feed a new strain of isolationism in public opinion', a sense of disillusionment driven not just by events in Iraq, but also by 'a wider pessimism and fatigue with the complex and seemingly intractable issues across the Middle East and in Afghanistan and elsewhere'.[72]

Despite sustained ministerial assertions about the immorality, not to mention the futility of attempting to engage in negotiations with the Taliban, officials were also now starting to consider the need for some form of political engagement. Outlining the shift in strategy, even if it was not explicitly advertised as such, Browne explained that the Taliban was not a 'generic, homogeneous organisation', and claimed that some of its members were 'capable of being persuaded' to participate in the democratic process. Attempting to spin the rising levels of violence as a sign of success, telling the Defence Committee that 'the nature of the insurgency' was 'a function of the progress that we have made', the Defence Secretary explained that '[p]art of what we are seeking to do is to create an environment where people can make that very transition'. '[T]here must be a place for them in a future Afghanistan', he said, 'It is what we call "reconciliation"'.[73] Thus:

> we need to accept that one of the measures of success in Afghanistan is going to be the political process's ability to get people to sign up to it and some of them will be people who at some stage signed up to one or other of the tiers of the Taliban movement.[74]

In December, the 'next stage' of the government's strategy in Afghanistan was formally unveiled by the Prime Minister. Insisting that coalition forces were 'winning the battle against the insurgency', Brown set out a wide-ranging battery of measures, mostly aspirational in form, ranging from a strengthening of the Afghan government's own security provisions, the promotion of political reconciliation, the development of local and provincial governance, extra funds for economic reconstruction, greater burden sharing by NATO allies and a drive to defeat the Taliban 'by isolating and eliminating their leadership'. Though ardently declaring that 'we will not enter into any negotiations with these people' (in the face of evidence suggesting that MI6 operatives had already held secret meetings with senior Taliban members during the summer),[75] the Prime Minister equally insisted that the door remained open, and that insurgents 'had a place' in legitimate Afghan society on the proviso that they renounced violence and agreed to abide by the rule of law.[76]

But the road to success for the government's strategy remained strewn with serious obstacles. Among the most notable of these, tensions with the Afghan government over the form and conduct of the military strategy threatened to derail any forward momentum, as did the increasingly public splits within NATO itself over the distribution of the burdens and responsibilities involved in the mission.[77] Warning members of the risks of continued disagreement, NATO's Secretary General, Jaap De Hope Scheffer, put the point bluntly. If the Taliban and its terrorist associates were not contained, he said, then their activities would invariably expand to Europe: the operation in Afghanistan was thus a 'necessity and not a choice'.[78] A similar point was made, albeit for domestic consumption, by the Foreign Secretary. Aiming to bolster public support for the campaign amidst growing talk of the need for a withdrawal and concerns as to whether the war could ever be won, Miliband insisted that while progress had been relatively slow, there was no question that Britain would baulk at its commitment to rehabilitate the country, and highlighted the dangers of allowing Afghanistan to revert to being a failed state and a safe haven for terrorists.[79] The state of Afghan public opinion, such as it was possible to discern, on the other hand, provided rare encouragement. According to one survey, the vast majority, amounting to some 85% of Afghanis, were supportive of the current national government, three-quarters considered the coalition's arrival in Afghanistan to have been 'mostly' to 'very good', and an overwhelming 92% declared themselves to be opposed to the Taliban, which, along with al-Qaeda and foreign fighters, was directly blamed by more than half of those asked (58%) for the current violence. Conversely, just 3% put the blame on Western forces.[80]

But the scale of the challenge remained daunting, even to the most fatally optimistic. In February 2008, a report from the International Institute of Strategic Studies warned that the Afghan government, still led by Hamid Karzai, continued to lack the requisite authority to function effectively, that international efforts to stabilise the country remained largely incoherent, and that Afghanistan risked becoming a 'failed state' once more if NATO operations proved to be unsuccessful.[81] At the same time, the US-based Afghanistan Study Group also warned that the situation was at a 'crossroads' and that Washington had yet to develop a 'clear and consistent comprehensive strategy',[82] while a report from the Senlis Council think-tank estimated that the Taliban had now managed to establish a permanent presence across more than half the country.[83] Although the US Director of National Intelligence, Mike McConnell, put the figure at a far lower level (at around 10% compared to the 54% being put out by Senlis), the poor position of Afghanistan's central government was clear nonetheless; controlling, in his estimation, little more than 30% of the country, with the rest falling under tribal control.[84]

Beyond the two obvious theatres of conflict, by this time the picture in the war on terror more generally was also far from salutary. On the positive side, signs of progress on the ideational front could now be seen. An international opinion poll conducted by Pew showed support for al-Qaeda and the popularity of Osama bin Laden to be in decline in Muslim countries (with a notable exception being Pakistan), and noted that the proportion of Muslims who considered suicide bombing to be a justified means of defending Islam had also fallen. That said, much of this shift owed less to the actions of the Western axis than to the negative effects of radical Islamic terrorism itself. With most victims of the al-Qaeda terror franchise since 9/11 having been Muslim, and with extremist Islamic organisations failing to offer any form of progressive social or political vision (and, indeed, with the aim being instead to impose backward and repressive Talibanesque 'Islamic' regimes), rising levels of alienation and anger towards al-Qaeda and its affiliates were now becoming increasingly evident across the Islamic world.[85] Supporting these findings, at the end of February a survey by Gallup, purporting to represent the views of 90% of the world's Muslims, showed the vast majority to be in support of Western-style democratic freedoms.[86]

On the negative side, though, studies into the ongoing threat of international terrorism reported mixed findings. Most favourably, a study from Simon Fraser University found there to have been a large drop in the number of fatalities from terrorist attacks (a 40% fall from 2001 to 2006, and a further fall in 2007), and noted a sharp decline in the scale of global terrorism as a result of more coordinated counter-terrorism efforts, doctrinal infighting between terrorist groups, and the growing rejection of terrorist violence by Muslims. Somewhat less palatable assessments, however, emerged from the US State Department, which reported a negligible change in the number of worldwide terrorist attacks from 2006 to 2007, and from the American Security Project, which claimed that the threat from al-Qaeda was not only 'more significant' than it had been prior to 9/11, but that there had been 'a massive and dramatic increase in Islamist terrorism since 2003', even excluding attacks in Iraq, Afghanistan and those related to the Israeli-Palestinian dispute.[87] Similar findings to this were also produced by RAND, which noted that al-Qaeda had been involved in a greater number of terrorist attacks in the post-9/11 period than in the history of the organisation prior to this point, and that these had been dispersed across a far wider geographical area. According to the Oxford Research Group, the current strategy in the war on terror was evidently failing, and that if al-Qaeda was to be defeated then this would require 'a change in policy at every level'.[88]

Conclusion

The shifting context for Britain's war on terror may have been accompanied by a change in its political leadership, but in terms of the underlying policy direction the New Labour government led by Gordon Brown retained strong lines of continuity with that ruled by Tony Blair. In this, the upholding of strong transatlantic ties, the reassertion of the Doctrine of No Responsibility and a renewed emphasis on the role of values and ideas all underpinned the new administration's approach to dealing with the threat from radical Islamic terrorism. But all the same, the impact of the contextual change was impossible to ignore. The divergent approaches being taken towards Iraq, where the new imperialist strategy of the Bush administration had now been abandoned in favour of a military surge, put the maintenance of a Blairite transatlantic bridge under growing strain, while the situation in Afghanistan was becoming progressively worse. Having been consistently ranked second in order of concern behind Iraq, and with the overall strategy of the war on terror having created the conditions for a Taliban resurgence, the centre of gravity for Britain's military operations was now moving decidedly towards Helmand province.

Notes

1   Evidence to the Defence Committee, 1 November 2005, Q. 11.
2   N. Temko and M. Townsend, 'Civil war raging in Iraq, says Allawi', *Observer,* 19 March 2006; M. Tempest and M. Oliver, 'Reid: Iraq civil war "not inevitable"', *Guardian,* 20 March 2006.
3   Monthly press conference, 23 January 2006.
4   Remarks in the House of Commons, *Hansard,* 26 January 2006, col. 1531.
5   I. Pannell, 'Where next for UK's Afghan mission?', BBC News, 16 August 2009, http://news.bbc.co.uk/1/hi/uk/8204071.stm, accessed 9 November 2010; M. Smith, 'UK troops "to spend 10 years" in Afghanistan', *Sunday Times,* 17 September 2006.
6   J. Starkey and D. McGrory, 'Escalating conflict in Afghanistan claims 22nd British victim', *The Times,* 29 December 2006.
7   Defence Committee (2006), para. 105; also see (2006a); National Audit Office (2006); Forster (2006).
8   R. Norton-Taylor, 'Britain's new top soldier: "Can the military cope? I say – just"', *Guardian,* 4 September 2006. Emblematic of this was the struggle over the town of Musa Qala. With the lack of resources undermining efforts to hold the town, in October commanders were forced to arrange a temporary ceasefire deal with the Taliban. The ceasefire lasted until February 2007, when the town was recaptured by Taliban fighters. It was subsequently retaken by coalition forces in December.
9   Evidence to the Liaison Committee, 4 July 2006, Q. 432, 434; also see S. Knight, 'Billions pledged to rebuild Afghanistan', *The Times,* 31 January 2006.
10 House of Commons, 27 February 2006, cols 2–3.
11 J. Booth, '"Afghanistan is tougher than we expected" says minister', *The Times,* 19 September 2006.
12 P. Riddell and P. Webster, 'Interview with Tony Blair', *The Times,* 2 September 2006.
13 Joint press conference with George Bush, 28 July 2006; Speech to the TUC conference, 12 September 2006.
14 O. King, 'PM admits divisions but says UN peace plan imminent', *Guardian,* 3 August 2006; J. Booth, 'Blair admits Lebanon violence could fuel extremism', *The Times,* 3 August 2006.
15 'Tony Blair's view of Britain's role in the world has left him vulnerable at home', *Economist,* 3 August 2006; also see M. Tempest and O. King, 'Blair returns to growing backlash on Lebanon', *Guardian,* 2 August 2006.
16 These and the following quotations are from: Speech to News Corps (Pebble Beach, California), 30 July 2006; Speech to the Los Angeles World Affairs Council, 1 August 2006.
17 Joint press conference, George Bush and Tony Blair, 28 July 2006.
18 Speech to the Labour Party conference, 25 September 2006.
19 P. Riddell, 'Best defence against terrorism is a split with US, say voters', *The Times,* 6 September 2006.
20 Speech to the Labour Party conference, 25 September 2006; Speech to the TUC conference, 12 September 2006.
21 Speech at Lord Mayor's Banquet, 13 November 2006.
22 See P. Webster, 'Labour paralysed as the poison spreads', *The Times,* 7 September 2006; BBC News, 'I will quit within a year – Blair', 7 September 2006, http://news.bbc.co.uk/1/hi/uk_politics/5322094.stm, accessed 9 November 2010.

23 S. Sands, 'Sir Richard Dannatt: a very honest General', *Daily Mail*, 12 October 2006.

24 M. Evans, 'Iraq and Afghan missions not clear, says field marshal', *The Times*, 23 October 2006; M. Evans and A. LeBor, 'Waging a war on two fronts is "cuckoo"', *The Times*, 30 October 2006.

25 General Sir Mike Jackson, Dimbleby Lecture, 7 December 2006.

26 Holloway (2009).

27 BBC News, 'General seeks Iraq withdrawal', 13 October 2006, http://news.bbc. co.uk/1/hi/6046332.stm, accessed 9 November 2010; 'Withdrawal from Iraq now would be disastrous – Blair', *Daily Mail*, 18 October 2006; B. Maddox, 'Blair's Iraq exit strategy seems to be out of the frying pan, into the fire', *The Times*, 28 November 2006.

28 House of Commons debate, *Hansard*, 31 October 2006, cols 171–2.

29 D. Summers, 'MPs reject call for Iraq war inquiry', *Guardian*, 31 October 2006.

30 'Iraq – Illustrative New Courses of Action', Memo by Rumsfeld, 6 November 2006, reprinted in *New York Times*, 3 December 2006.

31 S. G. Stolberg and J. Rutenberg, 'Rumsfeld resigns as Defense Secretary after big election gains for Democrats', *New York Times*, 8 November 2006.

32 See for example: E. MacAskill and I. Traynor, 'Iran nuclear crisis sent to security council', *Guardian*, 1 February 2006; P. Naughton, 'Iran now the key power in Iraq, says UK think-tank', *The Times*, 23 August 2006.

33 J. Borger, 'Britain stumbles in diplomatic dance with Iran', *Guardian*, 30 March 2007; T. Baldwin, D. Kennedy and D. Charter, 'EU refuses to back Britain over call to threaten exports freeze', *The Times*, 31 March 2007.

34 Address to the Nation, 10 January 2007.

35 BBC News, 'Blair announces Iraq troops cut', 21 February 2007, http://news.bbc. co.uk/1/hi/uk/6380933.stm, accessed 9 November 2010.

36 House of Commons Statement on Iraq and the Middle East, 21 February 2007.

37 P. Webster, 'We'll stay till the job is done, Blair tells Karzai', *The Times*, 15 February 2007.

38 BBC Press Office, 'Optimism fades in Iraq', 19 March 2007, http://www.bbc.co.uk/ pressoffice/pressreleases/stories/2007/03_march/19/iraq.shtml, accessed 9 November 2010; BBC News, 'Third "think Iraq war was right"', 20 March 2007, http://news. bbc.co.uk/1/hi/6467147.stm, accessed 9 November 2010.

39 Evidence to Home Affairs Committee, 13 December 2006; also see BBC News, 'Christmas attack "highly likely"', 10 December 2006, http://news.bbc.co.uk/1/hi/ uk/6166195.stm, accessed 9 November 2010.

40 'The International Terrorist Threat to the UK', speech by Eliza Manningham-Buller at Queen Mary's College, 9 November 2006.

41 Speech to the Labour Party conference, 25 September 2006.

42 'Security, Freedom and the Protection of Our Values', speech to DEMOS, 9 August 2006.

43 C. Dyer, 'There is no war on terror', *Guardian*, 24 January 2007.

44 Evidence to Joint Session of the FAC and the Defence Committee, 11 January 2007, Qs 36–7.

45 'Where Does Development Fit in Foreign Policy?', speech to the Center on International Cooperation, 16 April 2007.

46 Department for Communities and Local Government (2007).

47 M. Evans, 'Armed forces "stretched"', *The Times*, 7 March 2007; Speech in Plymouth, 12 January 2007.

48 Blair, Lecture on Public Life, 12 June 2007.
49 'Our Nation's Future', speech by Tony Blair, 12 January 2007; Evidence to the Liaison Committee, 18 June 2007, Q. 185.
50 Resignation speech in Sedgefield, 10 May 2007; Remarks in the House of Commons, 27 June 2007.
51 HMG (2007); T. Baldwin, 'Destructive power is no measure of a country's might, Britain tells US', 13 July 2007; BBC News, 'Speech not critical of US – Brown', 13 July 2007, http://news.bbc.co.uk/1/hi/uk_politics/6896797.stm, accessed 9 November 2010.
52 BBC News, 'PM defiant over "al-Qaeda threat"', 1 July 2007, http://news.bbc.co.uk/1/hi/uk/6258062.stm, accessed 9 November 2010.
53 Downing Street press conference, 23 July 2007; BBC News, 'Brown downplays Iraq terror link', 11 July 2007, http://news.bbc.co.uk/1/hi/6290882.stm, accessed 9 November 2010.
54 BBC News, 'Downing St rebuffs terror threat', 11 July 2007, http://news.bbc.co.uk/1/hi/uk/6290336.stm, accessed 9 November 2010.
55 Press conference at Camp David, 30 July 2007; also see Lord Mayor's Banquet speech, 12 November 2007.
56 Taken from: 'New Diplomacy: Challenges for Foreign Policy', speech to Chatham House, 19 July 2007; Speech to the Labour Party conference, 24 September 2007; Speech to the Fabian Society, 19 January 2008; 'The Democratic Imperative', Aung San Suu Kyi Lecture, Oxford University, 12 February 2008.
57 BBC News, 'UK agrees missile defence request', 25 July 2007, http://news.bbc.co.uk/1/hi/uk_politics/6916262.stm, accessed 9 November 2010.
58 R. Watts and T. Shipman, 'Gen Sir Mike Jackson's attack draws US ire', Daily Telegraph, 2 September 2007; F. Yeoman, 'Former army chief condemns US for "short-sighted" policy on Iraq', The Times, 1 September 2007.
59 BBC News, 'US "delayed UK Basra withdrawal"', 10 September 2007, http://news.bbc.co.uk/2/hi/uk_news/6986536.stm, accessed 9 November 2010.
60 Evidence to Defence Committee, 23 October 2007, Qs 10, 17, 18.
61 BBC News, 'UK Basra base exit "not a defeat"', 3 September 2007, http://news.bbc.co.uk/2/hi/6975375.stm, accessed 9 November 2010.
62 Defence Committee (2007), para. 41.
63 BBC News, 'Basra residents blame UK troops', 14 December 2007, http://news.bbc.co.uk/2/hi/middle_east/7144437.stm; 'UK troops return Basra to Iraqis', 17 December 2007, http://news.bbc.co.uk/1/hi/uk/7146507.stm, both accessed 9 November 2010.
64 BBC News, 'Majority believe Iraq war "lost"', 3 September 2007, .
65 BBC News, 'Ministers "failing UK soldiers"', 15 August 2007, http://news.bbc.co.uk/1/hi/uk_politics/6947770.stm; BBC News, 'Browne denies "failing" UK troops', 19 August 2007, http://news.bbc.co.uk/1/hi/uk_politics/6953500.stm, both accessed 9 November 2010; C. Moreton, 'Lord Guthrie: "Tony's General" turns defence into an attack', Independent, 11 November 2007; Edmunds and Forster (2007).
66 BBC News, 'UK troop reserves "almost gone"', 21 July 2007, http://news.bbc.co.uk/1/hi/uk/6909550.stm, accessed 9 November 2010; S. Rayment, 'Our forces can't carry on like this, says General Sir Richard Dannatt', Sunday Telegraph, 18 November 2007.
67 M. Mazetti, 'Intelligence chief says al Qaeda improves ability to strike in US', New York Times, 6 February 2008.
68 'Miliband appeals for calm amid Pakistani anger at Washington', The Times, 26 July 2007.
69 E. MacAskill, 'Wrong-footed Bush forced to rethink policy on Pakistan', Guardian,

29 December 2007.

70 C. Lamb, 'Britain's £1.5m bribes fail to buy Taleban peace deal', *Sunday Times*, 22 July 2007; BBC News, 'Soldiers "seize Taleban leaders"', 9 December 2007, http://news.bbc.co.uk/1/hi/world/south_asia/7134973.stm, accessed 9 November 2010.

71 Downing Street press conference, 8 October 2007; D. Loyn, 'Taleban "not a threat", says UK', BBC News, 29 November 2007; BBC News, 'Nato "must share Afghan burden"', 14 December 2007; also see F. Hamilton, 'Nato "lacking resources to fight Taleban"', *The Times,* 17 October 2007.

72 Speech at Oxford University's 3rd annual lecture for the Oxford-Leverhulme pro-gramme on the 'Changing Character of War', 9 May 2007; Speech to the Council for Foreign Relations, New York, 24 May 2007.

73 Evidence to the Defence Committee, 23 October 2007, Qs 54, 57, 74,

74 *Ibid.,* Q. 56.

75 T. Harding and T. Coghlan, 'Britain in secret talks with the Taliban', *Daily Telegraph*, 27 December 2007; A. Leithead, 'Why British-Afghan ties have hit a low', BBC News, 6 February 2008, http://news.bbc.co.uk/1/hi/world/south_asia/7231083.stm, accessed 9 November 2010.

76 Statement to the House of Commons, 7 December 2007.

77 As of December 2007 the top NATO contributing nations for the Afghanistan mis-sion were: US 15,038; UK 7,753; Germany 3,155; Italy 2,358; and Canada 1,730. See N. Childs, '"Failed state" warning on Afghanistan', BBC News, 5 February 2008, http://news.bbc.co.uk/1/hi/world/south_asia/7228680.stm, accessed 9 November 2010.

78 A. Haleem and L. Jing, 'NATO credibility in Afghanistan at stake if fails to curb militancy', ChinaView.cn, 28 February 2008, http://news.xinhuanet.com/eng-lish/2008-02/28/content_7687539.htm, accessed 9 November 2010.

79 M. Evans, '"We're doing all we can", British ministers tell Karzai', *The Times*, 4 February 2008; BBC News, 'Miliband defends Afghan presence', 11 February 2008, http://news.bbc.co.uk/1/hi/uk_politics/7238435.stm, accessed 9 November 2010.

80 M. Williams, 'The withdrawal of foreign troops would be a disaster for Afghanistan', *Guardian*, 12 February 2008.

81 N. Childs, '"Failed state" warning on Afghanistan', BBC News, 5 February 2008, http://news.bbc.co.uk/1/hi/world/south_asia/7228680.stm, accessed 9 November 2010.

82 Center for the Study of the Presidency (2008).

83 Senlis (2008).

84 BBC News, 'Taleban "run 10% of Afghanistan"', 28 February 2008, http://news.bbc.co.uk/1/hi/world/south_asia/7268467.stm, accessed 9 November 2010; CBS News, '70 percent of Afghanistan still lawless', 28 February 2008, www.cbsnews.com/stories/2008/02/28/world/main3885534.shtml, accessed 9 November 2010.

85 Pew (2008a); also see P. Bergen, 'Al-Qaeda: the cracks begin to show', *Sunday Times*, 8 June 2008; P. Bergen and P. Cruickshank, 'The unraveling: the jihadist revolt against bin Laden', *The New Republic*, 11 June 2008; J. K. Glassman, 'How to win the war of ideas', *Wall St. Journal*, 24 June 2008.

86 Esposito and Mogahed (2008).

87 D. Gollust, 'US Report: Iran world's most significant terrorism sponsor', GlobalSecurity.org, 30 April 2008, www.globalsecurity.org/security/library/news/2008/04/sec-080430-voa03.htm, accessed 9 November 2010; Finel and Gell (2007).

88 According to RAND the number of annual attacks rose from an average of fewer than 2 during 1995–2001 to more than 10 during 2001–08 (excluding attacks in Iraq and Afghanistan). See Jones and Libicki (2008); also see K. Kelland, 'Report says war on terror is fuelling al Qaeda', Reuters, 7 October 2007.

7

Brown's war

Washington's abandonment of a new imperialist strategy in favour of a military surge in Iraq was not only ambiguous in its effects, but clashed with the divergent move towards a military withdrawal that was now being pursued by the New Labour government. Uncertainty over the status of Britain's mission in Iraq was also reflected in growing confusion over the nature of the military campaign in Afghanistan, public support for which was now in steady decline. With the political fortunes of the Prime Minister facing a similar challenge, Brown turned to the issue of national security as a means of bolstering his leadership credentials. In particular, this focused on a new round of anti-terror legislation, central to which was a renewed attempt to extend the period of detention without charge for terrorist suspects. Being driven to a large degree by political concerns, the new proposals, along with renewed controversy over ministerial complicity in extra-legal measures, did little for the credibility and coherence of the government's 'values-based' approach to the war on terror.

A major strategic victory

While the outcome of the British operation in Iraq was proving to be distinctly ambivalent, so too were the results of the US surge. In September 2007, the US military commander in Iraq, General David Petraeus, delivered a report on the strategy to Congress, highlighting a dramatic fall in the overall level of violence in the country and hailing the approach as having been a notable success.[1] And, indeed, statistically, such an assessment appeared to be warranted. According to figures from Iraq's Interior Ministry, from June to November the number of car bombs in Iraq declined by two-thirds and casualties from roadside bombs had dropped by 80%, while figures from the US State Department showed that the level of violence had, by the spring of 2008, declined to levels not seen since late 2005.[2] Welcoming the downturn, President Bush used the occasion of his final State of the Union address in January to declare that the new approach had 'achieved results few of us could have imagined', and two months later claimed that the surge had 'done more than turn the situation in Iraq around' but had now 'opened the door to a major strategic victory in the broader war on terror'.[3]

But the situation was somewhat less than unequivocal. In August 2007 a US National Intelligence Estimate claimed that the results of the surge to date had been 'uneven', pointed out that overall levels of violence remained 'high', and noted that Iraqi leaders were still 'unable to govern effectively' due to internal political schisms and the prevailing level of instability across the country.[4] Concurring in this assessment, the International Institute of Strategic Studies also observed that while the surge had been effective in many ways, violence in Iraq remained high and political progress remained insubstantial.[5] Moreover, while the general level of violence may have fallen since the surge was initiated, the precise reasons for this were open to interpretation. As critics of the policy observed, much of the subsidence was due not to an increase in troop numbers, but to a combination of developments preceding the change in strategy, most notably the emergence of strong Sunni resistance to al-Qaeda's operations in Iraq, as well as the declaration of a ceasefire by one of Iraq's key militia leaders and the cumulative, if unquantifiable, war-weariness of Iraqis themselves.[6] To compound matters further, public opinion in Iraq was also mixed. By early 2008, while most Iraqis now believed their daily life to be improving, the issue of security remained the number one concern, with 70% stating that the US and the coalition generally had made a poor job of their responsibilities since the invasion, with more than half (53%) claiming that the surge had made security worse in the areas in which it had been deployed, and with up to 49% claiming that it had made security worse in Iraq as a whole. The number of people expressing confidence in the Iraqi government, despite a rise over the past twelve months, remained low (also at 49%), and while around two-thirds (63%) of Iraqis felt that US forces should only leave when the security and political situations had improved, almost two-fifths (37%) wanted an immediate withdrawal.[7]

In this context, the fifth anniversary of the invasion, in March 2008, gave scarce cause for celebration. Estimates for the civilian death-toll, though invariably imprecise, now ranged anywhere from a figure of 85,000 according to statistics from Iraq Body Count, to the 150,000 deaths formally accepted by the Iraqi government, up to an approximate 600,000 casualties according to a widely-cited medical study.[8] The number of military deaths, too, continued to rise, with 175 members of the British armed forces and almost 4,000 US troops having been killed during the course of the war to date. In addition, the humanitarian situation remained chronic, with around four million refugees having been displaced since the onset of hostilities, and with the Red Cross describing the situation as being 'among the most critical in the world'. Unsurprisingly, both economic and political reconstruction remained limited. For all the recent improvements in the security situation, with the strength of the Iraqi police and armed forces still well below that needed to take ownership of security matters, the country remained ranked as the world's single most violent and dangerous place.[9]

Against this backdrop, at the end of March there occurred a defining moment in the course of events. In an operation known as the Charge of the Knights, the Iraqi Prime Minister, Nouri al-Maliki, ordered an Iraqi army offensive to clear out Shia militia groups in Basra, providing a key test of its ability to act without the support of British troops. The results, however, were far from definitive, and instead the situation rapidly degenerated, with fighting spreading into surrounding areas, including parts of Baghdad, and with Iraqi troops and police proving unable to take control of the city amidst cases of desertion and refusals to fight. As the success of the mission hung in the balance, the Iraqi government opted to call for military assistance, though in so doing turned to US rather than British troops for support, with the latter remaining stationed at Basra airport before eventually being called on to provide air cover, surveillance and supplies.[10] Although the operation was ultimately successful, with most areas involved falling under the control of the Iraqi authorities by the end of April, it also revealed the extent to which the Iraqi government was still unable to enforce its will in Iraq's two biggest cities without calling on foreign firepower, and highlighted the strains in Britain's relationships with both the Iraqi government and the US.[11] Yet, in typical fashion, British officials presented the limited involvement of British troops as evidence of success; as having clearly illustrated the independence of the Iraqi army and the degree to which it had benefited from British training and expertise. In the world of the Ministry of Defence, the operation had been 'planned, implemented, and executed by the Iraqis', a degree of autonomy that was hailed by the Prime Minister's spokesman as 'a recognition of the training and support that they have been given in recent years'.[12] According to Sir Jock Stirrup, the course of events had been more propitious still. As he put it:

> far from being a divergence from the UK approach, Charge of the Knights was what we'd aimed for, worked for, and argued for over more than twelve months … And the outcome was what we had hoped for and what we had predicted.[13]

The fallout from the Charge, however, added further complications to the British position. While the less than convincing nature of the Iraqi victory led to a rapid postponement of plans for a reduction in British troop numbers, its eventual success raised the politically vexatious question of why it was that British troops should still remain in Iraq if the Iraqi army was, albeit problematically, capable of acting without them. The result was to leave Britain stuck in the worst of all possible worlds: unable to withdraw, unable to reinforce troop levels given the intense pressures on the military, and unable to do anything effective to improve matters in Iraq in the meantime.[14]

All this also served to exacerbate the politically contentious nature of the Iraq war itself, with the government remaining under pressure from the Conservatives for a full inquiry into its origins and conduct.[15] In fending this off, ministers continued to adhere rigidly to the existing line of defence, maintaining that while an inquiry would be held at some future point, the conditions for this were not yet right. As Brown put it, although an inquiry would be necessary in order 'to learn all possible lessons from the military action in Iraq and its aftermath', the present juncture was not an 'appropriate' time for such analysis given the 'fragile' nature of the situation. At this critical moment, he explained, it remained 'vital that the Government does not divert attention from supporting Iraq's development as a secure and stable country'.[16] While the notion that an inquiry would undermine troop morale or the security situation was rejected by several former leading defence figures, including Lord Craig, the former air marshal of the RAF, who remarked that an investigation would not have 'any psychological impact on the troops' and that it would be 'very timely to have an inquiry before memories fade',[17] the official line was also upheld by the Foreign Secretary. Despite conceding that the construction of a peaceful Iraq had been 'much more difficult' than had originally been expected, that 'the aftermath of the invasion had not gone to plan' and that it was 'evident that the mission has not been accomplished', Miliband nonetheless insisted that the war itself had been 'a remarkable victory' and that, overall, it had gone 'better than most people expected'. Nevertheless, he pertained, holding an inquiry now, given the ongoing events in Basra, would be 'a bizarre choice of priority'.[18]

Fundamental freedoms

If the new imperialist trajectory of the war on terror was proving to be volatile, then so too were domestic political affairs. Indeed, while party political concerns had fuelled the Brown government's initial drive to differentiate itself from its immediate predecessor, not dissimilar pressures had now ironically conspired to push it in the opposite direction. In October 2007, with Brown having encouraged speculation of a snap general election to reach feverish levels in the expectation of capitalising on a post-Blair bounce, the Prime Minister's disastrous strategic decision to abandon the plan amidst fears of a Conservative fightback attracted an intense hail of criticism. Centring on charges of personal weakness and vacillation, the attacks induced a dramatic and sustained fall in the opinion polls. By the spring of 2008 the Labour Party had slumped to its lowest poll ratings for a quarter of a century, and speculation was rife that Brown would soon face a leadership challenge as support for his premiership ebbed away.[19]

The Prime Minister's reaction to this unprecedented collapse was to try and recover lost ground by positioning himself as a strong, decisive and resolute leader; focusing, in particular, on the issues of national security and the war on terror. The opening round of Brown's fightback involved a series of new anti-terror measures, many of which had been in the pipeline from the dying months of the Blair administration. These were set out in November, being subsequently published as the Counter Terrorism Bill in January 2008, and endorsed a range of proposals including a removal of the prohibition on post-charge questioning for terrorist suspects, longer sentences, the creation of a monitoring register for individuals convicted of terrorism-related offences, increased scope for the retention and use of DNA and changes to the rules governing the use of 'intercept evidence'. The most controversial proposals, however, involved another extension to the period of detention without charge for terrorist suspects, with officials eventually settling, after an initial period of indeterminate ambiguity, on a figure of 42 days. The chief justification for instituting another extension so soon after the last one was based on a straightforward rehashing of the previously failed argument. Though ministers were forced to admit that there had been no cases in which it had been deemed necessary to go beyond the existing limit of 28 days, an extension was nevertheless said to be required due to the growing intricacy of terrorist plots, and the prospect that current provisions would prove to be insufficient at some unspecified future point. As the Home Secretary, Jacqui Smith, explained:

> investigations are becoming more complex … there is at least a possibility in the future that a terrorist suspect would need to be released because there was insufficient time in order to fully carry out the investigation and to charge them and to bring them to prosecution.[20]

As with previous floatations of anti-terror plans, the new measures were accompanied by renewed warnings, much repeated by ministers, about the nature of the terrorist threat. In a high-profile disclosure on the issue, the new Director General of MI5, Jonathan Evans, revealed that the intelligence services were currently watching 'at least 2,000' suspects, with the increase of 400 from the 2006 figures having been driven by 'a steady flow of new recruits'.[21] Taking his lead, Jacqui Smith reiterated that the threat from terrorism was both 'severe' and 'growing', warning that it was 'not some figment of the imagination' but 'a real risk and a real issue we need to respond to'.[22] Likewise, Brown also sought to impress the scale of the problem. Maintaining that the new anti-terror measures were designed to deal with a real threat, and that they were a necessity and not an optional extra, the Prime Minister was also forced to downplay suggestions that he was seeking to make political capital out of the issue, fervently denying that the proposals were merely 'a sort of political game in the House of Commons'.[23]

Unsurprisingly, the proposals proved to be highly contentious. Amongst those in favour of the plans, the independent reviewer of the government's anti-terrorism legislation, Lord Carlile, claimed that a move beyond 28 days was 'just common sense',[24] while the Chief Commissioner of the Metropolitan Police, Ian Blair, maintained that although there was not yet a need for a longer detention period, such a requirement would prove to be necessary at some future point, and that it would therefore be better to have the powers ready for use if needed than for Parliament to have to debate the issue 'in the aftermath of an atrocity'.[25] While supporters of the extension focused on arguments based around the need for extra security provisions, however, opponents centred both on the issue of civil liberties as well as security matters, claiming that the proposals constituted an unjust and unwarranted increase in the powers of the state and were only likely to exacerbate Islamic radicalism. Eric Metcalfe, the Director of human rights policy at JUSTICE, for example, pointed out that Britain already had 'the longest period of pre-charge detention of any country in the Western world',[26] Shami Chakrabarti warned that the measures would usher in 'a permanent emergency system on the basis that … there might well be an emergency one day',[27] and both the Home Affairs committee and the Joint Committee on Human Rights made clear their displeasure, with the latter stating that the government had yet to make 'a compelling, evidence-based demonstrable case' for an extension and that it was not at all clear that the terror threat had actually increased since the pre-charge detention limit was extended in 2006.[28] Indeed, the measures were attacked by a range of senior officials. Amongst them, the head of the Counter-Terrorism Division at the Crown Prosecution Service, Sue Hemming, claimed that '[w]e have not seen any evidence that we have needed beyond 28 days',[29] Lord Falconer (courtesy of a leaked email) maintained that it would only be valid to move beyond 28 days in the event of a 'major incident',[30] and the now-Baroness Manningham-Buller denounced the planned extension as lacking 'a practical basis, as well as a principled one'.[31] Highlighting the extent to which the plans would be completely at odds with the official 'values-based' discourse in which the war on terror was now embedded, Lord Goldsmith said that a 42-day limit would be 'a very serious incursion on our fundamental freedoms' and would help to destroy 'the very basis of free society that our ancestors fought so hard to create'.[32]

The government's attempts to rebut such charges further revealed the weakness of the foundations on which the case was built. In an embarrassing admission to the Home Affairs Committee, the Home Secretary was forced to concede that just 6 out of the 71 written responses to the government's original consultation document had supported an extension,[33] and a similar fate also befell the Security Minister, Lord West, who was forced to perform a humiliating U-turn in his public position on the issue, which swung from being not 'totally convinced' of the need for an extension to being 'personally convinced' within the space of a 30-minute period punctuated by a meeting with Gordon Brown.[34] Statistics from the Home Office hardly fought the government's corner either. These showed that of the 1,228 arrests that had been made under anti-terror laws from September 2001 to the end of March 2007, only 141 people had been charged with terrorism offences, and of these just 41 individuals had actually been convicted, with more than half (669) having been released without being charged with any offence whatsoever.[35] Moreover, according to Peter Clarke, the Deputy Assistant Commissioner and head of Anti-Terrorism Command, of the 204 people arrested under terrorism legislation since the 28-day detention period was introduced in July 2006, only 11 had been detained for longer than 14 days, eight of which were subsequently charged with terrorist offences.[36]

With the proposals coming under a fierce onslaught, at the beginning of June the government sought to save the measures, as well as ministerial face, by publishing a series of safeguards and amendments. Contained within these were provisions for use of the 42-day period to now require the approval of the Director of Public Prosecutions, a High Court judge and Parliament (following a debate in both Houses), and for this to be secured within a week of the limit coming into force and having to be renewed within 30 days.[37] Outlining the details of the shift, Smith explained that the mechanism for going beyond 28 days would now only become active in 'clear and exceptional' circumstances, though remained adamant that the measure itself was essential for national security and that it was 'important that we do what people expect us to do as a government'. 'It is not about the sort of government we want', she said, 'but about what it means to govern'.[38] Exactly what this meant was also clear in the political positioning which accompanied the changes. Ostensibly oblivious to the scale of the opposition, the Home Secretary, who accused the Tories of having been 'opportunistic' in their opposition to the measures,[39] stated that there was now a 'strong consensus' for addressing the detention issue, and claimed that 'most people now accept that 28 days in the future may be insufficient'.[40] According to Gordon Brown, on the other hand, the attempt to achieve consensus had already failed, and the government's resolve to press ahead was thus painted as a clear demonstration of his leadership qualities and of New Labour's resolve in dealing with the terror threat. Declaring it to be 'inevitable' that the 28-day limit would now need to be extended, the Prime Minister insisted that the government remained 'determined that we stick to our principles'.[41]

Ironically then, given that Brown's efforts to appear strong and principled on the issue of national security was largely motivated by a desire to bolster his hold on office, the eventual winning of the Commons vote on the issue was aided by the sheer anaemia of his position. With many Labour MPs fearful that any further erosion in the Prime Minister's standing would trigger his deposition and fuel irresistible pressure for a general election (with dire consequences for their own seats), the scale of backbench rebellion was significantly reduced, with just 37 Labour MPs choosing to defy the whip. But even so, the final vote delivered a wafer-thin majority of just 9 and was carried only with the support of the Democratic Unionist Party, amidst suspicions that the government had cut a deal for votes involving extra funds for Northern Ireland.[42] And all this, in any event, was ultimately to no avail. In October the measures were subsequently and overwhelmingly rejected by the House of Lords, forcing the government to abandon the planned extension rather than face another time-consuming, politically gruelling and energy-sapping trial in the Commons.[43]

More the bulldog

Running alongside the government's new anti-terror measures were other initiatives designed to improve Britain's security as well as showcase Brown's talents as a strong and decisive leader. The most notable of these was unveiled in March in the form of Britain's first National Security Strategy, which sought to bind together the various elements of New Labour's foreign and domestic policies. With the Prime Minister reissuing the warning that international terrorism remained 'the most serious and urgent' danger the country faced,[44] this set out a range of measures including tighter security provisions for public places, a programme of electronic border screening and greater resources for counter-terrorism and intelligence operations, with funding levels, which had already more than doubled to £2.5 billion since 2001, being set to rise to £3.5 billion by 2011.[45]

Accompanying this, steps to address the issue of radicalisation were also brought forward. The main features here involved the rolling-out of a nationwide, locally-driven de-radicalisation strategy designed to promote moderate Muslim opinion, including extra funding for community projects to tackle violent extremism, coupled with a further emphasis on the role of ideas and values as core weapons in the anti-terror fight.[46] Central to this latter dimension, too, was a further shift in the public discourse of the political debate away from the term 'war on terror'. At the Home Office, a counter-terrorism guide produced for internal use instructed civil servants to avoid any implication of an explicit link between Islam and terrorism, to avoid terms such as 'Islamist extremism' and to refer instead to the broader issue of global terrorism in terms of violent extremism and criminality. Describing the struggle with references to Islam, it explained, was often heard or interpreted by Muslims as a 'confrontation/clash between civilisations/cultures', when what was needed to enable communities to challenge the ideas of violent extremists robustly was to steer the discussion and the linguistics onto the platform of shared values and to 'avoid implying that specific communities are to blame'.[47] On the same theme, a briefing note by MI5's behavioural science unit, entitled: 'Understanding Radicalisation and Violent Extremism in the UK', also highlighted the potential value of promoting moderate Islamic opinion. Observing that there was no single pathway to extremism and that individuals becoming engaged in terrorism were 'demographically unremarkable', the paper claimed that a key point of weakness for many was 'religious naivety', and argued that fostering a well-established sense of religious identity could offer a useful defence against susceptibility to ideas of violent radicalisation.[48]

Although the emphasis on the promotion of moderacy was somewhat at odds with the potentially radicalising impact of the government's hard-line approach to foreign policy and anti-terror legislation, the necessity of dealing with radical Islamic ideas, especially in the younger generation, was nonetheless apparent. In July a report by the Centre for Social Cohesion found that one-third of Muslim students surveyed in British universities believed that killing in the name of religion was justifiable if the religion was under attack, that two-fifths supported the introduction of Sharia law into the British legal system, and that more than half (57%) held negative or uncertain views about the compatibility between Islam and secularism. While the report also highlighted several positive results, with more than three-quarters (78%), for example, agreeing that it was equally possible to be both British and Muslim, real social divisions over the issue of Islamic radicalism continued to widen.[49] In September, research conducted by Pew showed that opinions about Muslims in Britain were now becoming increasingly adverse, with negative perceptions having risen from 14% to 23% during the last three years.[50]

In this context, the government's anti-terror stance was caught in a double-bind. On the one hand, pursuing and maintaining a robust position risked producing counter-productive results; increasing a sense of alienation within Muslim communities, on whose shoulders the burden of tougher measures was likely to disproportionately fall, thus diminishing community support for anti-terror measures and thereby reducing the flows of intelligence about actual and potential elements of radicalism that would be essential to combat the problem. On the other hand, however, adopting an accommodating position and co-opting Muslim organisations into an anti-radicalisation partnership with the state ran alternative risks; namely, that state-approved organisations may lack credibility in their own communities, and that perceptions of ministerial oversensitivity to Muslim concerns may themselves exacerbate tensions by generating a heightened sense of separation and otherness between social groups. Although the effectiveness of the government's anti-terror strategy would clearly depend on Muslim support, the potential damage to social cohesion as a result of granting political power to divergent groups on the basis of their religious, ethnic and cultural affiliations, rather than on the constitutive basis of citizenship per se, could not be discounted. While there may well have been no easy or straightforward solution to this dilemma, the adoption of an approach that sought to enhance the influence of Muslim groups, and to grant them some form of insider status in terms of anti-radicalisation policy, but which, at the same time, impacted disproportionately on Muslims themselves through increasingly punitive legislation, risked producing the worst of both possible worlds.

While the government's appeal to Islamic moderacy and its emphasis on promoting 'core British values' as a central theme for dealing with the terror threat was compromised by the harsher legislative elements of its anti-terror position, the credibility of a 'values-based' approach itself was significantly undermined by the ongoing controversy surrounding British involvement in the extra-legal practices of the war on terror. A strong thematic persistence here involved the recurring issue of extraordinary rendition. Coinciding with Brown's ascension to office, in July 2007 a report on Britain's role in the process by the Intelligence and Security Committee purported to confirm the government's assertions on the matter, claiming to have found no evidence of any direct British involvement in extraordinary rendition, nor any use of British airspace by the CIA (the 1998 flights notwithstanding), but added that poor record-keeping by the government had made it difficult to properly establish the facts. The Committee also noted a distinct lack of regard for British concerns on the part of the US, recording that anxieties raised by British officials had 'not appear[ed] materially to affect its strategy on rendition', and warned, as a result, that this could have 'serious implications for the working of the relationship between the US and UK intelligence and security agencies'.[51]

Not for the first time, by the new year the situation on British involvement in extraordinary rendition had substantively changed. In stark contrast to the long series of official denials on the subject, in February 2008 David Miliband admitted to the House of Commons that, after a thorough search of its internal records, the US government had uncovered 'new information' showing that secret CIA flights had, in fact, used British territory, having twice taken advantage of the British military base on Diego Garcia to refuel in 2002. While this clearly rendered official statements on the matter intractably dubious, the Foreign Secretary also moved to reassure the House that although the flights had involved the transportation of a single detainee on both occasions (being neither a British national or resident), and that while one of the prisoners had subsequently ended up being incarcerated at Guantánamo Bay, the US government had now given its 'assurances' that neither had been subjected to torture during the interrogation process.[52]

Despite the obvious gap between public pronouncements and the reality in the air, ministers continued to refuse to accept that any wrongdoing had occurred, nor that there was any culpability to be borne by any member of the government for these events. As Gordon Brown maintained, it was simply 'unfortunate' that the information was not previously known, and 'unfortunate it happened without us knowing that it had happened'.[53] So too was the line held by Miliband. Insisting that ministerial assurances had all been made 'in good faith', the Foreign Secretary declared that the government 'would not allow any rendition through UK territory that would put us in breach of our international human rights obligations', and that it would now seek 'specific assurances' from the US about all flights in UK territory about which concerns had been expressed.[54] In July the Foreign Office produced a list of all such flights, amounting to almost 400 in number, with Miliband reporting that the US had now 'confirmed' that there had been no other instances of intelligence flights landing in UK territory with a detainee on board beyond the two cases in 2002. Attempting to turn the story to ministerial advantage, Lord Malloch-Brown sought to portray the government as an assiduous and ardent defender of human rights, and maintained that Britain was doing its best to dissuade the US from its more questionable practices. 'We are', he said, 'still more the bulldog than the poodle on this'.[55]

But not everyone was convinced by such asseverations of purity. In its ongoing criticism of the issue, the Foreign Affairs Committee warned that the government should not rely on US assurances concerning the use of torture, and pointed out that the Foreign Office list of suspect flights did not include those that had passed through UK airspace but which had not actually landed on its territory. Furthermore, the Committee also noted that all flight records from Diego Garcia covering the period in question had now been destroyed, and observed, somewhat understatedly, that the absence of such documentation made it 'very difficult' to ascertain the full extent of the use to which the base had been put. Allegations that it had been far more involved in rendition operations than was being publicly disclosed (including claims by the UN special rapporteur on torture, Manfred Novak, and the US General and former head of Southcom, Barry McCaffrey, that the US had actually held prisoners there) could not, therefore, be verified or refuted.[56] Governmental claims of innocence were also rapidly sullied by a series of related allegations about Britain's involvement in torture during the course of the war on terror. In January 2008, a report into alleged abuse of Iraqi prisoners by British troops (published after a two-year investigation by the Ministry of Defence) found no evidence of endemic mistreatment, but uncovered serious failings in army leadership, planning and training, and revealed that soldiers had been given 'scant' guidance by their superiors as to their obligations under international law.[57] On this, the Human Rights Committee were also critical, warning that the use of 'coercive interrogation techniques' (such as wall-standing, hooding, subjection to noise, and the deprivation of sleep, food and drink) may have been officially sanctioned, and that despite ministerial assurances that troops were aware that such techniques had been banned, the prohibition 'was not as clearly articulated to troops in Iraq as it might, and indeed should, have been'.[58] At the end of March, the Ministry of Defence admitted 'substantial breaches' of the European Convention on Human Rights over the torture and killing of several Iraqi civilians by British troops in September 2003, a case which led ultimately to the first ever conviction of a British soldier for war crimes.[59]

The forces of terrorism

For all his best efforts, Gordon Brown's attempt to make political capital out of the war on terror by positioning himself as decisive and principled on the issue of national security did nothing to alleviate his increasingly perilous standing in the polls. By the spring, personal approval ratings for the Prime Minister had experienced the largest collapse since records began in the 1930s. In response, Brown sought to frame his evident un-popularity as a governing virtue, presenting this as a demonstrable sign of strong leadership and of his determination to make the right long-term decisions for the country rather than court short-term popularity.[60] Along with this, the Prime Minister also sought to bolster his position by drawing on the political benefits of the special relationship with the US. Presenting himself as the arch-bearer of the transatlantic torch, Brown seized on the opportunity of a visit to Washington in April to state that Europe and the US were united by 'shared values' (namely '[t]he belief in liberty and freedom'), and to announce that: 'we want a better rela-tionship with America and I feel I can bring Europe and America closer together for the future'.[61]

But this too failed to produce any tangible benefits. On the contrary, with the trip being overshadowed by a simultaneous visit from the Pope, and with Brown being seen in the US (insofar as anyone knew of him at all) as a half-hearted and unreliable partner in the war on terror, given Britain's drawdown in Iraq and its reluctance to commit greater troop numbers to Afghanistan, the visit merely served to cement the prevailing sense of weakness.[62] To make matters worse, the question of a rift with the US also continued to bedevil the government. Despite flat rejections of any such thing from both Downing Street and Washington, with the Prime Minister's Official Spokesman claiming that there was 'absolutely no disa-greement' between the two countries, and with Bush praising Brown for being 'tough on terror', the discordance was there for all to see.[63] Indeed, schismatic tensions over Iraq grew wider still during the summer as the government's plans for a military drawdown gained pace. Despite refus-ing to set an 'artificial timetable' for a reduction in troop numbers, Brown continued to insist that 'enormous progress' had now been made on train-ing the Iraqi police and army, and told the House of Commons in July that he was expecting there to be a 'fundamental change of mission' in Iraq by the end of the year as this process neared its completion.[64] In December, the official announcement was made: the process of pulling out British troops would begin in March 2009, all military operations were to be completed by the end of May, and the withdrawal process (notwithstand-ing the retention of several hundred personnel for training purposes) was to be fully completed by the middle of the year.[65]

The ability of circumstances in Afghanistan to resist any discernible improvement, on the other hand, remained undiminished. The econo-my, such as it was (with at least half of Afghanistan's income deriving from the production of opium), now stood on the brink of collapse, with chronic poverty and unemployment continuing to be the norm, and with reconstruction efforts having been persistently thwarted by a lack of serious and well coordinated engagement from Western governments, not to mention the ongoing uncertainty and danger posed by the security situation. Signs of political success were equally sparse. The prevalence of corruption at every level of government, along with the widespread and persistent human rights abuses endemic to local warlordism, made a constant mockery of coalition claims to be working towards the establishment of a democratic state founded on equality before the rule of law. To further compound the matter, these obstacles stemmed not merely from the Gallionic attitude of the West or from the weakness of the central government in Kabul, but were connected to the very dynamics of Afghan society itself. At the same time as economic growth and development required substantial and long-term investment, the political circumstances necessary to create the prerequisite conditions for this, namely an environment of peace and stability, were themselves unlikely to emerge from conditions in which any semblance of national political cohesion required the support and the placation of rival warlords and mutually competitive and antagonistic tribal factions.[66]

To make matters worse, the scope and fervency of the Taliban resurgence continued to grow across the country. Marking this, in mid-October Taliban fighters mounted an audacious, if ultimately unsuccessful attempt to capture the provincial capital of Helmand, Lashkar Gah, the first time that it had come under enemy assault since the start of the war. More representative of its operations, though, was a notable shift in tactics away from directly confronting coalition forces, and towards the adoption of a discernibly Fabian mode of warfare.[67] Along with this, a large rise in the number of violent incidents, from an average of 700 a month during the first half of the year to an average of 900 to 1,000 from July to September, made the third quarter of the year, and indeed 2008 as a whole, the bloodiest for coalition forces since the invasion began.[68] By the end of the year, the total number of British personnel killed since the start of the invasion had reached 137, while the estimated death toll in Afghanistan as a whole during the course of the year, put at around 5,000 by the United Nations, was now some 40% higher than that for the previous twelve months.[69] The high incidence of civilian casualties naturally did little to aid coalition efforts in the so-called battle for the hearts and minds of the Afghan populace, and led to substantial criticism, not least from within Afghanistan, of its over-reliance on air strikes as a means of prosecuting the war effort. These points were well-noted by NATO itself, where concerns about the efficiency of military methods were becoming magnified, and where officials were becoming increasingly keen to strengthen public confidence in Afghanistan's own political institutions and to galvanise public support for the coalition – a goal, it explained, that made it essential to 'fight the information war as relentlessly as we fight the physical war'.[70]

With the situation threatening to spiral out of control, the Bush administration embarked on a concerted drive to change the dynamics of the conflict by repeating the Iraq strategy of a military surge. In this, the strength of US forces in Afghanistan was to be boosted by some 33,000 personnel, an increase of one-third over 2006 levels. Accompanying this, a more aggressive approach of proactively taking the fight to Islamic extremists in the border region with Pakistan was also adopted, including, much to the displeasure of Islamabad, the launching of cross-border attacks on suspected insurgents and terrorists.[71] The line from the British government on Afghanistan also remained resolute. Despite growing pressures over an absence of clear mission objectives and a definable exit strategy, in the summer Brown announced that British troop levels in the country were set to rise to a record height of more than 8,000, and claimed that the military situation was 'being transformed' by the coalition's more intensive strategy.[72] Reiterating the point, the International Development Secretary, Douglas Alexander, also maintained that the coalition was making 'real progress', both in the fight against the Taliban and in its efforts to reconstruct the country.[73]

Along with this, the official justification for Britain's continuing involvement in Afghanistan continued to draw heavily on the twin themes of humanitarianism and the dangers of radical Islam. Now portraying Afghanistan as a key front in the war on terror (even if the phraseology of this no longer formed part of the official lexicon), the Prime Minister ardently insisted that there was a direct link between the military endeavour and the threat of a destabilising al-Qaeda revival in the region. Confronting the Taliban, he maintained, was a core part of the ongoing struggle 'to defeat the forces of terrorism', and was essential to prevent 'terrorism coming to the streets of Britain'. 'We are utterly resolute in our determination to support this new democracy of Afghanistan', he explained, and the government would not 'relax our efforts to support and reconstruct Afghanistan because we understand that what happens in Afghanistan affects the rest of the world'.[74]

Doomed to fail

But not everyone was convinced that the prospects of success in Afghanistan were as sanguine as the official line portrayed. Putting the point bluntly, the British ambassador in Kabul, Sir Sherard Cowper-Coles, remarked that the current strategy was 'doomed to fail' and that a process of political engagement with the Taliban was now essential in order to convince those of its members not linked to al-Qaeda that they had a place in a legitimately negotiated settlement. The main aim of the coalition, he explained, should be 'to dismantle the insurgency by opening up a dialogue'. The same point was also made by Brigadier Gordon Messenger, the Commander of British forces in Helmand. Seeking to downgrade expectations of what it was possible to achieve, Messenger contended that the aim now should be for an outcome that could be regarded as 'good enough', adding that this was 'not second best, it's realistic'.[75] Re-emphasising the theme, the outgoing head of British forces in Afghanistan, Brigadier Mark Carleton-Smith, warned that the fight against the Taliban was one that simply could not be won in the conventional sense, and that expectations about what it was possible to achieve needed to be lowered. Hopes for a 'decisive military victory', he augured, would be 'unrealistic and probably incredible'. Instead, the suggested and revised objective was to aim for reducing the intensity of the war 'to a manageable level of insurgency that's not a strategic threat and can be managed by the Afghan army'.[76]

In addition to the strategic issue, the prospects for a successful British campaign in Afghanistan were also being undermined by the persistent under-resourcing, and consequent over-stretching, of the armed forces. On this, renewed calls by General Dannatt for more money to be spent on defence were accompanied by warnings from Sir Jock Stirrup that Britain's current operations had left its military 'stretched beyond the capabilities we have', and that talk of an Afghan surge in this context made him 'a little nervous'.[77] These concerns were reflected in the views of the armed services below the senior layer. A survey conducted by the Ministry of Defence during mid-2007 found that levels of morale were rated as being 'low' or 'very low' by 59% of Army members, 64% of those in the Royal Navy and 72% of the Royal Air Force. Indeed, the prospect of leaving the armed forces altogether was now being regularly contemplated by almost half of Britain's military personnel (some 47% of the Army and Royal Navy, and 44% of the RAF), with key sources of discontent being the frequency of tours, low levels of pay and the poor quality of equipment and housing.[78] The state of public opinion in general on the Afghan campaign offered no greater solace for the government. According to an ICM survey conducted in November, more than two-thirds of the British population (68%) now wanted British troops to be withdrawn from Afghanistan over the course of the next year.[79]

The manner in which New Labour met these pressures combined a typical mixture of positioning with efforts to mould the debate into a more favourable shape. While the Prime Minister insisted that the government would do 'everything in our power' to assist the armed forces,[80] Des Browne, following a series of high-profile attacks on the issues of army management and resourcing by coroners (one of whom accused the MoD of an outright 'breach of trust' over its failure to provide adequate equipment), sought to silence any further criticism by claiming that such remarks could indicate civil liability on the part of the Ministry of Defence and were therefore not permitted under coroner's rules.[81] Proposals for improving relations between the public and the armed forces, published in March 2008 by the now ex-Attorney General, Lord Goldsmith, were also politically tainted, with its core themes of promoting British values and citizenship directly echoing the official discourse on the war on terror and the domestic anti-radicalisation agenda.[82] The government's willingness to pour actual military resources into Afghanistan, on the other hand, remained limited. Though under pressure from the US to contribute more fully to the Afghan surge operation, the view in Whitehall was that the greater part of the load should instead be taken up by fellow NATO members. As Miliband put it, '[w]e want to make sure we're playing our full role, but equally we've got to make sure that all countries are bearing their fair share of the burden'. Moreover, any increase in troop numbers, he insisted, would also need to be part of a 'genuine comprehensive strategy' for dealing with Afghanistan, and that this would also require a 'civilian surge' focusing on political and economic reconstruction and reform in addition to the military effort.[83] The point was also made by Gordon Brown. Insisting that NATO's military campaign needed to be based on 'proper burden-sharing', and bemoaning that that the burden was 'not always shared equally', the Prime Minister called on Britain's NATO allies to step up their efforts, stating that it was 'vital that all members of the coalition contribute fairly'.[84]

Although such reluctance stood in contrast to ministerial assertions about the centrality of the mission to Britain's national security, as well as the existential necessity of defeating the Taliban and al-Qaeda, official proclamations on the subject remained bullish. Keeping the emphasis firmly on the link to the terrorist threat, Brown, citing intelligence from the security agencies, claimed that three-quarters of the most serious terror plots currently under investigation by British officials had links to Pakistan, and described the Afghan border region as forming part of 'a chain of terror' capable of reaching Britain if greater efforts were not made to address the threat it posed.[85] John Hutton, Des Browne's successor at the MoD from October, offered a particularly robust assessment.[86] While admitting that the military effort had been 'much tougher' than anyone expected, and that it was now necessary to accept that troops faced a 'long haul' in Afghanistan, the Defence Secretary insisted that the campaign was 'producing significant results' and warned that 'scuttling away' before the mission was completed would be 'profoundly dangerous' in the fight against terrorism. In sum, the scope of the fight in Afghanistan was equal to that which had been posed by the Second World War. It was, he said, 'a struggle against fanatics that may not challenge our borders but challenges our way of life in the same way the Nazis did'. Moreover, with success in Afghanistan providing 'the test of NATO credibility in this new post cold war age', the stakes could not have been higher. Thus, as he put it:

> Withdrawal would confirm Al Qaida propaganda that Britain, like the Soviet Union before, bombed and then bolted. We would be portrayed as either wrong, callous or weak. And the lesson our friends, vulnerable states, potential aggressors and terrorists would take is that ... we would give up and go home.

But invoking the spectre of Fascism and equating the Taliban to the Nazis sat uneasily with the non-military side of the government's strategy for Afghanistan; namely, the emphasis on a push for political reconciliation. Indeed, despite the obvious contradiction, this too was a call that Hutton was keen to echo. At the same time as the West was said to be engaged in a historic battle to the death against 'those who fight every advance for democracy, every expression of free choice, every manifestation of individual rights', there could, he explained, nevertheless be 'no long term solution to any conflict without a political settlement'.

Unethical or immoral

By the end of 2008 the Bush administration was entering its final days. The circumstances of its passing, however, proved to be far from smooth. With the US facing a steep global recession and an unprecedented financial crisis, with Bush's approval ratings amongst the lowest in modern US history, and with Washington's extra-legal conduct in the war on terror continuing to make headlines following an admission from the convenor of the military appeals process at Guantánamo Bay, Susan Crawford, that the US had used 'torture' against a detainee accused of being involved in the 9/11 attacks, controversy continued to dog the leadership.[87] Those atop the outgoing regime, though, remained defiant in the face of adversity. Declaring that he felt 'very good about what we did', Dick Cheney claimed that the detentions at Guantánamo and the use of extraordinary renditions had been 'absolutely essential' in the fight against terrorism, and defiantly maintained that 'it would have been unethical or immoral for us not to do everything we could in order to protect the nation'.[88] Bush himself, describing the war on terror as a 'generational conflict' akin to the Cold War struggle against Communism, insisted that the actions of his government had 'made the world freer', and cautioned against any attempt to change direction. 'America's future leaders', he warned, 'must always remember that the war on terror will be won on the offense – and that is where America's military must stay'.[89]

But behind the political machismo, the reality of the war on terror was far from auspicious. In seven years of fighting, the central assumptions of Washington's new imperialist strategy – that quick, limited and hi-technology warfare could produce a rapid transition to free market democracy – had been comprehensively abandoned in favour of a military surge in Iraq, with similar pressures now coalescing around Afghanistan. Moreover, in contrast to the declared goal of defeating terrorism, the threat from the al-Qaeda brand remained undiminished. In yet another consecutive annual increase in terrorist attacks from radical Islamic groups, figures from the American Security Project showed that the number of incidents during 2008 had risen to 670, excluding Iraq, Afghanistan and the Israeli/Palestine dispute.[90] With particular hotspots now being located in Pakistan and Somalia, and with the role of Sudan as a breeding ground for extremism increasingly in the spotlight too, concerns were also rising about the spreading influence of al-Qaeda in Africa as well as in the Middle East.[91] That the terror threat itself was still very much alive was aptly demonstrated at the end of November, as terrorists launched a series of coordinated attacks in the Indian city of Mumbai, killing more than 170 people.

Public perceptions about the course of the war on terror also remained less than impressive. According to a poll of 23 countries conducted for the BBC World Service, 29% of respondents believed that it had produced no discernible effect on terrorism, a similar number (30%) claimed that the war had actually strengthened al-Qaeda, and 49% contended that neither the US nor al-Qaeda could be said to be winning.[92] On this, the view of the British public was in accord. Two-fifths now felt that the war on terror had made al-Qaeda stronger, more than a third (36%) believed that it had produced no effect at all, and three-quarters felt that neither side was on course for victory. While only 5% believed that al-Qaeda were currently out in front, the proportion who felt the US to be winning, at just 11%, was hardly encouraging.[93] And for all this, the financial costs of fighting the war on terror had, by this point, reached staggering proportions. For Britain, the total outlay for the Iraq and Afghan campaigns to date had exceeded £13 billion, a not insubstantial sum, even if this was dwarfed by the bill of $1 trillion that had been incurred by the US by mid-2009.[94]

The new imperialist attempt to establish US credibility and to reshape a world order conducive to the maintenance of US interests had also palpably failed. Alongside a rise in geopolitical instability in the Middle East, with the US military remaining stretched and bogged down in two major theatres of war, and with the prospect of opening up a third looking highly unlikely, the possibility of any more deviant regimes attracting a military response from Washington, and hence the incentive to remain on the right side of the US, had been considerably reduced. Accompanying the risk of political collapse in Pakistan, with all the attendant danger of nuclear weapons capability falling into the hands of Islamic extremists, the continuation of nuclear programmes by the radiological rogue states of North Korea and Iran provided a clear demonstration of the limits to US power and influence.[95] The boundaries of US (and indeed Western) authority on the world stage were also exposed by the eruption of military conflict between Russia and Georgia in August 2008. Triggered by a Georgian attempt to assert control over secessionist regions with sizeable Russian minorities, the response from Moscow was both swift and brutal. Within a matter of days the Georgian army lay defeated, and the most pro-Western state in Eastern Europe, and a much-vaunted beacon of democratic change in the region, stood ignominiously humiliated.[96] The action also served notice of Russian intent for a reassertion of international strength following the interregnum caused by the collapse of the Soviet Union, and posed a direct challenge to US geo-strategy, most notably its plans for securing Georgian membership of NATO and for housing a controversial missile defence system in the Czech Republic and Poland.[97]

As with the Iranian kidnapping crisis of 2007, the episode also revealed the extent to which New Labour's goal of elevating Britain's influence on the world stage had been undermined by its unflinching support for the US in the war on terror. While the actions of the US remained carefully limited to a symbolic deployment of troops for delivering humanitarian supplies, the response from London was more circumscribed still.[98] Ministerial exhortations, such as Miliband's call for Russia's 'immediate withdrawal', and Brown's appeal for NATO members to 'intensify our support to Georgia and others who may face Russian aggression',[99] amounted to little more than protests from the sidelines and served to highlight the Prime Minister's lack of brio in the foreign policy arena. This stood in marked contrast to the diplomatic vivacity shown by the French President, Nicholas Sarkozy, whose successful marshalling of a European initiative played an instrumental role in the eventual ceasefire.[100]

A similar case of rhetoric over substance characterised the government's response to the second major international crisis of the year; an intensive assault on Gaza by the Israeli army in November following the cessation of a six-month truce with the Palestinian politico-paramilitary organisation, Hamas. While the scale of international outrage over the conflict echoed that of the 2006 Lebanon crisis, the reaction of New Labour officials was this time markedly different. Instead of siding wholeheartedly with the Israelis, the Foreign Secretary pressed for an immediate suspension of hostilities, while Brown called openly for an 'urgent ceasefire'.[101] But the appearance of a more engaged and humanitarian position again underlined the government's lack of any real influence over the situation. In contrast to Blair's refusal to call for a ceasefire during the 2006 conflict, an action which stood not as a passive response but as a testimony to his avowed desire to stand with the US and facilitate a reordering of the Middle East, the government's stance on this occasion was symbolic for its impotence. In Washington, the only Western power that counted, the view of the outgoing administration remained staunchly pro-Israeli, with the departing President Bush refusing to countenance any response that might undercut or in any way limit the military operation.[102]

Conclusion

By 2007 the dynamics of the new imperialist strategy launched by the US under the guise of a war on terror had proved to be a spectacular failure. Reflecting this, with levels of violence rising in both Iraq and Afghanistan, the small, limited and arm's-length military approach in the former was replaced by an intensive troop surge. Although the success of this policy was far from clear-cut, by the end of 2008 the model of an expansive military deployment had been replicated in Afghanistan, where a Taliban resurgence had undermined the cogency of the NATO effort. For New Labour, the centre of politico-military gravity had by this point also shifted to the Afghan campaign, public uncertainties about which saw ministers deploying the threat from international terrorism in an increasingly desperate attempt to re-legitimise Britain's involvement. Assertions about a direct link between British foreign policy and the threat from radical Islamic terrorism in this context, however, sat uneasily with the government's repeated denials of any such connection through the Doctrine of No Responsibility. At the same time, the parallel insistence on the necessity of promoting a values-based approach also clashed with other elements of government policy. Politically contentious anti-terror legislation, as well as controversy surrounding ministerial complicity in extra-legal practices, did much to undermine the kind of liberal freedoms and civil rights that the war on terror was purportedly being fought to defend. A series of international crises involving Iran, Russia and Israel further highlighted the sense of failure, illustrating the loss of US credibility as well as the decline of New Labour's attempt to increase Britain's standing and influence on the world stage. The continuation of these themes would characterise the final months of the Brown administration.

Notes

1 T. Baldwin, 'Turning point for America in Iraq', *The Times,* 11 September 2007.
2 T. Baldwin, D. Haynes and A. Stroman, 'Iraq surge brings hope for a day without death', *The Times,* 3 November 2007; US Department of State (2008).
3 State of the Union Address, 28 January 2008; 'Global War on Terror', speech at the Pentagon, 19 March 2008.
4 'Prospects for Iraq's Stability', National Intelligence Estimate, August 2007.
5 N. Childs, '"Failed state" warning on Afghanistan', BBC News, 5 February 2008, http://news.bbc.co.uk/1/hi/world/south_asia/7228680.stm, accessed 9 November 2010.
6 Jones and Libicki (2008); also see M. Fletcher, 'Al-Qaeda leaders admit: "We are in crisis. There is panic and fear"', *The Times,* 11 February 2008.
7 'Iraq Five Years Later: Where Things Stand', poll conducted for ABC News, BBC, ARD and NHK by D3 System, Va., and KA Research, 17 March 2008.
8 Burnham, Drocy, Dzeng *et al* (2006).
9 BBC News, 'Bleak picture of Iraq conditions', 17 March 2008, http://news.bbc.co.uk/1/hi/7299914.stm, accessed 9 November 2010.
10 See for example: R. Norton-Taylor, 'Battle for Basra', *Guardian,* 26 March 2008; J. Hider and M. Evans, 'British warplanes fire on Basra as civil war looms with Shia militia', *The Times,* 29 March 2008; M. Townsend and G. Hinsliff, 'British army joins battle to control Basra', *Observer,* 30 March 2008; E. Stewart, 'Plans to cut UK troops in Iraq put on hold', *Guardian,* 1 April 2008; D. Haynes and M. Evans, 'Iraq snubbed Britain and calls US into Basra battle', *The Times,* 10 April 2008.
11 R. Beeston, 'What a difference a month makes', *The Times,* 25 April 2008; S. Jenkins, 'The occupation has frozen Iraq', *Guardian,* 3 May 2008.
12 P. Cockburn, 'Iraq implodes as Shia fights Shia', *Independent,* 27 March 2008; R. Norton-Taylor, 'American warplanes join Iraqi troops in taking the fight to Shia militia', *Guardian,* 29 March 2008.
13 Speech to Royal United Services Institute, 1 December 2008.
14 R. Fox, 'In Basra without a paddle', *Guardian,* 10 April 2008.
15 BBC News, 'Tories in new Iraq inquiry call', 17 March 2008, http://news.bbc.co.uk/1/hi/uk_politics/7300631.stm, accessed 9 November 2010.
16 A. Grice and N. Morris, 'There WILL be a public inquiry into Iraq, says Brown', *Independent,* 17 March 2008.
17 C. Brown, 'Former defence chiefs reject claim soldiers do not want Iraq inquiry', *Independent,* 29 March 2008.
18 R. Norton-Taylor, 'Building peace in Iraq harder than expected, says Miliband', *Guardian,* 21 March 2008.
19 D. Smith and J. Oliver, 'Support for Labour hits 25-year low', *The Sunday Times,* 16 March 2008.
20 Evidence to the Home Affairs Committee, 11 December 2007, Qs 39, 177.
21 'Intelligence, Counter-Terrorism and Trust', address to the Society of Editors, 5 November 2007.

22 BBC News, 'Terror threat to UK "is growing"', 13 April 2008, http://news.bbc.co.uk/1/hi/7344925.stm, accessed 9 November 2010.

23 BBC News, 'Brown vows to "win" over 42 days', 15 May 2008, http://news.bbc.co.uk/1/hi/uk_politics/7402242.stm, accessed 9 November 2010; P. Wintour, 'Brown signals retreat on 42 day detention', *Guardian,* 16 May 2008.

24 A. Sparrow, 'Terror watchdog backs 42-day detention bill', *Guardian,* 24 January 2008.

25 Evidence to the Home Affairs Committee, 9 October 2007, Q. 1.

26 *Ibid.,* 11 October 2007, Q. 157.

27 *Ibid.,* Q. 121.

28 Joint Committee on Human Rights (2007), para. 101.

29 *Ibid.,* Q. 119.

30 P. Wintour and M. White, 'Former lord chancellor joins critics of detention beyond 28 days', *Guardian,* 13 December 2007.

31 B. Russell, 'Former head of MI5 says 42-day detention plan is "unworkable"', *Independent,* 9 July 2008.

32 P. Goldsmith, 'We shouldn't hold terror suspects for 42 days', *Daily Telegraph,* 1 June 2008.

33 Evidence to the Home Affairs Committee, 11 December 2007, Q. 23.

34 BBC News, 'West denies terror limit U-turn', 14 November 2007, http://news.bbc.co.uk/1/hi/uk_politics/7094438.stm, accessed 9 November 2010; J. Kirkup and G. Cleland, 'Security minister opens rift on terror laws', *Daily Telegraph,* 4 November 2007.

35 R. Ford, 'Terror police to track capital's cars', *The Times,* 17 July 2007.

36 S. O'Neill, 'Met chief calls for stronger anti-terror law', *The Times,* 9 October 2007

37 Joint Committee on Human Rights (2007).

38 D. Summers and D. Batty, 'Smith talks up terror threats in push for 42-day law', *Guardian,* 24 January 2008; P. Wintour and N. Watt, 'Brown says 42-day detention vote is not a confidence issue', *Guardian,* 3 June 2008.

39 P. Wintour, 'Smith rounds on Tories over terror laws', *Guardian,* 12 December 2007.

40 Evidence to the Home Affairs Committee, 19 February 2008, Qs 154, 169.

41 A. Travis, P. Wintour and J. Percival, 'Brown remains defiant on 42 days', *Guardian,* 2 June 2008.

42 BBC News, 'Brown wins crunch vote on 42 days', 11 June 2008, http://news.bbc.co.uk/1/hi/7449268.stm, accessed 9 November 2010.

43 BBC News, 'Ministers shelve 42-day detention', 13 October 2008.

44 Statement to the House of Commons, 19 March 2008.

45 Cabinet Office (2008).

46 BBC News, 'New advice on tackling extremism', 3 June 2008, http://news.bbc.co.uk/1/hi/uk_politics/7432051.stm, accessed 9 November 2010.

47 A. Travis, 'Whitehall draws up new rules on language of terror', *Guardian,* 4 February 2008.

48 A. Travis, 'MI5 report challenges views on terrorism in Britain', *Guardian,* 20 August 2008; A. Travis, 'The making of an extremist', *Guardian,* 20 August 2008.

49 Thorne and Stuart (2008).

50 Pew (2008).

51 ISC (2007), para. 137.

52 Statement to the House of Commons, 21 February 2008.

53 BBC News, 'UK apology over rendition flights', 21 February 2008, http://news.bbc.

co.uk/1/hi/uk_politics/7256587.stm, accessed 9 November 2010.

54 Statement to the House of Commons, 21 February 2008.

55 House of Lords debates, *Hansard*, 21 February 2008, col. 352.

56 FAC (2008). Asked if detainees were being held on Diego Garcia, the Principal Deputy Assistant Secretary of Defence, Laurence Di Rita, replied that: 'I don't know. I simply don't know'. See Defence Department Operational Update Briefing, 14 July 2004; FAC (2009); Interview with *Deborah Norville Tonight*, MSNBC, 6 May 2004; J. Doward, 'British island "used by US for rendition"', *Observer*, 2 March 2008; 'Labour government gags "extraordinary renditions" whistleblower', ukwatch.net, 5 March 2008.

57 Aitken (2008).

58 Joint Committee on Human Rights (2008), para. 13.

59 K. Sengupta, 'MoD admits human rights breaches over death of tortured Iraqi civilian', *Independent,* 28 March 2008. This was followed, in July 2009, by the establishment of an independent inquiry into claims that up to 20 Iraqis had been tortured and killed by British troops in May 2004 (an event known as the 'Battle of Danny Boy') after a flawed investigation by the MoD. See R. Norton-Taylor, 'Judges attack Ministry of Defence over bid to suppress Iraq information', *Guardian,* 10 July 2009.

60 Kettell and Kerr (2008).

61 N. Watt, 'Brown adopts Blair's "bridge" strategy in US relations', *Guardian,* 15 April 2008.

62 N. Gardiner, 'We'd rather have a Winston', *The Sunday Times,* 13 April 2008.

63 A. Sparrow, 'Downing Street denies rift with Bush over withdrawal of troops from Iraq', *Guardian,* 16 June 2008; A. Sparrow, 'Brown announces Afghanistan troops to increase during "final" Bush visit to Downing Street', *Guardian,* 16 June 2008.

64 N. Hines, 'Gordon Brown predicts major Iraq troop withdrawal by 2009', *The Times,* 22 July 2008.

65 BBC News, 'UK troops to leave Iraq "by July"', 17 December 2008, http://news.bbc.co.uk/1/hi/7787103.stm, accessed 9 November 2010.

66 P. Beaumont, 'Fear, disillusion and despair: notes from a divided land as peace slips away', *Observer,* 8 June 2008; J. Borger, and R. Norton-Taylor, 'US faces downward spiral in Afghan war, says leaked intelligence report', *Guardian,* 10 October 2008.

67 R. Norton-Taylor, 'Troops who hoped they would not fire a shot mourn 100th comrade', *Guardian,* 9 June 2008; T. Coghlan, 'Taleban stage audacious "Tet-style" attack on British HQ city', *The Times,* 13 October 2008.

68 S. Shah and S. Goldenberg, 'Nine US troops die in Taliban assault on Afghan base', *Guardian,* 13 July 2008; C. Lamb, 'Taliban revival sets fear swirling through Kabul', *The Sunday Times*, 28 September 2008.

69 C. Wyatt, 'Bloodiest year so far in Afghanistan', BBC News, 6 October 2008, http://news.bbc.co.uk/1/hi/uk/7648020.stm, accessed 9 November 2010; M. Weaver, 'Royal Marine killed in Afghanistan at end of worst year for British deaths', *Guardian,* 1 January 2009; S. Shah, 'Taliban rivals unite to fight US troop surge', *Guardian,* 3 March 2009.

70 ISAF (2008), para. 11.

71 I. Wilkinson, 'Pakistan to defend borders against US military incursions', *Daily Telegraph,* 11 September 2008; BBC News, 'US "must target Pakistan havens"', 11 September 2008, http://news.bbc.co.uk/1/hi/world/south_asia/7609073.stm, accessed 9 November 2010; R. Whitaker, 'Afghanistan: Pakistan fury at US cross-border attacks', *Independent,* 14 September 2008.

72 A. Lloyd, 'Tell us why our soldiers must die in Afghanistan', *The Times,* 10 June 2008; A. Sparrow, 'Brown announces Afghanistan troops to increase during "final" Bush visit to Downing Street', *Guardian,* 16 June 2008.

73 T. Coghlan, 'Western forces' latest Afghanistan losses overtake Iraq death toll', *The Times,* 2 July 2008.

74 Press conference with Hamid Karzai, 21 August 2008.

75 C. Lamb, 'War on Taliban cannot be won, says army chief', *The Sunday Times,* 5 October 2008; G. Alagiah, 'New realism in Afghanistan rhetoric', BBC News, 25 November 2008, http://news.bbc.co.uk/1/hi/uk/7747145.stm, accessed 9 November 2010.

76 T. Coghlan and M. Evans, 'We can't defeat Taleban, says Brigadier Mark Carleton-Smith', *The Times,* 6 October 2008.

77 M. Smith, 'SAS chief resigns over lack of kit', *The Sunday Times,* 8 June 2008; F. Elliott and B. Quinn, 'Sir Jock Stirrup: forces too stretched to cope with Iraq and Afghanistan', *The Times,* 25 June 2008; M. Evans, 'Sir Jock Stirrup warns against troop move to Afghanistan', *The Times,* 9 November 2008.

78 M. Evans, 'Half of all British servicemen say they want to quit', *The Times,* 10 July 2008.

79 BBC News, 'Britons call for troop withdrawal', 13 November 2008, http://news.bbc. co.uk/1/hi/uk/7725228.stm, accessed 9 November 2010.

80 BBC News, 'Brown makes pledge on forces' pay', 5 June 2008, http://news.bbc. co.uk/1/hi/uk/7437014.stm, accessed 9 November 2010.

81 BBC News, 'MoD criticised for soldier deaths', 15 February 2008, http://news.bbc. co.uk/1/hi/england/7245533.stm, accessed 9 November 2010; BBC News, 'Better UK troop protection urged', 19 February 2008; P. Naughton, 'High Court rejects MoD attempt to "gag" outspoken coroners over defence failures', *The Times,* 11 April 2008; Provisions to allow ministers to call secret inquests in the interests of national security were pushed through parliament in November 2009. See R. Verkaik, 'Labour forces secret inquests Bill through the Commons', *Independent,* 10 November 2009.

82 Bar Council (2008).

83 BBC News, '"No Afghan move" for UK troops', 9 November 2008, http://news. bbc.co.uk/1/hi/uk_politics/7718464.stm, accessed 9 November 2010; BBC News, 'Miliband denies UK troops claim', 25 November 2008.

84 Remarks in the House of Commons, *Hansard,* 15 December 2008, cols 815–16.

85 BBC News, 'Pact targets Pakistan terror link', 14 December 2008, http://news.bbc. co.uk/1/hi/uk/7782125.stm, accessed 9 November 2010..

86 The following remarks are taken from: Speech at the International Institute of Strategic Studies, 11 November 2008; Speech at the Berlin Security Conference, 27 November 2008; and A. Thomson and R. Sylvester, 'Interview with John Hutton', *The Times,* 20 December 2008.

87 B. Woodward, 'Detainee tortured, says US official', *Washington Post,* 14 January 2009.

88 J. Ward, 'Cheney defends war on terror's morality', *Washington Times,* 18 December 2008; also see FOX News, 'Cheney on *FOX News Sunday*', Transcript, 22 December 2008, www.foxnews.com/story/0,2933,470706,00.html, accessed 9 November 2010.

89 Speech to Veterans of Foreign Wars National Convention, 20 August 2008; Remarks on Security at US Army War College, Pennsylvania, 17 December 2008.

90 Finel and Dehn (2009).

91 See M. Fletcher, 'How the "war on terror" pushed Somalia into the arms of al-Qaeda',

The Times, 18 November 2008; P. Salopek, 'War on terror's hidden front', *Chicago Tribune*, 18 November 2008.

92 BBC News, 'Al-Qaeda not weakening', 29 September 2008, http://news.bbc.co.uk/1/hi/7638566.stm, accessed 9 November 2010.

93 BBC Press Office, 'US "war on terror" has not weakened al Qaeda, says global poll', 28 September 2008, www.bbc.co.uk/pressoffice/pressreleases/stories/2008/09_september/29/poll.shtml, accessed 9 November 2010; R. G. Khouri, 'A failing war', *International Herald Tribune*, 2 October 2008.

94 M. Evans, 'British cost of Iraq and Afghanistan reaches £13bn', *The Times,* 26 November 2008; M. Thompson, 'The $1 trillion bill for Bush's war on terror', *Time Magazine*, 26 December 2008; ABC News, 'US "war on terror" spending hits $1 trillion', 10 May 2009.

95 See for example, R. Wright, 'Iran a nuclear threat, Bush insists', *Washington Post*, 21 March 2008.

96 A. Hamilton, 'We are still fighting the Cold War', *Independent*, 14 August 2008.

97 R. Beeston, 'Analysis: why the Russia-Georgia conflict matters to the West', *The Times,* 8 August 2008.

98 R. Beeston, 'Echo of Cold War as US flexes its muscles in the Russia/Georgia conflict', *The Times*, 14 August 2008; S. Milne, 'This is a tale of US expansion not Russian aggression', *Guardian*, 14 August 2008.

99 BBC News, 'Miliband demands Russian retreat', 16 August 2009, http://news.bbc.co.uk/1/hi/uk_politics/7565739.stm, accessed 9 November 2010; BBC News, 'UK warns over "Russia aggression"', 31 August 2009.

100 For example, see M. Portillo, 'A world role for Britain slips away', *The Sunday Times*, 17 August 2008.

101 J. Hider. 'Death toll at least 310 as Israel's Gaza assault in third day', *The Times,* 29 December 2008; BBC News, 'Israel rejects Gaza truce calls', 31 December 2008, http://news.bbc.co.uk/1/hi/7805558.stm, accessed 9 November 2010.

102 BBC News, 'Israeli troops enter Gaza Strip', 4 January 2009, http://news.bbc.co.uk/1/hi/7809959.stm, accessed 9 November 2010.

8

Elysian fields

The end of the Bush regime, and its replacement by a new Democrat administration headed by Barack Obama, was hailed as a sign of positive directional change in the war on terror. Yet despite key areas of difference, continuities in US policy remained apparent. The most significant of these centred on the war in Afghanistan, where the shifting nature of the military strategy was accompanied by an increasing escalation in the conflict. In Britain, where domestic support for the campaign remained weak, ministers continued to emphasise the national security imperatives of defeating the Taliban in an ever more forlorn attempt to justify the mission with reference to the fight against international terrorism. Alongside these events, domestic anti-terror measures also continued to feature strongly on the political agenda. Central to this was the publication of a new counter-terrorism framework, the main theme of which again focused on promoting moderate values within Britain's Muslim community and eschewed any causal role for foreign policy. On a similarly recurrent note, the government's attempt to foster a values-based approach to the war on terror was further undermined by controversy over Britain's role in its extra-legal practices. The political consequences of these various issues also proved to be substantial, helping to send New Labour down to a heavy defeat in the General Election of May 2010.

Misleading and mistaken

The demise of the Bush administration and the historic election to the US Presidency of Barack Obama augured the start of a new era in both US and international politics. But despite the arrival of a fresh and untainted regime in Washington, the strategic approach adopted by the Democrats towards the war on terror contained elements of continuity as well as change with that of their Republican predecessors. The main departures in this regard were obvious: a prohibition on the use of secret

146

CIA prisons and harsh interrogation methods was accompanied by moves to close Guantánamo Bay within a year, by an avowed desire for a more multilateral approach towards global affairs, and by the cancellation (formally announced in September 2009) of the missile defence programme in Eastern Europe.[1] In addition to this, the organising phrase of a 'war on terror' itself was also sidelined, with Obama now referring instead to an 'enduring struggle against terrorism and extremism' and describing US actions in Iraq and Afghanistan as 'overseas contingency operations'.[2] Beyond this, however, much of the Obaman approach remained a variation on a Bushian theme. In Iraq, where conditions were tentatively continuing to stabilise, the process of handing control of security provision over to government forces was maintained, while in Afghanistan the ongoing drive for a military surge was both intensified and extended. Notwithstanding a greater emphasis on issues of governance, development and reconciliation, the core aspect of the new 'AfPak' strategy, designed to tackle insurgents in the border region with Pakistan, involved a doubling of the US troop presence by the end of 2009.[3]

For the New Labour leadership Obama's election was regarded with a sense of both fortune and anxiety. On the one hand, the arrival of a new and popular President provided the beleaguered Brown with an opportunity to bolster his domestic frailties by linking himself to the star-spangled bandwagon. After winning the race to become the first European leader to meet the new man at the White House, the forefront of the Prime Minister's efforts centred on trying to catch some of the reflective allure by presenting himself as the architect of plans for reconstructing the international financial system following its near meltdown earlier in the year, and by making repeated references to his close working partnership with the President on this issue. On the other hand, undercurrents of paranoia that the new regime might seek to downgrade the status of the special relationship as part of its broader repositioning of the US ship of state were also evident. Not helped by the indignity of having the traditional Rose Garden press conference relegated to an indoor press availability event on Brown's inaugural meeting with Obama, as snowstorms swept across the US capital, such concerns were only slightly assuaged by the President's subsequent description of the transatlantic relationship as 'special and strong', and by his affirmation that Britain remained one of the 'closest and strongest allies' of the US.[4]

Anxious to remain close to the new US administration, the government also sought to mirror its handling of the now phraseologically defunct 'war on terror'. One of the central elements here was a reiterated rejection of the term as an accurate conceptual framework for current operations against al-Qaeda. Reprising the argument set out by Hilary Benn in 2007, the Foreign Secretary explained that while the phrase may have been useful as a means of capturing the nature of the threat in the immediate aftermath of 9/11, continuing with its use would be both 'misleading and mistaken', creating the impression that the West faced a unified transnational enemy when, in fact, 'the forces of violent extremism remain diverse'. Drawing the battle lines in terms of 'a simple binary struggle between moderates and extremists or good and evil', Miliband pointed out, was thus only likely to 'play into the hands of those seeking to unify groups with little in common', to 'magnify the sense of threat' and to help sustain al-Qaeda's propaganda concerning the global oppression of Muslims by Western powers. Moreover, describing the campaign as a 'war' also carried the problematic implication that a militaristic solution to the issue remained possible. Reiterating the core tenets of the government's values-based approach, Miliband maintained that what was actually required was a concerted drive to promote a 'politics of consent', and to 'uphold our commitments to human rights and civil liberties both at home and abroad'.[5]

In like fashion, the unveiling of a new strategy for Afghanistan at the end of April also bore more than a passing resemblance to the plans set out by the US. Belying its international consistency, however, the sheer breadth and diversity of the stated objectives undercut ministerial assertions to be presenting a clear and coherent vision. Amongst the veritable mix of objectives now on offer included increased levels of economic development, improvements in poverty reduction, progress on human rights, a diminution in the production of narcotics, better local and national governance, greater democracy, enhanced regional stability, an increase in the security capabilities of the Afghan army, and a reduction in the level of the Taliban insurgency and terrorist activities more generally in the border region.[6] But as laudable as these aims may have been, the task ahead for achieving even a minimal degree of success remained hideously daunting. While rising numbers of civilian casualties continued to undermine NATO efforts at winning the hearts and minds of the Afghan people, the results of the humanitarian and reconstruction drive remained distinctly limited. According to a report from Oxfam/Acbar, less than half of the $39 billion that had been originally pledged for reconstruction had by this point been disbursed, and of this some 40% had found its way back to donor countries themselves in the form of consultancy fees and profits for private firms. Statistics from the United Nations, showing that Afghanistan remained mired at the foot of the world's human development index (being ranked 181 out of a total of 182 countries), were also damnable.[7] And highlighting the inadequacy of the coalition effort further, findings from the Brookings Institution placed Afghanistan second from bottom in a league table of the world's weakest states, a position that was currently surpassed only by Somalia.[8]

Against this backdrop, support for the coalition was unsurprisingly now starting to fall. Although a majority of Afghans continued to approve of the military presence, according to a survey conducted by the Afghan Center for Socio-Economic and Opinion Research little more than a third (37%) now expressed confidence in the NATO operation (down from 67% in 2006), just two-fifths believed that the country was moving in the right direction (down from 77% in 2005), and only 18% supported the US strategy of dispatching yet more troops throughout the country.[9] To make matters worse, the scale of the insurgency also continued to escalate. As the death toll for coalition troops rose sharply, with the number of casualties during the first quarter of the year exceeding that for the same period in 2008 by some 78%, Taliban fighters embarked on one of their most audacious moves to date, capitalising on internal disorder in Pakistan to mount a cross-border assault on the Swat valley in the north-west of the country.[10] Clearly highlighting the deficiencies of the Pakistani military, which remained primarily geared to deal with the potential threat from India in the South, the attack, and the subsequent Pakistani counteroffensive in May, displaced almost two million people, creating a pronounced and destabilising humanitarian crisis.[11]

Strategic stalemate

At the end of May, British combat operations in Iraq formally came to an end with the transfer of military authority in Basra to the US. This was accompanied by the establishment of a long-awaited independent inquiry into the war, the apparent aim of which, as Brown put it, was 'to learn the lessons' of its 'complex, and often controversial events'. But controversy also surrounded the terms of the inquiry. With ministers decreeing that it would only hear evidence in private, that it would not be tasked with apportioning any blame for the conflict, and that its report would not be published until after the next general election (set to take place by the summer of 2010), the decision prompted a strong public, parliamentary and media backlash. Critical ire was further aroused by the composition of the inquiry team. Headed by Sir John Chilcot, a career civil servant and former member of the Butler review, and with two of the three supporting members on record as having been supportive of Blair's approach to foreign policy, the prevailing suspicion was that the inquiry would be conspicuously unable to provide any kind of robust and forthright examination of the issues. Moreover, with Chilcot himself known to be displeased about the level of secrecy being imposed by Downing Street, the credibility of the entire exercise was called into question. Alive to the danger, ministers performed a rapid and abrupt U-turn. Highlighting the need for there to be 'full public confidence' in the process, Brown dispatched a letter to Chilcot pointing out the importance of balancing openness in the hearing of evidence with the interests of national security, and said that it would now be up to the members of the inquiry itself to decide how 'these objectives can best be met'.[12]

While the ongoing fallout from Iraq continued to provide a rich source of ministerial bedevilment, events in Afghanistan were now threatening to swamp the domestic political agenda altogether. In June, following a steady build-up of US forces, coalition troops launched a concerted offensive against Taliban fighters in the Helmand River valley, aiming to seize and hold large swathes of territory and to bring heavily populated areas under NATO control ahead of a Presidential election in August.[13] The British element of the offensive, known as Operation Panther's Claw, was dogged from the outset by controversy over the size and resourcing of the mission. With the government rebuffing calls from military chiefs for an extra 2,000 troops, ostensibly on the grounds of cost – the annual bill for British military operations in Afghanistan having grown by more than 300% over the previous two years (to £2.6 billion compared with £750 million in 2006/7) – frustrations with ministerial reluctance spilled out into public view.[14] Matching criticism from the House of Commons Defence Committee, which claimed that Britain's operational abilities were being undermined by a lack of helicopters,[15] General Dannatt warned that success in the fight against the Taliban was 'not discretionary' and that the scale and intensity of the mission was such that 'more boots' were needed on the ground'.[16] 'We should be under no illusion', he said: 'we are at war and if we want to succeed, which we must, we must get on to a war-like footing … even if not everyone in our nation realizes that'.[17]

While ministers naturally denied that troop numbers were a problem, and indeed maintained that the British presence would actually be reduced after the Afghan election, the sight of Gordon Brown making renewed appeals for extra support from fellow members of the NATO alliance did little to convince the public that all was well.[18] Moreover, as the operation in Helmand proceeded throughout the summer, so the level of military casualties steadily increased. As they did so, and as the number of British fatalities now surpassed those from the Iraq war for the first time, the tendons of public support became increasingly strained. According to a poll by ICM, by mid-July British public opinion on the matter was split directly down the middle, with 47% of respondents declaring their opposition to the war, and with 46% stating their continued support.[19]

To a significant degree, public disquiet over the campaign owed as much to the prevailing uncertainty about its exact purpose, and to the lack of a clear end-point, as it did to concerns about the government's handling of the military effort. Doubts about whether 'success', however it be defined, could now actually be achieved, were also rising.[20]

Though initially anxious to distinguish itself from the New Labour governments of the Blair era, and despite having renounced the conceptual framework of a 'war on terror', throughout 2009 the Brown administration's defence of the war in Afghanistan remained rooted in a discourse of national security. The key theme here, involving a more intensive promulgation of the government's current line on the issue, was that the military campaign was essential in order to prevent the Taliban and al-Qaeda from re-establishing a secure base from which to plan and launch attacks against the West. In this, ministers hoped to bolster public support for the mission and to undercut political criticism by drawing a direct link between the actions of British troops in a far-off land and the security of British citizens in their everyday lives. Describing Afghanistan and Pakistan as the 'epicentre' of the global terror threat, and repeatedly citing the intelligence claim that three-quarters of the most serious terrorist plots under investigation by British security agencies had links to the border region, the Prime Minister insisted that the mission remained 'vital to preventing al-Qaeda once again using Afghanistan as a base for terrorist attacks against Britain and other countries'.[21]

The case was further put by a range of senior figures. Amongst them, Lord Malloch-Brown, while admitting that the government had been 'surprised' by the strength of the insurgency, warned that failure 'would mean that there would be nothing stopping al-Qaeda operating again in Afghanistan';[22] David Miliband warned of a 'strategic stalemate' with the Taliban and insisted that the campaign was essential in order 'to deny Al Qaeda a base from which to launch attacks of the kind we saw on 9/11';[23] and John Hutton claimed that Afghanistan was now the central front in 'the worldwide campaign against terrorism', a fight which he again described as 'one of the defining struggles of our time'.[24]

But ministerial assertions about the nature of the threat and the consequences of failure were also coupled with renewed assertions about the limits of military action, and, reflecting the lack of progress in the mission, by a subtle downgrading of the criteria by which 'success' could now be adjudged. This was accompanied by a renewed insistence on the need to broker a political solution that involved the Taliban itself. Though little headway had been made here either, Brown explained that a key part of the mission was to 'persuade Taliban leaders to come over and resist the Taliban and at the same time embrace democratic politics',[25] while the new Defence Secretary, Bob Ainsworth (replacing John Hutton in June), cautioned that the conflict was 'not winnable in the short term' and that success could only be achieved by 'encouraging reintegration and reconciliation so that insurgents renounce violence in favour of legitimate Afghan-led political processes'.[26] On this, the Foreign Secretary was equally clear. Claiming that the majority of those fighting against the coalition were being driven by pragmatic motives, such as a desire for money or political advantage, and that the insurgency amounted to 'a wide but shallow coalition of convenience', Miliband said that the 'vast majority' of insurgents had 'absolutely no ideological affiliation with al Qaeda' and that the goal of the campaign was now to establish a political climate conducive to drawing them into the political arena.[27] Expanding on the theme, Malloch-Brown pointed out that the objective of the campaign was to strengthen the Afghan government in order that the coalition could engage in reconciliation from a position of strength, and conceded that 'we cannot have a definition of success beyond a containment strategy'. 'We will not prevail and win militarily', he said, 'if the success of a military win is eliminating all Taliban from Afghan soil and keeping it that way – that is not our definition of success'.[28]

Difficult circumstances

In addition to the rising political tumult surrounding the British mission in Afghanistan, ministers also spent much of 2009 under renewed pressure over the extra-legal dimension to the war on terror. Foremost amongst a series of allegations to emerge during the course of the year about the collusion of British security officials in the rendition and torture of terrorist suspects, was the high-profile case of Binyam Mohamed,[29] a British resident and Muslim convert who had been captured as a suspected terrorist in Pakistan in 2002. Having been questioned by MI5, Mohamed was subsequently passed over to US agents and rendered to Morocco, where he was allegedly tortured for several months before being taken to Guantánamo Bay. With all terrorist charges against him being eventually dropped, Mohamed duly took the British authorities to court claiming that MI5 had colluded in his mistreatment.[30] In February, the controversy over the case erupted as High Court judges blocked the release of information provided by the US that, they believed, 'gave rise to an arguable case of torture or cruel, inhuman or degrading treatment', after the Foreign Office claimed that its release would endanger US-British relations. This was followed by a supportive declaration from the US State Department, having been asked by the Foreign Office to set out its position on the matter, which confirmed that public disclosure would 'result in serious damage to US national security and could harm existing intelligence information-sharing arrangements between our two Governments'.[31]

David Miliband's explanation for this, while denying that the US statement amounted to any sort of a 'threat', was that intelligence relations depended on mutual trust, and that this required that the confidentiality of any information provided by the US be respected.[32] Two months later, however, the government was forced to apologise to the High Court after an internal review uncovered no fewer than thirteen new documents relating to the case that had not previously been disclosed. In October, a further High Court ruling came down in favour of allowing the US documents to be released given the 'overwhelming' public interest involved, and in January 2010, following a failed appeal by the Foreign Office, the information was duly made public. This showed that Mohamed had indeed been subject to practices involving torture, and that the British authorities had been aware of this mistreatment at the time that it was taking place.[33]

Following a steady stream of allegations, by the summer of 2009 the British intelligence agencies stood accused of complicity in torture in four separate countries: Morocco, Bangladesh, Pakistan and the United Arab Emirates.[34] Under growing pressure, officials pushed out a series of caveated and nuanced rebuttals. At the end of May, Sir Richard Dearlove, the now-former head of MI6, stated that agents were unlikely to have been involved in 'questionable practices' such as the abuse of terror suspects without ministerial approval, and maintained that while the intelligence service was 'sometimes asked to act in difficult circumstances', it was always sure to seek 'political cover' for its actions.[35] Denials from the current heads of MI6 and MI5, John Scarlett and Jonathan Evans, made headlines too. The line from the former was that there had been 'no complicity in torture' by the British secret service, and that its officers were 'as committed to the values and the human rights values of liberal democracy as anybody else'. But the refutation, nonetheless, was also qualified. Despite rejecting any wrongdoing, Scarlett was sure to add a defensive clause to his argument, pointing out that the security services 'have the responsibility of protecting the country against terrorism', and imploring that 'these issues need to be debated and understood in that context'.[36] The defence proffered by Evans ran on similar lines. Despite insisting that 'the security service does not torture people, nor do we collude in torture or solicit others to torture people on our behalf', the head of MI5 was keen to point out that agents were acting in 'difficult and at times dangerous circumstances', and maintained that the situation in the aftermath of 9/11 involved activities 'in parts of the world where the standards and practices of the local security apparatus were very far removed from our own'. Nonetheless, he asserted, MI5 would have been 'derelict in our duty' had it not dealt with foreign security services '[g]iven the pressing need to understand and uncover al-Qaeda's plans', adding, for good measure, that this cooperation had stopped 'many attacks'.[37]

At the ministerial level, the allegations were also formally rejected. In March, Gordon Brown declared that torture had 'no place in a modern democratic society', and insisted that the government would not condone it and '[n]or will we ever ask others to do it on our behalf'. The Prime Minister also announced that new rules would be published determining how the security and intelligence agencies would be allowed to interrogate suspects, including strict guidance banning the use of torture. Three months later, however, the government refused to publish guidelines covering the period to which the allegations about British collusion in torture referred, with Miliband bizarrely claiming that to do so could 'give succour to our enemies'. In mid-November, the government made a consolidated version of its latest guidelines available to the Intelligence and Security Committee, although the earlier guidance remained secret.[38] Adding their names to the mix, the Foreign and Home Secretaries also mounted a staunch public defence. In a jointly written article in August, Miliband and Alan Johnson (the ministerial replacement for Jacqui Smith from June), reiterated that the government was 'firmly opposed' to the use of torture, as well as cruel, inhuman and degrading treatment or punishment, and maintained that there was 'no truth' in the allegations that it was official policy to either 'collude in, solicit, or directly participate in abuses of prisoners'. In like fashion to the formal denials from the agencies, though, the ministers also remained anxious to emphasise that Britain faced a 'serious terrorist threat', that 'difficult judgments and hard choices' had to be made, and that the 'sensitive nature' of the work in which the agencies engaged necessitated 'a different set of checks and balances from other parts of government'. Furthermore, readers were reminded that while individuals detained in the UK would be well treated, the same guarantees could naturally not be made about those held by foreign authorities.[39]

A similar situation arose over the issue of Britain's role in extraordinary rendition. In February, John Hutton was forced to admit, contrary to the government's repeated insistence that Britain had not been involved in rendition operations, that this was, in fact, not strictly true. Rather, another internal review of the government's records had revealed that two terrorist suspects who had been detained by British forces in Iraq in 2004 had been handed over to US forces and subsequently rendered to a prison in Afghanistan, where they currently remained. It also transpired from this that both Jack Straw and Charles Clarke had been aware of the case when Home Secretary, but that their officials had not sought to 'highlight its significance'.[40] The former Prime Minister, Tony Blair, on the other hand, insisted that he had possessed no knowledge of any involvement in extraordinary rendition operations whatsoever during his time in office, and once more rounded on the media for sensationalising the issue. 'I didn't know about those things', he retorted, and: 'It's only ever journalists who ask me questions about issues like that'.[41]

These events and their surrounding concerns also attracted numerous calls for further investigation. Amongst them, pressure groups such as Amnesty, CagePrisoners and Human Rights Watch claimed that there was now enough credible evidence of wrongdoing to warrant a full-scale inquiry into the role played by British intelligence and security agents, with the latter maintaining that it was 'inconceivable' that officials could not have known about the use of torture in Pakistan, and that this would have amounted to 'a significant failure of British intelligence' given the close security relationship between the two countries.[42] The call for an inquiry was also supported by a range of high-profile figures and bodies. Amongst these were General Lord Guthrie, the now-ex Director of Public Prosecutions, Sir Ken Macdonald, and the government's own independent watchdog on anti-terror legislation, Lord Carlile, who accused ministers of having provided a 'limited' explanation of Britain's participation in such matters.[43] Adding its weight to the campaign, the Joint Human Rights Committee also claimed that there had now emerged a 'disturbing number of credible allegations' of British complicity in torture, and lamented that 'none of the existing accountability mechanisms have come anywhere close to answering the questions raised or ensuring that the relevant information is placed in the public domain'. The government, it said, appeared 'determined to avoid parliamentary scrutiny' about its knowledge of events.[44] Lambasting the government, too, a hard-hitting report earlier in the year from Martin Scheinin, the exotically titled UN Special Rapporteur on the Protection of Human Rights while Countering Terrorism, accused officials of breaching human rights and abusing state secrecy provisions in an attempt 'to conceal illegal acts' committed in the war on terror. Noting, *inter alia*, that the presence of British interrogators at Guantánamo Bay could 'be reasonably understood as implicitly condoning' torture and ill-treatment, the report also laid bare the vacuity of the official defence that it was not formal policy to commit or solicit the use of torture, and that it was impossible to know the precise conditions under which information had been gathered by other countries. As he put it, such a defence was nothing more than a thin and convenient veneer designed 'to give intelligence services the possibility of denying responsibility for the use of information that has been obtained in breach of international law'.[45]

Other people's secrets

The war on terror's negative impact on civil liberties was not confined to terrorist suspects. Indeed, one of the main features of the domestic anti-terror debate at this time centred on the role of state surveillance for the general population. Plans, justified in part with recourse to the terror threat, for an expansion of Britain's national DNA database (already the world's largest, and containing details of more than a million people) were stopped only after a ruling from the European Court of Human Rights that retaining the DNA details of innocent people was unlawful.[46] Similarly, Home Office plans to collect and store information on all phone calls and e-mails passing through Britain also faced severe criticism, despite a downgrading of the initial scheme from a centrally-housed database to a requirement for the information to be retained by internet service providers and telecommunications companies. Amidst worries about the social and political impact of the proposals, the information commissioner, Richard Thomas, cautioned that the process of 'creeping surveillance' had now gone 'too far, too fast' and was at risk of undermining British democracy.[47] On the same point, the House of Lords Select Committee on the Constitution also expressed concerns, calling for the British public to be given greater protection from 'over-zealous state surveillance' and warning that the erosion of privacy 'weakens the constitutional foundations on which democracy and good governance have traditionally been based in this country'.[48] More dramatically still, the former head of MI5, Dame Stella Rimington, accused ministers of having cynically exploited the fear of terrorism in order to restrict civil liberties to the point where the British people were now 'living in fear and under a police state'.[49]

In their inevitable refutation, government officials once more turned to the supposed trump card of national security. Attacking opponents of the plans for taking 'an approach to rights which puts the right of privacy above a pretty fundamental right for us to be safe', Jacqui Smith (prior to her unseating from the Home Office) warned that people needed to wake up to 'the scale of what it is we're facing',[50] a view that was also emphasised by Jonathan Evans, who warned that there remained 'a significant number' of individuals in Britain who were 'in active sympathy' with al-Qaeda, and that the threat of a terrorist attack was real and present.[51] David Omand, the Cabinet Office's former security and intelligence coordinator, made the case with an alarmingly casual level of frankness. As he explained, providing the security services with access to a broad range of personal data was essential in order to successfully counter the threat from global terrorism. Thus:

> Finding out other people's secrets is going to involve breaking everyday moral rules ... Modern intelligence access will often involve intrusive methods of surveillance and investigation, accepting that, in some respects this may have to be at the expense of some aspects of privacy rights.[52]

In the event, it was the state of Britain's economy rather than the opinions of its citizenry that finally undid the plans. In November, with the country struggling against the deepest recession since the Second World War, and with concerns about the high costs involved in pursuing the project playing negatively for the government, the Home Office announced that the scheme was to be put on hold, at least until such time as the economic situation improved on the other side of the general election.[53] Delayed too, were plans to introduce ID cards, with Brown telling the Labour Party conference in September that compulsory cards would not be introduced 'in the next parliament'.[54] Other initiatives, though, proved to be more durable. In March the government unveiled its latest strategic framework for dealing with the threat from terrorism, known as Contest2. Reiterating that the scale and nature of the threat were qualitatively 'quite different' from anything that had gone before, and disclosing that the security forces had disrupted more than a dozen terrorist plots since 2001, this warned that while support for al-Qaeda had been substantially eroded by the killing of Muslims in terrorist attacks, and that while the network was 'likely to fragment and may not survive in its current form', the threat from radical Islamic terrorism itself would nonetheless remain as the various groups affiliated to the al-Qaeda terror brand diversified and became more autonomous in their operations. The ideology behind al-Qaeda, it predicted, would 'outlive changes to its structure'.[55]

The main feature of the new strategy was a shift in focus to deal more attentively with the process of domestic radicalisation, placing a core emphasis on the need for preventative action. Observing that radicalisation was a complex phenomenon, and one driven by 'a range of causes', the framework was also notable for its continuity with the government's generic inability to accept any role in this for causes linked to British foreign policy. Instead, the analysis again centred on 'perceptions' about foreign policy on the part of British Muslims, many of whom, it was stated, considered the West (principally, of course, the US and Britain) to have either caused conflicts in the Islamic world, or (as in the case of 'perceived western inaction in Palestine') to have 'done too little to resolve them'. In addition, it was also argued that many Muslims felt aggrieved about the 'alleged support' given by the West to authoritarian regimes, as well as its hypocritical position on human rights issues given the circumstances surrounding Guantánamo Bay, extraordinary renditions, detainee abuse and so on. Unsurprisingly, with such grievances being deemed to be 'misinformed', the primary focus of the anti-radicalisation effort fell not on the need for any alterations in foreign policy, but, as before, on countering radicalism by challenging it at the level of ideas. In practical terms, however, this amounted to nothing more than a pallid rehashing of previous governmental efforts. Among the measures on offer included an emphasis on the need to promote 'Britishness' and to tackle 'un-British' views, to distinguish between mainstream Islam and 'violent extremist ideologies', to present extremist activity as a criminal justice matter (it being noted that '[d]escribing terrorists as criminals and murderers deglamorises terrorism'), and to engage with Muslim communities more broadly, involving a shift away from sustaining close institutional ties to umbrella organisations, such as the hitherto favoured Muslim Council of Britain, and towards the provision of greater funds and access to a more diverse range of community groups.[56]

Unsurprisingly too, the new approach remained deeply flawed. An obvious starting point here was that the attempt to address the issue of identity conflict by promoting the idea of 'Britishness' ran up against the immediate problem of exactly how to define an inclusive version of the term that most people could comfortably subscribe to. Given that much of this involved ambiguous concepts such as 'tolerance', 'fairness' and 'responsibility', as well as the more inglorious elements associated with (typically English) parochial nationalism, the absence of any recognisable consensus on the matter raised obvious doubts about the entire point of the exercise. Beyond this, the drive to promote 'British values' also risked exacerbating the very problem that it purportedly set out to solve. Since many young Muslims had turned to religion largely as a source of identity and group belonging in response to feelings of alienation and rejection from British society, promoting the idea that they should now aim to cultivate a greater sense of Britishness carried the prospect of driving the wedge deeper still. The attempt to directly link the anti-terror drive to broader notions about social cohesion and the integration of Muslims into a 'British' way of life were further undercut by the nature of the government's funding regime. With financial support for Islamic groups now being made dependent on expressions of state-sanctioned 'core British values', awkward questions were raised about precisely which groups and bodies officials would now choose to engage with, and about how the potential loss of credibility within Muslim communities that any state-approved groups might endure would impact upon their ability to serve as effective anti-radicalising agents.[57]

Problematic as well was the ideological geography of Islam within Britain. Characterised by sectarian divisions, by the inherently conservative nature of many grassroots Islamic organisations, and by the absence of a well established, organised and critical liberal voice within the Muslim mainstream, the prospect of any progressive movement gaining traction as a result of the government's plans remained correspondingly weak.[58] To the extent that the development of such a movement (rather than state-sponsored value-promoters) was essential to bridge the gap between 'traditionalists' and modernity, and to challenge the more dogmatic interpretations of the radical fringe, then the overall aims of the government's strategy were also likely to go unfulfilled.[59] In this context, the Contest2 framework itself risked exacerbating the alienation of Muslims from British society, and hence of hampering the growth of progressive elements, precisely by constructing and stigmatising Muslims as a 'suspect community'.[60] Add to this the suspicion that government-funded groups were being placed under pressure to pass information about suspected non-conformists to the police, and the danger was that the entire project would prove to be counterproductive: stifling political debate, marginalising progressive Muslim groups and undermining community relations by fostering greater social divisions.[61]

A noble struggle

But for all the difficulties with the government's domestic anti-terror stance, the latter half of the year was dominated by the growing crisis in Afghanistan. A defining moment in this proved to be the presidential election in August. Marred by allegations of corruption and vote-rigging on the part of the incumbent, Hamid Karzai, who eventually secured re-election in October following the withdrawal of his primary opponent, the debacle intensified the pressures on the coalition, for whom the establishment of democracy had been one of the celebrated aims of the mission. At the end of August the US Commander of NATO forces in Afghanistan, General Stanley McChrystal, called for the adoption of a new military approach. Reporting that a successful outcome would now require 'a revised implementation strategy' involving extra troops and resources, the General warned that any failure to seize the initiative risked producing 'a longer conflict, greater casualties, higher overall costs, and ultimately, a critical loss of political support'. The end result, he concluded, would be 'an outcome where defeating the insurgency is no longer possible'.[62]

With the rising death toll in the country now making 2009 the worst year for fatalities among British service personnel since the Falklands conflict of the early 1980s, support for the war in Britain continued to fall. According to a Populus survey, by September half the British public were of the view that the Afghan campaign was not reducing the threat from terrorism, while a survey conducted by GFX/NOP in November showed that four-fifths rejected the official account of the mission, with 46% also claiming that the presence of British forces was actually making the terror threat worse.[63] At the same time, a ComRes poll for the BBC indicated that almost two-thirds (64%) of the public now felt the war to be 'unwinnable', an increase of six points from July.[64]

Under mounting pressure, and rapidly losing control of the narrative, ministers turned to a panoply of arguments in an attempt to breathe new legitimacy into the mission. A core element in this involved a further reassertion of the argument from national security. Centring on three primary points, officials repeatedly re-emphasised claims of a link between terrorist plots in Britain and the tribal border region; warned of the dangers of allowing Afghanistan to fall back into the hands of the Taliban (and hence al-Qaeda); and highlighted the dangers that a precipitate withdrawal or defeat would have for the credibility of NATO and the West in general.[65] According to Bob Ainsworth, the mission in Afghanistan was vital for 'the stability of the whole region and the credibility of the NATO alliance', David Miliband insisted that the campaign was 'essential to our security at home' and that to leave 'would be risking the next 9/11 or 7/7', while Brown, warning that failure would hand al-Qaeda free reign in Afghanistan, also highlighted the longer-term implications of defeat 'for the credibility of NATO and the international community, and for the stability of this crucial region and for global stability'.[66] Keen not to underplay his hand, the Prime Minister also sought to make explicit the terror connection, insisting that 'al-Qaeda has links to the Afghan and Pakistan Taliban', and even went as far as to erroneously describe the 7/7 bombings as having been 'al-Qaeda led attacks'.[67] Aligned to these arguments was a renewed emphasis on the need for a political strategy designed to detach moderate elements of the Taliban and to draw them into the political process. Highlighting the need for reconciliation, an internal Foreign Office memo called for the development of a 'tactical reintegration programme' based on a mixture of incentives and coercion, and underlined the need to 'weaken and divide the Taliban if we are to reduce the insurgency to a level that can be managed and contained by the Afghan Security Forces'.[68] Making the case publicly, the Foreign Secretary maintained that the core strategic necessity for the coalition was to decouple the 'vast majority' of the Taliban who were not Islamic extremists from the 'hard core' elements driving the insurgency, and to integrate them into the political system as swiftly as possible.[69]

The latter months of the year were dominated by a prolonged and dramatic wait for Barack Obama to reach a settled decision on the future course of US strategy in Afghanistan. By November, with rumours abounding that the President would opt for a more expansive military deployment, Brown pre-empted the decision by announcing the adoption of a more vigorous British approach. One of the main components of this involved taking a visibly tougher line against both Islamabad and Kabul. Accusing Pakistan of having done too little to deal with extremists in the border region, Brown also put pressure on Hamid Karzai to increase the capacity of the Afghan army and to adopt robust and credible anti-corruption measures, announcing that a conference on the situation was to be held in London during 2010 and that benchmarks for measuring the progress of the Afghan government were to be set. British troops, he warned, would not continue to be put in harm's way 'for a Government that does not stand up against corruption'.[70] In addition to this, Brown also announced the deployment of an extra 500 British troops, taking the total number above 10,000, and predicted that responsibility for sections of Helmand province could start to be handed over to Afghan forces during the course of the next year.[71] In this, the Prime Minister's announcement reflected broader moves to discursively reframe the goals of the mission. Increasingly, the long-standing objective of constructing a democratic state was now being downplayed, with the emphasis instead being placed on the need to speed up the development of Afghanistan's own security provision and to ensure a degree of political stability sufficient to allow the coalition to withdraw. Though insisting that the government would not be 'deterred, dissuaded or diverted' from the mission by rising casualty figures, Brown was nonetheless keen to point out that 'we will have succeeded when our troops are coming home because the Afghans are doing the job themselves'.[72]

At the beginning of December, Obama duly confirmed the rumours about his decision on Afghanistan by announcing the largest escalation of the US military presence in the country since the war began. Involving a surge of some 30,000 extra US troops (being supported by a NATO pledge to provide a further 7,000), the new plan would take the total number to around 100,000 by the middle of 2010, though was also accompanied by an intention to initiate a gradual withdrawal from July 2011, a measure designed both to placate domestic US opinion and to put pressure on the Afghan government to gear-up its own security capabilities.[73] In justifying the expansion, the President also sought legitimacy with recourse to the humanitarian as well as the security aspects of ensuring that the Taliban could not return to power. Drawing on the self-image of the US as an anti-imperialist beacon of liberty in the world, Obama insisted that the US had no interest in a long occupation, and was keen to see a move to self-governance as soon as was practicably possible. '[U]nlike the great powers of old', he adjured, 'we have not sought world domination', but were 'heirs to a noble struggle for freedom'.[74]

A new world

Noble or not, the fate of foreign ventures in the war on terror continued to shape events into the new year. Although the promotion of democracy had unofficially been allowed to lapse as one of the core criteria for the Afghan mission, the theme of democratic governance remained a key source of division between this and the campaign in Iraq. In the latter, progress on the slow and steady, if still bloody path to democracy was maintained with successful elections in March, leading to a change of government despite significant instances of violence, intimidation and fraud. Conditions in the former, on the other hand, remained fraught with concerns over the outcome of the Presidential election. Following the launch of the largest offensive against the Taliban since the start of the war (known as Operation Moshtarak), discernible tensions between Hamid Karzai and the US saw the Afghan President round on the NATO coalition. Blaming Western powers for the fraudulent conduct of the election, Karzai accused the Americans of trying to keep him quiescent, and threatened to join the Taliban if he came under too much pressure.[75]

Questions of democratic governance also dominated on the home front, where the forthcoming general election was now colouring events with its own particular hue. But while the core issues throughout the campaign revolved around the poor state of the economy, and particularly the need to deal with Britain's record deficit following a huge financial stimulus in the face of recession, the key themes of the war on terror also continued to percolate throughout the political agenda. Indeed, in a reminder of the ongoing reality of the terrorist threat, in January the official alert status was raised from 'substantial' to 'severe', indicating that an attack was now 'highly likely'.[76] One of the most prominent themes of this period, however, centred on the transgressions of the British government and the security forces as the case of Binyam Mohamed returned to the headlines. In this, the prevailing controversy surrounding the publication of US documents relating to the use of torture was heightened following revelations that the Foreign Office had successfully persuaded the senior judges presiding over the case to water-down their final judgment by removing a paragraph critical of the security services.[77] Following a media outcry over the omission, an amended version of the paragraph was subsequently reinserted (with the original text also being published for comparison), revealing the judges' concern about MI5's lack of respect for human rights, its attitude towards the use of coercive interrogation techniques, and the fidelity of its claims about terror detainees; the judges noting that there was 'an obvious reason for distrusting any UK Government assurance, based on SyS advice and information, because of previous "form"'. Both the Foreign Office and the secret services, they maintained, had 'an interest in the suppression of such information'.[78] The response from the Home Secretary, in completely rejecting these claims and denying that either the government or its agencies had 'any interest in suppressing or withholding information from ministers or the courts', was itself dissimilatory.[79] A subsequent (and failed) attempt by both MI5 and MI6 to use secret evidence in the ongoing court case against them, was paralleled by the actions of the government, whose decision to finally publish the current guidelines issued to agents on the use of torture (though not earlier versions) was duly reversed at the last minute, with government lawyers and members of the Intelligence and Security Committee complaining that the revised procedures contained too many 'ambiguities'.[80]

Accompanying these controversies, ministers also found themselves under pressure on broader issues of anti-terror policy. In March, a report from the Communities and Local Government Committee set out a highly critical assessment of the ongoing Contest2 strategy, claiming that its emphasis on prevention and its focus on Muslims had been detrimental to social cohesion, and had generated feelings of 'alienation and stigma' amongst many British Muslims while fostering 'deep resentment' in non-Muslim communities about unequal treatment in terms of funding. Calling on the government to abandon its attempt to socially engineer a moderate and politically acceptable form of Islam (and for it to cease 'promoting and funding only those groups which conform to this model'), the Committee called for greater attention to be devoted to other factors leading to radicalisation, such as poverty, alienation, identity conflicts and foreign policy, and warned that significant resources had 'been wasted on unfocused or irrelevant projects'.[81] At the same time, a report from the Joint Committee on Human Rights was also scathing. Amongst a veritable array of criticisms to be levelled against the government, the Committee expressed concerns about the way in which exceptional measures to deal with the terrorist threat had become normalised; raised doubts about the validity of the official claim that Britain had been in a state of public emergency for eight years; and called, as a matter of urgency, for a 'thoroughgoing, evidence-based review' of all anti-terror measures introduced since 9/11. Warning, too, of a 'serious democratic deficit in the making of counter-terrorism policy', the Committee took a particularly dim view of Jonathan Evans's refusal to give evidence before it in public, describing this as 'unacceptable in a democracy' and noting that this was somewhat at odds with the Director General's evident willingness to engage in public lectures on the matter.[82] On the subject of Britain's complicity in torture, the Committee's findings were similarly reproachful. Reiterating calls for an independent inquiry into the current spate of allegations, the report sharply attacked the government's position on the receipt of intelligence from foreign agencies (namely, that this 'should not occur where it is known or believed that receipt would amount to encouragement to the intelligence services of other States to commit torture'), eruditely observing that this had no actual basis in law given that complicity 'does not require active encouragement', and concluding that the particular form of words chosen had been 'carefully designed' to allow the government to deny complicity when it knowingly received intelligence that may have been obtained through torture.[83]

With the consequences of Britain's role in the war on terror continuing to play badly for the government, at the end of January the ex-Prime Minister, Tony Blair, returned to the public eye to give evidence before the ongoing Chilcot inquiry. Taking the opportunity to launch a strident and resolute defence, not merely of Britain's role in the Iraq war, but of the entire course of New Labour's foreign policy, Blair reprised the familiar narrative of rogue states, WMD and global terrorism, and effused the need for a vigorously hawkish stance on issues of international security. On the specific case of Iraq, Blair, posing 'the 2010 question', insisted that failure to have taken military action would have left Saddam Hussein free to reconstitute a weapons capability with which to menace the region and beyond, and that this, in all likelihood, would have led to a competitive nuclear arms race with Iran, whose own weapons ambitions were highlighted as one of the foremost threats to world peace.[84]

The appearance before the inquiry of the former Prime Minister was followed shortly thereafter by that of the current incumbent. Here, Gordon Brown held to a carefully crafted narrative, the core element of which was that, as Chancellor, he had been at the centre of the policy-making process over Iraq, but not too central as to have actually been aware of, and hence implicated in any of the most controversial decisions, discussions and meetings. In a similar fashion to Blair, Brown also took advantage of the opportunity to restate the key features of New Labour's geopolitical strategy, re-emphasising the importance both of positioning Britain as a transatlantic bridge, and of upholding a hard line on security issues. Declaring his determination to have 'the strongest possible relationship between Europe and America', and describing this as 'the basis of the international order of the future', the Prime Minister defended the decision to invade Iraq as having been an issue of credibility, bound up with a broader restructuring of world affairs. '[W]e were in the midst of creating the institutions and the practices of a new world', he explained, and 'if the international community did not act here, then the international community would find it difficult to gain credibility for acting in other areas, and this new world order that we were trying to create was being put at risk'.[85]

By this time, however, proclamations about the need for Britain to maintain a global role, and assertions about the vitality of the 'special relationship' as well as the transatlantic bridge approach to foreign affairs, were becoming increasingly problematic. Not least was this due to the shifting strategic interests of the United States, now moving under President Obama to cultivate a broader network of alliances beyond Europe, and to establish closer and deeper links with new and emergent powers such as China, India and South Africa. Concerns about the waning importance of Europe were not helped by remarks from the US Defense Secretary, Robert Gates, who directly criticised the lack of military spending by European nations as having gone from being 'a blessing in the 20th century to an impediment to achieving lasting peace in the 21st'.[86] The changing nature of the special relationship, and, indeed, the changing nature of Britain's international position as a whole, was also highlighted by a critical report from the Foreign Affairs Committee. Describing the notion of a peculiarly 'special' transatlantic relationship as nothing more than a political fiction, the FAC warned that the continuing use of the phrase carried 'unrealistic expectations' and 'should be avoided', and lamented that perceptions of British subservience to the US over the Iraq war had been 'deeply damaging' both to Britain's reputation abroad as well as to its broader national interests. Moreover, with the extent to which Britain's military commitments furnished it with a degree of influence over US geopolitical decision-making being 'likely to diminish' in forthcoming years, the Committee also called for a broad reassessment of its position in global affairs, concluding that Britain would be 'unlikely to be able to influence the US to the extent it has in the past'.[87]

For all this, the issues surrounding the war on terror were largely absent from the general election campaign. With this being dominated by questions about the economy and by the impact of newly introduced televised leadership debates, the closest the issue of national security came to breaking through as an election issue was over Liberal Democrat proposals to replace Trident with a cheaper alternative, an idea that was rapidly disparaged by the Conservative and Labour parties as being certain to put the country at risk. While the outcome of the election offered no side a decisive victory, with the pragmatics of a hung parliament leading ultimately to the formation of a coalition government between the Conservatives and the Liberal Democrats, the result was nonetheless a resounding defeat for New Labour. Even if the scale was not as bad as many in the party had at one point feared, the loss of more than 90 seats and the heavy slump in Labour's share of the vote, which now fell to its lowest point since the electoral disaster of 1983, ensured that Gordon Brown's tenure as Prime Minister ended in calamitous fashion.

Conclusion

While the political guard at Washington may have changed, the contours of the war on terror remained familiar. Having discarded the failings of the new imperialist approach, the model of a military surge, following its apparent success in Iraq, was now hailed as the most effective means of placating an increasingly tempestuous insurgency in Afghanistan. Eight years after the initial invasion, the escalation of the conflict and the persistence of political and economic dilapidation throughout the country were both a damning indictment and a bitter legacy of the Bush regime. The course taken by New Labour remained close to that being charted by the US. Keen to bask in the halo effect of President Obama, and having invested extensive political capital in the necessity of defeating the Taliban, ministers upheld a robust stance on the war in the face of declining public support. The narrowing of the campaign objectives, designed to create conditions that would facilitate the onset of a withdrawal over the course of the next two years, marked a political expediency that reflected the unpopularity of the conflict as well as the diminishing prospects for success. Controversy over the domestic anti-terror agenda also continued to plague the government. Allegations of collusion in extra-legal practices refused to abate, as did disquiet over the imbalance of power in the relationship between the citizen and the state. The adoption of a new counter-terror framework, too, highlighted a distinct lack of prescience. Continuing to rely on a values-based approach that foreclosed consideration of foreign policy issues, the effectiveness of the strategy as a means of coping with radicalisation remained doubtful. The political effect of these events, though impossible to quantify with precision, undoubtedly proved to be negative for New Labour. After 13 years in power, two-thirds of which had been dominated by the events of the war on terror, the party's removal from office was chastening in the manner with which it was delivered.

Notes

1   In the event, the plan to close Guantánamo became sidelined by political wrangling over the precise details of the closure, and by the end of 2010 the camp remained open.

2   D. Sevastopulo and J. Blitz, 'Obama begins overhaul of "war on terror"', *Financial Times,* 21 January 2009; S. Wilson and A. Kamen, '"Global war on terror"', is given new name', *Washington Post,* 25 March 2009.

3   A. Gillian, 'Obama would welcome talks with Taliban moderates', *Guardian,* 8 March 2009; Barack Obama, speech at the White House, 27 March 2009; S. Salahuddin, 'Taliban say US reconciliation offer "lunatic"', Reuters, 1 April 2009; I. Traynor, 'Nato summit: Europe resists US pressure on Afghanistan "surge"', *Guardian,* 3 April 2009.

4   P. Naughton, 'White House cancels Brown press conference in Rose Garden', *The Times,* 3 March 2009; A. Sparrow, 'Special relationship as strong as ever, Obama tells Brown', *Guardian,* 3 March 2009.

5   'After Mumbai, Beyond The War On Terror', speech by Miliband in Mumbai, 15 January 2009.

6   Cabinet Office (2009).

7   United Nations (2009).

8   G. F. Will, 'Time to get out of Afghanistan', *Washington Post,* 1 September 2009.

9   S. Waterman, 'Costs of war: The civilian casualty issue', ISN Security Watch, 17 February 2009; S. G. Jones, 'Going the distance: the war in Afghanistan isn't doomed. We just need to rethink the insurgency', *Washington Post,* 15 February 2009.

10 R. Omaar, 'Why the West should fear the Taliban and al-Qaeda's hold on Pakistan', *Daily Telegraph,* 19 March 2009; R. Norton-Taylor, 'British troops take brunt of huge rise in Taliban attacks in Afghanistan', *Guardian,* 11 June 2009.

11 M. Qadri, 'Pakistan's army: as inept as it is corrupt', *Guardian,* 3 May 2009; J. Perlez and P. Z. Shah, 'Taliban losses are no sure gain for Pakistanis', *New York Times,* 27 June 2009.

12 G. Cordon, 'Downing Street signals u-turn in Iraq war inquiry row', *Independent,* 18 June 2009; A. Grice and K. Sengupta, 'Brown forced to open Iraq inquiry to public scrutiny', *Independent,* 19 June 2009.

13 R. A. Oppel Jr, 'U.S. marines try to retake Afghan valley from Taliban', *New York Times,* 1 July 2009; T. Shanker and R. A. Oppel Jr, 'In tactical shift, troops will stay and hold ground in Afghanistan, *New York Times,* 2 July 2009.

14 FAC (2009), para. 214.

15 BBC News, 'MoD budget "harm" claims denied', 23 August 2009, http://news.bbc.co.uk/1/hi/uk/8217172.stm, accessed 9 November 2010.

16 M. Evans and T. Coghlan, 'Dannatt calls for rethink on Afghan resources as troop deaths mount', *The Times,* 15 July 2009; N. Hines, 'Dannatt warns of strategic failure in Afghanistan as 16th soldier dies in a month', *The Times,* 17 July 2009.

17 Speech to International Institute of Strategic Studies, 30 July 2009.

18 P. Webster and M. Evans, 'Generals rebuffed in plea for more Helmand forces', *The Times,* 13 July 2009; J. F. Burns, 'Britain urges Afghan political effort', *New York Times,* 28 July 2009.

19 R. Norton-Taylor, J. Glover and N. Watt, 'Public support for war in Afghanistan is firm, despite deaths', *Guardian,* 13 July 2009.

20 J. F. Burns, 'Criticism of Afghan war is on the rise in Britain', *New York Times,* 11 July 2009.

21 BBC News, 'Pact targets Pakistan terror link', 14 December 2008, http://news.bbc. co.uk/2/hi/uk_news/7782125.stm, accessed 9 November 2010; R. Henry, 'Gordon Brown insists Afghan war being won', *The Times*, 11 July 2009.

22 Evidence to the FAC, 14 May 2009, Qs 183 and 186.

23 Speech to the Munich Security Conference, 7 February 2009; 'UK and allies face "strategic stalemate" in Afghanistan, admits David Miliband', *Daily Mail*, 20 March 2009.

24 R. Norton-Taylor, 'Hutton attacks European allies over lack of support in Afghanistan', *Guardian*, 15 January 2009; also see speech to the Institute for Public Policy Research, 27 April 2009.

25 Downing Street press conference, 22 July 2009.

26 Speech at Chatham House, 8 July 2009; R. Norton-Taylor and I. Cobain, 'Eight British soldiers killed in bloodiest day of Afghan mission', *Guardian*, 10 July 2009.

27 'Our Shared Future: Building Coalitions and Winning Consent', speech at the Oxford Centre for Islamic Studies, 21 May 2009; Speech at NATO Headquarters, Brussels, 27 July 2009.

28 Evidence to the FAC, 14 May 2009, Qs 199, 204.

29 See for example: M. Taylor, 'Smith faces questions on MI5 torture collusion', *Guardian*, 4 February 2009; S. Swann, 'Fresh UK torture collusion claims', BBC News, 22 April 2009, http://news.bbc.co.uk/1/hi/uk/8013444.stm, accessed 9 November 2010; I. Cobain, 'Further evidence that Pakistan tortured suspects for Britain', *Guardian*, 9 July 2009.

30 BBC News, 'MI5 telegrams "fed interrogation"', 7 March 2009, http://news.bbc. co.uk/1/hi/uk/7930708.stm, accessed 9 November 2010.

31 R. Ford and F. Elliott, 'UK judges accuse Obama administration of suppressing torture claim', *The Times*, 5 February 2009; R. Winnett, 'Torture row: David Miliband denies US threatened to stop sharing intelligence', *Daily Telegraph*, 5 February 2009; P. Harris and M. Townsend, 'Foreign Office link to torture cover-up', *Observer*, 15 February 2009.

32 'David Miliband is wrong on the war on terror', *Daily Telegraph*, 15 January 2009; R. Winnett, 'US accused of threatening Britain over terrorism "torture evidence"', *Daily Telegraph*, 4 February 2009.

33 See D. Rose, 'Government makes "unprecedented" apology for covering up Binyam torture', *Daily Mail*, 19 April 2009; BBC News, 'Ban on "torture documents" lifted', 16 October 2009, http://news.bbc.co.uk/1/hi/uk/8311075.stm, accessed 9 November 2010; I. Cobain, 'Top judge: Binyam Mohamed case shows MI5 to be devious, dishonest and complicit in torture', *Guardian*, 10 February 2010.

34 I. Cobain, 'MI5 faces fresh torture allegations', *Guardian*, 26 May 2009; H. Carter, 'Torture – new claim of secret UK complicity', *Guardian*, 26 July 2009.

35 J. Soal and I. Cobain, 'British agents would have had ministers' OK for collusion in torture – ex-MI6 chief', *Guardian*, 31 May 2009.

36 G. Corera, 'MI6 "is not complicit" in torture"', BBC News, 10 August 2009, http:// news.bbc.co.uk/1/hi/uk/8188307.stm, accessed 9 November 2010.

37 See BBC News, 'MI5 does not collude in torture', 16 October 2009, http://news. bbc.co.uk/1/hi/uk/8309919.stm, accessed 9 November 2010; A. Barrowclough, 'MI5 chief defends "torture intelligence"', *The Times*, 16 October 2009.

38 Human Rights Watch (2009); Joint Committee on Human Rights (2010); also see D. Gardham, 'David Miliband refuses to publish old MI5 guidelines on interrogation', *Daily Telegraph*, 16 June 2009.

39 D. Miliband and A. Johnson, 'We firmly oppose torture – but it is impossible to eradi-

cate all risk', *Sunday Telegraph,* 8 August 2009.

40 F. Elliott and M. Evans, 'Britain admits rendition of terror suspects', *The Times,* 27 February 2009.

41 J. Merrick, 'Britain and rendition: wait for the facts, says Tony Blair', *Independent,* 31 May 2009.

42 CagePrisoners (2009); Public statement by Amnesty, 10 August 2009; Human Rights Watch (2009).

43 D. Leppard, 'Terror watchdog calls for inquiry into MI5 "torture role"', *Sunday Times,* 1 March 2009; I. Cobain, '"Cruel, illegal, immoral": Human Rights Watch condemns UK's role in torture', *Guardian,* 24 November 2009.

44 Joint Committee on Human Rights (2009).

45 Report of the Special Rapporteur on the Promotion and Protection of Human Rights and Fundamental Freedoms while Countering Terrorism, February 2009.

46 A. Hirsch, 'Devoted to the DNA database', *Guardian,* 27 February 2009; A. Travis, 'Home Office climbs down over keeping DNA records on innocent', *Guardian,* 19 October 2009.

47 A. Mostrous and R. Ford, 'Information Commissioner Richard Thomas warns of surveillance culture', *The Times,* 27 February 2009.

48 House of Lords (2009), paras 162 and 14.

49 K. Sengupta, 'Terrorist threat "exploited to curb civil liberties"', *Independent,* 17 February 2009; M. Weaver, 'Former MI5 chief: government exploits terror fears to restrict civil liberties', *Guardian,* 17 February 2009.

50 Interview in *Daily Telegraph,* 27 March 2009.

51 R. Norton-Taylor, 'MI5 chief: al-Qaida threat diminished, but not yet over', *Guardian,* 7 January 2009; D. Gardham, 'MI5 chief warns of threat from global recession', *Daily Telegraph,* 7 January 2009.

52 N. Cecil, 'Privacy sacrificed in war on terror, says spy chief', *London Evening Standard,* 25 February 2009.

53 Digital Rights in Britain, 'UK Home Office steps back in the project to intercept communications', EDRi-gram, No. 7.22, 18 November 2009.

54 Speech to Labour Party conference, 29 September 2009.

55 HMG (2009).

56 *Ibid.*

57 S. Saggar, 'In a muddle on terror', *Guardian,* 24 March 2009.

58 Abbas (2005, 2007); Archer (2009).

59 S. Hundal, 'Is Contest 2 talking to the right people?', *Guardian,* 24 March 2009.

60 In December 2009, the Communities Secretary, John Denham, admitted that the Contest2 strategy lacked clarity and needed to be altered. See D. Casciani, 'Terrorism strategy lacks clarity, says minister', BBC News, 8 December 2009, http://news.bbc.co.uk/1/hi/uk/8400734.stm, accessed 9 November 2010.

61 Kundnani (2009).

62 P. Steinhauser and B. Woodward, 'McChrystal: more forces or "mission failure"', *Washington Post,* 21 September 2009.

63 'Afghanistan conflict not stopping terrorism, say almost half of Britons', *Daily Telegraph,* 12 September 2009; K. Sengupta and N. Morris, 'Afghan war is bad for security, voters say', *Independent,* 11 November 2009.

64 C. Lamb, J. Oliver and S. Grey, 'Army wants to retreat in Afghanistan', *Sunday Times,* 8 November 2009.

65 See for example: 'Gordon Brown defends the role of British troops in Afghanistan', *Daily Telegraph,* 5 November 2009.

66 P. Reynolds, 'New emphasis on exit from Afghan war', BBC News, 4 September 2009; BBC News, 'UK considers Afghan troops boost', 1 October 2009, http://news.bbc.co.uk/1/mobile/uk_politics/8283989.stm, accessed 9 November 2010.

67 Lord Mayor's Banquet speech, 16 November 2009.

68 G. Corera, 'UK "backs Taliban reintegration"', BBC News, 13 November 2009, http://news.bbc.co.uk/1/hi/8357972.stm, accessed 9 November 2010.

69 A. Sparrow, 'Miliband calls for majority of Taliban to be reintegrated into Afghan society', Guardian, 17 November 2009; BBC News, 'UK considers Afghan troops boost', 1 October 2009, http://news.bbc.co.uk/1/mobile/uk_politics/8283989.stm, accessed 9 November 2010.

70 E. Schmitt and D. E. Sanger, 'U.S. asks more from Pakistan in terror war', New York Times, 15 November 2009; R. Henry, 'Gordon Brown announces Afghan conference to decide exit strategy', Sunday Times, 28 November 2009; S. Jaggar, 'Gordon Brown demands Pakistan "take out" bin Laden', The Times, 29 November 2009. The London conference was held at the end of January. For details see: http://afghanistan.hmg.gov.uk/en/conference/, accessed 9 November 2010.

71 BBC News, 'Brown commits 500 more UK troops to Afghanistan', 30 November 2009, http://news.bbc.co.uk/1/hi/8385539.stm, accessed 9 November 2010.

72 Speech and Q&A at the International Institute of Strategic Studies, 4 September 2009; BBC News, 'UK considers Afghan troops boost', 1 October 2009; BBC News, 'Afghan mission will go on', 6 November 2009, http://news.bbc.co.uk/1/hi/uk_politics/8346038.stm, accessed 9 November 2010; Lord Mayor's Banquet speech, 16 November 2009.

73 CBS News, 'July 2011 is locked in for Afghanistan withdrawal', 2 December 2009, www.cbsnews.com/8301-503544_162-5868282-503544.html, accessed 9 November 2010; E. MacAskill, 'Barack Obama sets out final push in Afghanistan', Guardian, 2 December 2009; P. Walker, 'Clinton admits US is "war weary" as Nato pledges more Afghan troops', Guardian, 4 December 2009.

74 Afghanistan war strategy address at US Military Academy at West Point, 4 December 2009.

75 C. McGreal, 'US concern after Hamid Karzai blames west for Afghanistan election "fraud"', Guardian, 2 April 2010; G. Whittell, 'President Karzai: pressure me and I might join Taleban', The Times, 6 April 2010.

76 '"War on terror" to last as long as Cold War', Daily Telegraph, 9 February 2010.

77 See D. Rose, 'Government makes "unprecedented" apology for covering up Binyam torture', Daily Mail, 19 April 2009; BBC News, 'Ban on "torture documents" lifted', 16 October 2009, http://news.bbc.co.uk/2/hi/uk_news/8311075.stm, accessed 9 November 2010; Letter to the Appeals Court from Jonathan Sumption QC, 8 February 2010; R. Norton-Taylor and I. Cobain, 'Top judge: Binyam Mohamed case shows MI5 to be devious, dishonest and complicit in torture', Guardian, 10 February 2010; F. Gibb and S. O'Neill, 'Judges persuaded to curtail MI5 criticism', The Times, 11 February 2010.

78 'Binyam Mohamed case: full texts of Paragraph 168 – and how they changed', The Times, 26 February 2010; R. Booth and A. Hirsch, 'Torture ruling passages critical of MI5 are restored', Guardian, 26 February 2010.

79 R. Verkaik, 'MI5 can't be trusted to tell truth, senior judge suggested', Independent, 27 February 2010.

80 R. Norton-Taylor, 'Gordon Brown breaks promise over torture guidelines', Guardian, 18 March 2010; R. Norton-Taylor, 'Government cannot use secret evidence in Guantánamo torture case, court rules', Guardian, 4 May 2010.

81 Communities and Local Government Committee (2010).
82 Joint Committee on Human Rights (2010), especially paras 16, 24, 107 and 120.
83 *Ibid.*, especially paras 33, 41 and 48.
84 Evidence to the Chilcot inquiry, 29 January 2010.
85 Evidence to the Chilcot inquiry, 5 March 2010.
86 Speech to National Defense University, Washington, 23 February 2010.
87 FAC (2010), especially paras 48, 91, 192, 215 and 230.

9

Decline and fall

A significant change

The launching of the war on terror in September 2001 was shaped by two immediate factors: the new imperialist trajectory adopted by the US from the end of the Cold War, and the specific form and character of the George W. Bush administration. Seeking to craft a new world order more conducive to US interests, Washington's response to the al-Qaeda attacks of 9/11 was driven by military measures designed to expand free market democracy in the Middle East and to establish a credible willingness to use force in defence of its interests. In this, the Bush regime was assisted by a New Labour government anxious to elevate Britain's power and influence on the world stage. In reality, the primary means of achieving this, by positioning the British state as a transatlantic bridge between Europe and the US, became one of unflinching and uncritical support for the actions of the US. The one-dimensional character of New Labour's handling of the war on terror more generally was also problematic in a number of ways. Bluntly refusing to admit to any form of wrongdoing, or to accept any responsibility for the subsequent course of events, the government's approach not only hampered any critical analysis of the underlying causes of radical Islamic terrorism, but acted to sustain the very conditions on which it thrives.

Considered even on its own terms, by the start of 2010 the results of the war on terror had been considerably less than propitious. More than eight years after its inception, levels of geopolitical instability in the Middle East had increased, and hopes for extending democracy and free markets within the region had deteriorated markedly. In Afghanistan, a Taliban resurgence continued to defy coalition attempts to impose order, the situation in Pakistan remained volatile and conditions in Iraq were far from settled. The initial tenets of the new imperialist project itself had by now also been comprehensively discredited. The model of capitalising on the advantages of high-tech weaponry to produce rapid, flexible and limited interventions had been replaced by military surges in both Afghanistan and Iraq, while the prevailing expectation that regime change in the latter would be followed by a pain-free transition to democratic governance had led directly to an absence of planning for the aftermath of the invasion. The result of this had been to set the conditions for an outbreak of widespread chaos, culminating in a vicious and bloody insurgency. With the war in Iraq having also served to divert resources and attention from the situation in Afghanistan, where Western involvement following the initial invasion was already characterised by a disinterested, arm's-length approach to political reform and reconstruction, the critical loss of momentum provided the space for both the Taliban and al-Qaeda to reorganise and regenerate their capabilities.

Belying the aim of expanding the global influence of the US, one of the main effects of the war on terror had also been to diminish its power in international affairs. With its military tied down in Iraq and Afghanistan, and with a war-worn US public becoming increasingly leery about the prospect of further military interventions, Washington's credible willingness to use military force against deviant regimes was patently undermined. Reflecting this, growing bellicosity from North Korea, a renewed Russian assertiveness in Eastern Europe and ongoing efforts by Iran to develop nuclear weapons technology in the face of international condemnation all pointed towards the emergence of a more variegated and volatile international landscape. While one should be careful not to overstate the extent of US decline in these circumstances, the fact that these limits to US influence were revealed at a time when competitor states such as India, Brazil, South Africa and China were poised to strengthen their own regional and global authority, augured a significant change in international politics, suggesting a shift to a multipolar world and the end of unbridled US supremacy.

The financial and human costs of the war on terror were also high. By 2010, US expenditure in Afghanistan and Iraq stood in excess of $1 trillion, with the combined outlay for Britain running into tens of billions, a cost, with spending set to rise further as operations against the Taliban intensified, that would only become more difficult to bear in a context of deep global and domestic recessions. So too, the toll of lives lost and broken. Statistics for military deaths in the two main theatres of war, with the total number of coalition fatalities by this point exceeding 6,300, were dwarfed by the civilian casualty figures, estimates for which now ran into several hundreds of thousands, and with many more people having been displaced.[1] Against this backdrop, the conduct of the war on terror had also undermined attempts to embed it within a justificatory discourse of humanitarianism. Controversies over the use of extra-legal practices, including a programme of extraordinary renditions and detainee abuse at Guantánamo Bay and elsewhere, had all been enormously detrimental to any notions of Western beneficence, as had been the distinct lack of humanitarian concerns revealed in the post-war planning and reconstruction arrangements for both Afghanistan and Iraq, as well as the politically motivated use of the threat from terrorism to engage in the domestic pursuit of eroding civil liberties.

In a related fashion, the opportunity costs of waging the war on terror had also been hugely significant. Absorbing resources that could have been put to genuine humanitarian use elsewhere, the militaristic pursuit of geo-strategic objectives in the Middle East had served to push a range of non-related issues down the global political agenda. Among these, meaningful steps to tackle global inequality, promote sustainable development, dismantle unjust systems of trade and finance, reduce poverty, hunger and disease, confront the international flow of arms and face up to the millenarian challenges posed by climate change, would have done immeasurably more to erode the sources of terror that confront millions on a daily basis.[2] And for all this, the threatening glow from radical Islamic terrorism, particularly that conducted under the al-Qaeda brand, remained undimmed. Despite having suffered heavy losses to its leadership, despite the absence of another global 'spectacular' since 9/11, and despite declining levels of support throughout the Muslim world, the core threat from al-Qaeda, along with that from associational groups located within Western countries, remained a potent one.[3]

The consequences of Britain's engagement in the war on terror were also substantial. In international terms, one noteworthy, if paradoxical, effect of this was to undermine New Labour's goal of elevating Britain's influence on the world stage. Having broken the precepts of the transatlantic bridge strategy by choosing to side so comprehensively with the US, the prospects of Britain successfully pursuing a more engaged relationship with Europe, an increasing necessity for influence in Washington as well as on the Continent, had been significantly weakened. At the same time, US suspicions about British inconstancy in dealing with the terror threat, fuelled by issues such as the drawdown in Iraq, a reluctance to commit extra troops to Afghanistan and the problems of domestic radicalisation also had a negative impact.[4] And Britain's influence in the world beyond Europe and the US was unsettled as well. Having given uncompromising support to the new imperialist designs of one of the world's most divisive regimes, having expended its stocks of moral authority and political capital in the process, and with more countries now showing signs of being willing to challenge Western ambitions, any hopes that Britain could continue to hold a place at the high table of world politics looked set to become increasingly forlorn.

In terms of domestic politics, the impact of the war on terror had been more dramatic still. The scars on the political landscape resulting from the invasion of Iraq, in particular, remained deep and indelible, with the controversies surrounding the war having soiled the legacy of Tony Blair, undermined trust in New Labour and tainted the British political system as a whole. While the fallout from the war continued to shape the political agenda, the ongoing military campaign in Afghanistan also remained prominent, with disputes about the rationale and conduct of the mission continuing to surface under the new coalition government, whose approach towards the Afghan war appeared to be little different from that of its predecessor. Political tensions over an array of other matters, including the effective resourcing of the armed forces, the balance between security and civil liberties and the open questions that had still to be answered about British complicity in extra-legal practices, remained equally visible. Alongside this, the theme of domestic radicalisation also continued to animate public concerns. Indeed, at the same time as New Labour had played the terrorist threat for all it was worth, the dangers posed remain very real. Aptly demonstrating the point, a series of high-profile incidents during the latter months of 2009, including the trial and conviction of a jihadist cell for having plotted to blow up numerous transatlantic aircraft, and an unrelated attempt to detonate explosives on board a transatlantic flight on Christmas Day, served as a chilling reminder of the fact that the threat had yet to pass.

New Labour's ability to deal with the challenge from radical Islamic terrorism, however, was compromised by the core elements of its approach to the war on terror. Most notably, ministerial adherence to the Doctrine of No Responsibility and the promulgation of an ostensibly values-based framework for dealing with radicalism, was particularly problematic. A central flaw here was the uncompromising denial of any possible connection to Western (especially British) foreign policy, a political compulsion in the wake of the Iraq war and the 7/7 bombings that foreclosed any prospect of critical analysis and substantive policy change. While it is certainly true that foreign policy is not a singular driver of radicalism, and thus equally the case that radicalism would not therefore be stopped by changes to this alone, the fact remains that the foreign policy activities of the British state, not least those conducted under the geopolitical orchestrations of the war on terror, were a key part of the causal mix. That said, although the wars in Afghanistan and Iraq, along with the corresponding impression of Western powers acting with impunity against the views and legal frameworks of the international community, had an obvious impact, the events associated with military action in the Middle East were merely the latest additions to what was already a lengthy roll-call of dubious activities in the field of foreign affairs. Accompanying these, Britain's long-standing history of imperial disregard for human rights, along with its interventions and support for repressive regimes, found contemporary resonance in New Labour's diplomatic support for states with dire records on humanitarian issues and democratic governance (such as China, Turkey, Russia, Indonesia and Saudi Arabia), its continued role as a leading player in the global arms trade (remaining the world's second largest exporter after the US), its lack of substantive action on issues such as climate change and nuclear disarmament, and its continuing desire to promote a global political and economic order based on the anti-human and discredited principles of neo-liberal, free market capitalism.

To the extent that such behaviour acts as a contributory factor in fostering Islamic extremism (and naturally does little for the credibility of a values-based approach to the war on terror), changes to the direction of foreign policy would logically appear to be in order. Particularly apposite here, then, is the need for a recalibration of Britain's overall role and position in the world. Given the increasingly evident futility of continuing to chase the status of a leading world power, the adoption of a more streamlined and realistic position as a middle-order post-Imperial nation, is one that now appears to be not only necessary, but eminently desirable for a host of reasons. Giving up delusions of international grandeur would not only provide benefits in terms of financial savings and the stirring up of grievances, but would also open the way for a more progressive, focused and pragmatic vision of Britain's future; allowing the armed services to be reshaped along smaller and more effective lines, facilitating a closer and more constructive position within the European Union, and freeing up resources for more socially productive uses, both internationally and domestically, including investment in health and education, the development of alternative energy and sustainable technologies, and the creation of a more equitable and human-centric society.

A damning indictment

This said, much of how the course of events in the war on terror plays out will be determined by what happens in Afghanistan during the next few years. At the present time the tone of public debate in Britain is increasingly marked by strong opposition to the war, with its continuation being seen at best as an act of folly, and at worst as driven by the collective vanities of a political class unable to admit the error of its ways. From this perspective the official argument from national security, based on the need to prevent Afghanistan from once more becoming a base for terrorists, is deemed by opponents to be questionable on several counts. Al-Qaeda's successful relocation to the border region with Pakistan, for example, and hence the lack of any obvious need for it to re-establish a base elsewhere, is seen to clearly demonstrate the confusion at the heart of the campaign, as does the assumption that a re-empowered Taliban regime would permit al-Qaeda to return to Afghanistan given the not inconsiderable inconvenience to have resulted from their previous sojourn. In addition to this, the global nature of the al-Qaeda brand is also regarded as something of a problem for claims that the defeat of terrorism requires military action in any one particular place. As has been well noted, the largest and most high-profile attacks against Western countries, including 9/11 as well as the Madrid and London bombings, had been planned and executed in the West. Beyond this, critics also highlight the futility of the military campaign itself. Not only is the idea of driving out the Taliban and establishing a national democratic government where none has existed before deemed to be fanciful in the extreme, but the prolongation of the conflict is derided as being a course of action that will only make matters worse; fuelling radicalisation by creating the impression of a war against Islam, and driving ever more numbers of Afghans into the arms of the insurgency as civilian casualties rise.[5]

Against this, however, while such points are persuasive and compelling, it remains the case that arguments are not wrong by virtue of their origin. Indeed, for all of New Labour's transgressions, it remains far from certain that a rapid cessation of the war effort would actually yield a more positive outcome, either for the Afghan people, the Middle East as a region, Western states, or the world in general. On the contrary, it is arguable that the potential consequences of such action would likely be far worse than those to be endured by remaining on the current trajectory. While there is no doubt that the continued presence of coalition forces in Afghanistan will exacerbate radicalisation, it is equally true that withdrawing before sufficient political stability and security provisions are established would also have a dramatic effect, giving a boost to the self-confidence of Islamic extremists and providing them with the ready propaganda coup of a famous victory over the West.[6] In addition to this, it is also far from clear why al-Qaeda, despite their geographical relocation, would have no interest in re-establishing a presence in Afghanistan (not least given that it would provide an operating environment free from the encumbrances of the Pakistan army), nor that the Taliban themselves would refuse permission for them to do so, especially since the Western threat to their rule would by this point have been repelled, and since the prospect of a re-invasion to oust them for a second time would be extraordinarily unlikely. A further factor here is the risk of increased political instability in Pakistan. Given that a coalition withdrawal would alleviate the pressure in the border region and thus allow al-Qaeda and the Taliban to turn their attentions eastward, and given the boost that this would provide to radical streams within Pakistan itself, already suffering from high levels of extremist violence, the risks of a deeper and broader overspill cannot be discounted.[7]

In humanitarian terms too, the case for ensuring that the Taliban do not return to power, or that Afghanistan does not relapse into a state of civil war, is a strong one. Indeed it is not unreasonable to assume that the human consequences of withdrawal, which would effectively signal the abandonment of any humanitarian pretensions on the part of Western states and leave the Afghan people to their fate at the hands of a backward and repressive regime, would be far worse than the current state of affairs. Similarly, the impact of withdrawal on the credibility of Western states cannot be understated either. The implications of this for any genuine humanitarian interventions in the future (the prospects of which would be far reduced in any event) would be serious and significant; compromising the odds of success by providing a source of inspiration and psychological strength to opposition forces, not to mention a model of action for them to follow. The likely results would be to prolong the length, cost and human suffering of any conflict. All this said, however, given the deterioration of conditions within Afghanistan, it stands as a damning indictment of the course of the war on terror thus far that the goals of the current strategy, having been reduced to enforcing a sufficient degree of political stability and security that will allow coalition forces to withdraw, and with diminished goals in terms of development and democratic governance, are now probably the best that can be reasonably hoped for.

The prospects of success in the broader war on terror are no more propitious. Indeed, one of the difficulties of defeating al-Qaeda in any outright fashion are highlighted by the findings of a recent and comprehensive study of terrorist campaigns by RAND. One of the key points to emerge from this is the unlikelihood of being able to achieve a military solution. Of all the terrorist campaigns to have been conducted since 1968, just 7% have been stopped by the use of military force, with the vast majority having been brought to an end by the killing or arrest of key leadership figures, or because group members more broadly had been persuaded to join the political process (these accounting for 40% and 43% of all cessations respectively).[8] Given the hydra-like nature of the al-Qaeda terror brand and the impossibility of a political solution in the face of its sheer ideological opposition to the West, neither of these factors would appear to offer much in the way of viable options. To compound matters further, terrorist organisations that have been driven by religious motives, in contrast to groups driven by other factors such as a desire for territorial autonomy, have proved to be by far the most resilient and difficult to stop. While 62% of all terrorist campaigns over the course of the last forty years have been eliminated in one fashion or another, only 32% of those that have been fuelled by religion have been shut down.[9]

That said, while it remains impossible to eliminate terrorism as a method of warfare altogether (and thus, by extension, to eradicate the al-Qaeda form of terrorist violence), and notwithstanding the dangers of an extreme localised attack, such as the nightmare scenario, however unlikely, of a chemical, biological or radiological/nuclear strike on a metropolitan centre, the long-term threat to the West from radical Islamic terrorism contains several self-limiting dynamics. One important point here is the detrimental effect of the very method employed. With the indiscriminate killing of Muslims in terrorist atrocities themselves having greatly damaged support for extremism in countries across the Muslim world, the longer and more intensive the global jihadi campaign, barring a grossly disproportionate and highly radicalising response from Western states, the more likely it is to erode the very support it needs for long-term survival. Related to this is the self-limiting nature of radical Islamic dogma itself. Incapable of offering any sort of progressive vision for human society, and, indeed, unable to offer any form of vision at all beyond the repugnant oppressions of a Talibanesque theocracy, the prospect of radical Islam establishing itself as a movement with mass appeal is slim at best. The situation, as Devji explains, is that '[t]he global jihad has no coherent vision for the future and thus no plan of action to bring it about'.[10] Further still, beyond the problems of support in Muslim countries, radical Islamic terrorism in the West itself faces an even greater difficulty. With the radicalisation process proving to be most effective in young, alienated and conflicted Muslim males, the result is to produce small, inward-looking and individualistically motivated jihadi groups that, by definition, remain socially isolated and disconnected. As such, self-starter and leaderless jihadi groups are unable to propagate more broadly without adopting the kind of formal organisational structures that are capable of being detected and destroyed by intelligence agencies.[11]

The road ahead

While New Labour's foreign policy approach helped to perpetuate and sustain grievances conducive to radical Islamic extremism, its domestic conduct in the war on terror was also problematic. A central theme here concerned the government's approach to anti-terror legislation. This was based on a zero-sum conception of civil rights and security, in which the latter was considered to be enhanced by a diminution of the former. Not only is this a false dichotomy, but the reality is actually the obverse. While it may of course be necessary to curtail civil freedoms in times of grave emergency, an effective anti-terror strategy demands that such reductions be tempered by a non-negotiable commitment to human rights, due process and equality under the rule of law. Indeed, such qualities are not merely valued ends in and of themselves, without which there is little point in fighting the challenge from radical Islamic extremism, or indeed from any other form of threat, but are also crucial for promoting the levels of mutual trust and cooperation between citizens and the state on which a purposeful and cogent counter-terror strategy must ultimately depend. In contrast, New Labour's approach proved in many ways to be a counter-productive one; aiding the stigmatisation of Muslims, undermining community relations and eroding public trust. Moreover, with civil liberties having been progressively debased, and with the powers available to the government having been progressively enhanced, the threat to liberal values and individual freedoms proved to be not limited to the al-Qaeda terror brand, but to derive also from the actions of an overweening and overly intrusive state.[12]

In addition to the problems of anti-terror legislation, the government's anti-radicalisation agenda was also a source of some difficulty. Alongside the incongruity of founding a values-based approach on the essentially amorphous nature of 'British values' themselves, tensions surrounding the government's commitment to a multiculturalist agenda rooted in the pursuit of social diversity as an intrinsically valued end in its own right, was also contentious. Having fostered the growth of an identity politics based on ascribed ethno-cultural and religious characteristics, this has led to an ossification of cultural boundaries, has strengthened conservative forces within immigrant communities, and has entrenched a sense of 'otherness' that has served to exacerbate social mistrust and suspicion. In so doing, this has helped to create and sustain the very circumstances in which the kind of identity crises that are central to the radicalisation process can thrive.

Part of the problem in this concerns the very notion of 'Britishness' itself. While the indeterminacy and ambiguities inherent in the concept provide sufficient flexibility for it to co-exist alongside, and without impinging upon, other forms of identity, be they national, cultural or religious in nature, the same qualities (and the more so given the assertions of 'sub-British' nationalisms in the wake of devolution) also mitigate against the prospect of Britishness being able to provide any form of strong and meaningful identity on its own. Essentially comprising a 'light' form of identity, open and amenable to differing content and meanings, a core dilemma facing those who would wish to promote the term as a means of engendering national unity is that there cannot be said to exist any single or true form of 'Britishness' at all.[13] In terms of the debate surrounding multiculturalism, the issue is also pronounced. While evidence suggests that ethnic and religious minorities have no trouble feeling British, or regarding themselves as such (although some individuals, mostly belonging to the younger generation, certainly do),[14] the primary issue is not so much a lack of 'British' feelings, as the inadequacy of Britishness as a means of providing an overarching and substantive form of identity above and beyond other constitutive elements of identity that individuals may possess. As these sub-, or extra-British dimensions to identity have become more intense in recent years, so political clashes over the nature of identity have come increasingly to the fore.

In this context, debates about multiculturalism that centre on the dichotomy between assimilation and diversity, on the need for greater integration of ethnic and religious minorities or a greater respect for difference, thus fall wide of the mark. For the former, the simple question of 'integration into what?' is one that provides a major stumbling block given the ambiguous and fluid nature of British national identity, while for the latter, the claim that greater awareness, tolerance and rights for differing ethno-cultural and religious groups would create a more harmonious and cohesive society cannot credibly be sustained given that this would merely compound the underlying problem of defining identity in terms of separateness and otherness.[15] Indeed, since both assimilationist and multiculturalist schools of thought place the politics of identity at the centre of their conceptions of the public sphere, neither is capable of effectively addressing social problems that are driven by competing visions of identity rights, and thus neither is able to provide a compelling solution to the current predicament concerning the issue of radicalisation.[16]

This is not, of course, to suggest that the multicultural agenda has been the sole cause of problems surrounding radicalisation, though nor is it to accept, as Abbas claims, that to highlight the tensions raised by identity politics is to revert to 'a culturalist socio-pathological argument' in which victims are blamed for their own plight.[17] To be critical of a policy approach designed to promote social diversity for its own sake is not to automatically argue in favour of an opposing and illiberal assimilationist position. Rather, a core challenge in dealing with these issues, as Saggar notes, is 'to foster a more credible language of common bonds and shared values' that is capable of bridging walls of difference between social groups while at the same time fostering (within liberal parameters) a tolerance and respect for other ways of life.[18] Given that the conditions for radicalisation in the West are, to a large degree, grounded in issues of alienation and identity conflict, it seems evident that such an approach must not only address prevailing levels of social inequality and empower a progressive stream within the Muslim community, but must also aim to de-emphasise the presently prevailing fetish for a form of politics based on identity, and promote instead a politics based on the principles of inclusion and human solidarity.

Clearly this is a difficult and complex task, and one that requires greater consideration than can be given here, but the broad outlines of the road ahead, if not the exact details, are at least discernible. One important, and increasingly necessary step towards achieving this end would be the establishment of an avowedly secular constitution. While this would no doubt be seen in many quarters as an attack on religious freedom, the fact remains that a public sphere divest of religious accoutrements, and a state overtly committed to impartiality in matters of faith, offers the best guarantor of religious freedom by virtue of ensuring equal rights for all citizens regardless of their personal beliefs.[19] A commitment to upholding the rights of individuals on the basis of their human rights per se, rather than their membership or otherwise of any particular social group, is the best, and indeed the only means by which meaningful provisions of equality and plurality can be sustained. Such a move would be far from a panacea, however, and along with this wide-ranging political reforms designed to assert a more participatory and accountable form of democracy are also long overdue. Measures to bridge the ever widening gap between the British public and their elected representatives, and to foster a real sense of common ownership over the processes of government, are valuable ends in themselves, but such reforms are also important given that much of what has occurred in relation to Britain's role in the war on terror has taken place due to the unaccountable, unresponsive and opaque nature of its political system. With New Labour having persistently acted without regard for (and indeed, in the face of) domestic public opinion; having sought to deceive and manage the electorate through the routinised use of spin and manipulation; having superciliously misled the country over the invasion of Iraq; having given its support for (and having yet to fully answer ongoing and serious questions about) British complicity in extra-legal practices; and having systematically sought to erode civil liberties for party political advantage in the name of fighting terrorism, it cannot be said that the British system of government is one that has served its people well.

Such reforms that are required in this respect have been outlined before, and the arguments in their favour have been well rehearsed. They include a written constitution, a Bill of Rights with enshrined protections for civil liberties, a greater social democratic commitment to reducing inequality and strengthening public services, as well as greater mechanisms of public control over the political system, such as fixed-term parliaments, a fully elected second chamber, a greater number of free votes in the Commons, the ability to recall MPs, a fairer system of elections and more robust and wide-ranging rights of access to official information. Unfortunately, in the present political climate there is little appetite, at least from the political class, for such a programme of far-reaching and progressive change. While the avowed intentions of the new coalition government are in many of these respects worthy of support, not least its proposals to reform the upper chamber and to repeal many of New Labour's obtrusions on civil liberties (including the abolition of identity cards and the holding of an inquiry into British involvement in the torture of terrorist suspects), much of its ostensibly 'progressive' vision remains half-hearted and politically tainted. Its commitment to hold a referendum on the use of the Alternative Vote system for Westminster elections, for example, amounts to the feeblest form of electoral change imaginable, its plans for fixed-term parliaments, in erring on the longest time possible of five years, appear to be motivated more by a desire to retain power rather than enhance accountability, and its plans to re-examine Britain's adherence to the European Human Rights Act and to introduce swingeing cuts in public services in order to help reduce Britain's deficit, do not appear to bode well for any prospect of addressing inequalities and promoting social cohesion. The implications of this for the continued unfolding of events under the war on terror, or whichever phraseological device is contrived to replace it over the course of the next few years, are disturbingly clear. Although the idea of fighting a 'war on terror' may have been mistaken and misconceived, the issues it has raised are serious, and the challenges posed remain very real. The threat from radical Islamic terrorism may not be a civilisational one, but nor will it go quietly into the night. If the challenge is to be effectively addressed then extensive changes both in Britain's foreign policy as well as its domestic political and social life will need to be made. If the response falls short then Britain, and others beyond its shores, will continue to reap the consequences.

Notes

1   Statistics for the number of fatalities are often variable and imprecise, and there are no definitive figures available. Useful sources and analyses can be found at: www.iraqbodycount.org, www.antiwar.com and www.icasualties.org.
2   On this point see Elworthy and Rogers (2001); Rogers (2007).

3 Hoffman (2008).
4 Relations were further damaged by the Scottish Parliament's decision to release the Lockerbie bomber in August 2009.
5 On these points, see for example: S. Jenkins, 'This trial tells us it's policing, not war, that stops terrorists', *Guardian*, 8 September 2009; 'End the nightmare of the Afghan war', *Socialist Worker*, 24 October 2009; 'Why we must leave Afghanistan', *Independent*, 8 November 2009; D. Gardham, 'Is the "war on terrorism" better fought at home?', *Daily Telegraph*, 9 November 2009; M. Hasan, 'Two sides of the Coin', *New Statesman*, 26 November 2009; S. Milne, 'Only pressure to withdraw can stop this blood price', *Guardian*, 27 January 2010.
6 The effects of this would be particularly strong following the initial demoralisation of Islamic extremists after the fall of the Taliban in 2001. See Cook (2003).
7 D. Walsh, 'Pakistan suffers record number of deaths due to militant violence', *Guardian*, 11 January 2010.
8 The remaining 10% of terrorist campaigns ended in the successful achievement of their aims, although no group had achieved this since 1968.
9 See Jones and Libicki (2008).
10 F. Devji, 'Spectral brothers: al-Qaida's world wide web', OpenDemocracy.net, 18 September 2005, accessed 9 November 2010.
11 Roy (2008); Sageman (2008).
12 See Buzan (2006); Saggar (2009).
13 See Kiely, McCrone and Bechhofer (2005); Uberoi and McLean (2007); Archer (2009).
14 For example see Georgiadis and Manning (2009).
15 From this perspective see Runnymede Trust (2000); Modood and Ahmad (2007); Saggar (2009).
16 Kelly (2005).
17 Abbas (2007), p. 119; also see Abbas (2007a).
18 Saggar (2009), p. 227.
19 See for example Kelly (2005); Baggini (2006); Habermas (2006).

References

Official Reports

Aitken, R. (2008), 'The Aitken Report: An Investigation into Cases of Deliberate Abuse and Unlawful Killing in Iraq in 2003 and 2004'. HM Army.

All Party Parliamentary Group on Extraordinary Rendition (2005), 'Briefing: Torture by Proxy: International Law Applicable to "Extraordinary Renditions"', APPG-01-05.

Butler, Lord (2004), 'Review of Intelligence on Weapons of Mass Destruction', HC898, HMSO, London.

Cabinet Office (2008), 'The National Security Strategy of the United Kingdom', Cm. 7291, TSO, Norwich.

Cabinet Office (2009), 'UK Policy in Afghanistan and Pakistan: The Way Forward', HMSO, Norwich.

Communities and Local Government Committee (2010), 'Preventing Violent Extremism', Sixth Report of Session 2009–10. HC 65. HMSO, London.

Defence Committee (2006), 'The UK deployment to Afghanistan', Fifth Report of Session 2005–06, HC 558, HMSO, London.

Defence Committee (2006a), 'Ministry of Defence Annual Report and Accounts, 2004–05', Sixth Report of Session, 2005–06, HC 822, HMSO, London.

Defence Committee (2007), 'UK Land Operations in Iraq, 2007', First Report of Session 2007–08, HC 110, HMSO, London.

Department for Communities and Local Government (2007), 'Preventing Violent Extremism: Winning Hearts and Minds', HMSO, London.

Foreign Affairs Committee (2003), 'The Decision to go to War in Iraq', Ninth Report of Session 2002–03, HC 813. HMSO, London.

Foreign Affairs Committee (2005), 'Foreign Policy Aspects of the War Against Terrorism', Sixth Report of Session 2004–05, Vol. I, HC 36-I, HMSO, London.

Foreign Affairs Committee (2007), 'Visit to Guantánamo Bay', Second Report of Session 2006–07, HC 44, HMSO, London.

Foreign Affairs Committee (2007a), 'Human Rights Annual Report 2006', Third Report of Session 2006–07, HC 269, HMSO, London.

Foreign Affairs Committee (2008), 'Human Rights Annual Report 2007', Ninth Report of Session 2007–08, HC 533, HMSO, London.

Foreign Affairs Committee (2009), 'Human Rights Annual Report 2008', Seventh Report of Session 2008–09, HC 557, HMSO, London.

Foreign Affairs Committee (2010), 'Global Security: UK–US Relations', Sixth Report of Session 2009–10, HC 114 (incorporating HC 1100-i), HMSO, London.

HMG (2002), 'Iraq's Weapons of Mass Destruction: The Assessment of the British Government', HMSO, London, 24 September.

HMG (2003), 'Iraq – Its Infrastructure of Concealment, Deception, and Intimidation', February.

HMG (2005), 'Foreign Policy Aspects of the War Against Terrorism: Response of the Secretary of State for Foreign and Commonwealth Affairs', Cm. 6590, HMSO, Norwich.

HMG (2005a), 'The Government's Reply to the Sixth Report from the Home Affairs Committee, Session 2004–05', HC 165, Cm. 6593, HMSO, Norwich.

HMG (2007), 'The Governance of Britain', Cm. 7170, HMSO, London.

HMG (2009), 'The United Kingdom's Strategy for Countering International Terrorism', Cm. 7547, TSO, Norwich.

Home Affairs Committee (2004), 'Identity Cards', Fourth Report of Session 2003–04, Vol. I, HC 130-I, HMSO, London.

Home Affairs Committee (2005), 'Terrorism and Community Relation', Sixth Report of Session 2004–05, Vol. I, HC 165-I, HMSO, London.

Home Affairs Committee (2006), 'Terrorism Detention Powers', Fourth Report of Session 2005–06, Vol. I HC 910-I, HMSO, London.

Home Office (2001), 'Community Cohesion: A Report of the Independent Review Team', HMSO, London.

Home Office (2002), 'Entitlement Cards and Identity Fraud: A Consultation Paper', Cm. 5557, TSO, Norwich.

Home Office (2003), 'Identity Cards: The Next Steps', Cm. 6020, TSO, Norwich.

Home Office (2004), 'Strength in Diversity: Towards a Community Cohesion and Race Equality Strategy', Home Office Communication Directorate.

Home Office (2005), 'Preventing Extremism Together', Working Group Reports.

Home Office (2006), 'Countering International Terrorism: The United Kingdom's Strategy', Cm. 6888, HMSO, Norwich.

House of Lords (2009), 'Select Committee on the Constitution. Second Report of Session 2008–09, Surveillance: Citizens and the State', Vol. I, HL 18-I, HMSO, London.

House Committee on the Judiciary (2009), 'Reining in the Imperial Presidency: Lessons and Recommendations Relating to the Presidency of George W. Bush', Majority Staff Report to Chairman John Conyers, Jr., Washington DC.

Intelligence and Security Committee (2003), 'Iraqi Weapons of Mass Destruction: Intelligence and Assessments', Cm. 5972, HMSO, London.

Intelligence and Security Committee (2005), 'The Handling of Detainees by UK Intelligence Personnel in Afghanistan, Guantánamo Bay and Iraq', Cm. 6469, HMSO, Norwich.

Intelligence and Security Committee (2006), 'Report into the London Terrorist Attacks on 7 July 2005', Cm. 6785, HMSO, Norwich.

Intelligence and Security Committee (2007), 'Rendition', Cm. 7171, HMSO, Norwich.

ISAF (2008), 'Afghanistan Theatre Strategic Communications Strategy', October 2008.

Joint Committee on Human Rights (2006), 'The UN Convention Against Torture (UNCAT)', Nineteenth Report of Session 2005–06, Vol. I, HC 701-I, HMSO, London.

Joint Committee on Human Rights (2007), 'Counter-Terrorism Policy and Human Rights: 42 Days. Second Report of Session 2007–08', HC 156, HMSO, London.

Joint Committee on Human Rights (2008), 'UN Convention Against Torture: Discrepancies in Evidence Given to the Committee About the Use of Prohibited Interrogation Techniques in Iraq', Twenty-Eighth Report of Session 2007–08, HC 527, HMSO, London.

Joint Committee on Human Rights (2009), 'Allegations of UK Complicity in Torture', Twenty-third report of session 2008–09, HC 230, HMSO, London.

Joint Committee on Human Rights (2010), 'Counter–Terrorism Policy and Human Rights (Seventeenth Report): Bringing Human Rights Back In', Sixteenth report of Session 2009–10, HL 86, HC 111, HMSO, London.

National Audit Office (2006), 'Recruitment and Retention in the Armed Forces', HMSO, London.

National Commission on Terrorist Attacks Upon the United States (2004), 'Final Report of the National Commission on Terrorist Attacks Upon the United States', US Government Printing Office.

Office of Management and Budget (2009), 'Historical Tables: Budget of the US Government', US Government Printing Office, Washington DC.

Privy Counsellor Review Committee (2003), 'Anti-Terrorism, Crime and Security Act 2001 Review', HC 100, HMSO, London.

Runnymede Trust (2000), 'The Future of Multi-Ethnic Britain: The Parekh Report', Profile Books, London.

United Nations (2009), 'Human Development Report 2009', United Nations Development Programme, Palgrave, New York.

US Department of State (2008), 'Country Reports on Terrorism', US Department of State Publication Office of the Coordinator for Terrorism.

US Senate Committee on Intelligence (2004), 'Report on the US Intelligence Community's Prewar Intelligence Assessments on Iraq', Washington DC.

Books and Articles

Abbas, T. (2005), 'Muslims in Britain after 7/7: The problem of the few', openDemocracy. net.

Abbas, T. (2007), 'A theory of Islamic political radicalism in Britain: Sociology, theology and international political economy', *Contemporary Islam*, 1(2): 109–22.

Abbas, T. (2007a), 'Ethno-religious identities and Islamic political radicalism in the UK: A case study', *Journal of Muslim Minority Affairs*, 27(3): 429–42.

Ahmed, N. M. (2003), *Behind the War on Terror: Western Secret Strategy and the Struggle for Iraq*, Clairview, East Sussex.

Al-Lami, M. (2009), 'Studies of Radicalisation: State of the Field Report', Royal Holloway University, Department of Politics and International Relations Working Paper, No. 11.

Alleyne, B. (2002), 'An idea of community and its discontents: Towards a more reflexive sense of belonging to multicultural Britain', *Ethnic and Racial Studies*, 25(4): 607–27.

Amin, S. (1977), *Imperialism and Unequal Development*, Monthly Review Press, New York.

Amnesty (2006), 'USA: Below the Radar: Secret Flights to Torture and "Disappearance"', Index No. AMR 51/05/2006.

Archer, T. (2009), 'Welcome to the Umma: The British state and its Muslim citizens since 9/11', *Cooperation and Conflict*, 44(3): 329–47.

Ashton, N. (2005), 'Harold Macmillan and the "Golden Days" of Anglo-American relations revisited, 1957–63', *Diplomatic History*, 29(4): 691–723.

Ayers, A. (2009), 'Imperial liberties: Democratisation and governance in the "new" imperial order', *Political Studies*, 57(1): 1–27.

Azubuike, S. (2005), 'The "poodle theory" and the Anglo-American "special relationship"', *International Studies*, 42(2): 123–39.

Back, L., M. Keith, A. Khan, K. Shukra and J. Solomos (2002), 'New Labour's white heart: Politics, multiculturalism and the return of assimilation', *Political Quarterly*, 73(4): 445–54.

Baggini, J. (2006), 'The rise, fall and rise again of secularism', *Public Policy Review*, 12(4):

204–12.

Bamford, B. W. C. (2004) 'The United Kingdom's "war against terrorism"', *Terrorism and Political Violence*, 16(4): 737–56.

Bar Council (2008), 'The Governance of Britain: Lord Goldsmith QC's Citizenship Review', Report of a Working Group of the Bar Council.

Baran, P. A. and P. A. Sweezy (1968), *Monopoly Capital: An Essay on the American Economic and Social Order*, Penguin, Harmondsworth.

Barkawi, T. and M. Laffey (2002), 'Retrieving the imperial: Empire and international relations', *Millennium*, 31(1): 109–27.

Barrow, C. W. (2005), 'The return of the state: Globalization, state theory, and the new imperialism', *New Political Science*, 27(2): 123–45.

Baylis, J. (1997), *Anglo-American Relations Since 1939: The Enduring Alliance*, Manchester University Press, Manchester.

Beitel, K. (2005), 'The US, Iraq and the future of empire', *Historical Materialism*, 13(3): 163–92.

Belasco, A. (2009), 'The Cost of Iraq, Afghanistan, and Other War on Terror Operations Since 9/11', Congressional Research Service.

Bello, W. (2005), *Dilemmas of Domination: The Unmaking of the American Empire*, Zed, London.

Bello, W. (2006). 'Humanitarian intervention: Evolution of a dangerous doctrine', *Focus on the Global South*, 19 January 2006.

Biddle, S. (2002), 'The new way of war?', *Foreign Affairs*, May/June, www.foreignaffairs.com/articles/58015/stephen-biddle/the-new-way-of-war.

Blair, T. (2002), 'The power of world community', in *Re-Ordering the World*, Foreign Policy Centre.

Blix, H. (2004), *Disarming Iraq: The Search for Weapons of Mass Destruction*, Bloomsbury, London.

Blum, W. (2006), *Rogue State: A Guide to the Word's Only Superpower*, Zed, London.

Blunkett, D. (2006), *The Blunkett Tapes*, Bloomsbury, London.

Bogdanor, V. (2005), 'Footfalls echoing in the memory. Britain and Europe: The historical perspective', *International Affairs*, 81(4): 689–701.

Boot, M. (2003), *The Savage Wars of Peace: Small Wars and the Rise of American Power*, Basic, New York.

Bose, P. (2007), '"New" imperialism? On globalisation and nation-states', *Historical Materialism*, 15(3): 95–120.

Bowman, S. (2003), 'Iraq: U.S. Military Operations', Congressional Research Service Report for Congress, The Library of Congress, 4/8/03.

Bremer, P. (2006), *My Year in Iraq: The Struggle to Build a Future of Hope*, Simon and Schuster, London.

Brenner, R. (2001), 'The world economy at the turn of the millennium: Towards boom or crisis?', *Review of International Political Economy*, 8(1): 6–44.

Brenner, R. (2006), 'What is, and what is not, imperialism?', *Historical Materialism*, 14(4): 79–105.

Brewer, A. (1990), *Marxist Theories of Imperialism: A Critical Survey*, second edition, Routledge, London.

Brighton, S. (2007), 'British Muslims, multiculturalism and UK foreign policy: "Integration" and "cohesion" in and beyond the state', *International Affairs*, 83(1): 1–17.

Bromley, S. (2005), 'The United States and the control of world oil', *Government and Opposition*, 40(2): 225–55.

Bukharin, N. (1929), *Imperialism and World Economy*, International Publishers,

London.

Burke, J. (2004), *Al-Qaeda: The True Story of Radical Islam*, Penguin, London.

Burnham, G., S. Doocy, E. Dzeng, R. Lafta and L. Roberts (2006), 'The Human Cost of the War in Iraq', Bloomberg School of Public Health, Johns Hopkins University, Baltimore, and School of Medicine, Al Mustansiriya University, Baghdad.

Burrach, R. and J. Tarbell (2004), *Imperial Overstretch: George W. Bush and the Hubris of Empire*, Zed, London.

Bush, B. (2006), *Imperialism and Postcolonialism*, Pearson, London.

Buzan, B. (2006), 'Will the "global war on terrorism" be the new Cold War?', *International Affairs*, 82(6): 1101–18.

CagePrisoners (2009), 'Fabricating Terrorism: British Complicity in Renditions and Torture', London.

Caldwell, A. (2006), 'Empire and exception', *New Political Science*, 28(4): 489–506.

Callinicos, A. (2002), 'The actuality of imperialism', *Millennium*, 31(2): 319–26.

Campbell, A. (2007). *The Blair Years: Extracts from the Alastair Campbell Diaries*, Hutchinson, London.

Center for the Study of the Presidency (2008), 'Afghanistan Study Group Report: Revitalizing our Efforts, Rethinking our Strategies', second edition, Washington DC.

Chatham House (2005), 'Security, Terrorism and the UK', ISP/NSC Briefing Paper 05/01.

Chatterjee, P. (2004), *Iraq, Inc. A Profitable Invasion*, Seven Stories Press, New York.

Chesnais, F. (2007), 'The economic foundations of contemporary imperialism', *Historical Materialism*, 15(3): 121–42.

Chibber, V. (2004), 'The return of imperialism to social science', *European Journal of Sociology*, 45(3): 427–41.

Chomsky, N. (2003), *Hegemony or Survival: America's Quest for Global Dominance*, Penguin, London.

Chomsky, N. (2003a), *Power and Terror: Post 9/11 Talks and Interviews*, Turnaround, London.

Chomsky, N. (2008), 'Humanitarian imperialism: the new doctrine of imperial right', Monthly Review, 60(9), www.monthlyreview.org/080908chomsky.php.

Clarke, R. A. (2004), *Against All Enemies: Inside America's War on Terror*, Free Press, New York.

Coates, D. and J. Krieger (2004), *Blair's War*, Polity Press, Cambridge.

Coen, D. (2005), 'The G8, globalisation and the not-so-new imperialism', Socialist Outlook, May, www.isg-fi.org.uk/spip.php?article277.

Coker, C, (1992), 'Britain and the new world order: The special relationship in the 1990s', International Affairs, 68(3): 407–21.

Coll, S. (2005), *Ghost Wars: The Secret History of the CIA, Afghanistan and Bin Laden*, Penguin, London.

Colman, J. (2004), *A 'Special Relationship'? Harold Wilson, Lyndon B. Johnson and Anglo-American Relations 'At the Summit', 1964–68*, Manchester University Press, Manchester.

Cook, D. (2003), 'The recovery of radical Islam in the wake of the defeat of the Taliban', *Terrorism and Political Violence*, 15(1): 31–56.

Cooper, R. (2002), 'The Post Modern State', *Re-Ordering the World*, Foreign Policy Centre.

Cox. M. (2004), 'Empire, imperialism and the Bush doctrine', *Review of International Studies*, 30(4): 585–608.

Cox. M. (2005), 'Empire by denial: the strange case of the United States', *International*

References

Affairs, 81(1): 15–30.

Cox, R. (2004), 'Beyond empire and terror: critical reflections on the political economy of world order', *New Political Economy*, 9(3): 307–23.

Croft, S. (2007), 'British jihadis and the British war on terror', *Defence Studies*, 7(3): 317–37.

Diamond, L. (2004), 'What went wrong in Iraq?', *Foreign Affairs*, September/October 2004, www.foreignaffairs.com/articles/60095/larry-diamond/what-went-wrong-in-iraq.

Dickie, J. (1994), *Special No More. Anglo-American Relations: Rhetoric and Reality*, Weidenfeld and Nicolson, London.

Dimbleby, D. and D. Reynolds (1988), *An Ocean Apart: The Relationship Between Britain and America in the Twentieth Century*, Random House, New York.

Dobson, A. P. (1988), *The Politics of the Anglo-American Economic Special Relationship 1940–1987*, Wheatsheaf, Sussex.

Dobson, A. P. (1995), *Anglo-American Relations in the Twentieth Century*, Routledge, London.

Donnelly, T. (2002), 'The past as prologue: an imperial manual', *Foreign Affairs*, July/August.

Doyle, M. W. (1986), *Empires*, Cornell University Press, Ithaca, NY.

Dumbrell, J. (2001), *A Special Relationship: Anglo-American Relations in the Cold War and After*, Macmillan, London.

Dumbrell, J. (2006), *A Special Relationship: Anglo-American Relations From the Cold War to Iraq*, Palgrave, London.

Edmunds, T. and A. Forster (2007), 'Out of Step: The Case for Change in the British Armed Forces', DEMOS.

Eland, I. (2002), 'The empire strikes out: the "new imperialism" and its fatal flaws', *Policy Analysis*, 459: 1–127.

Eland, I. (2008), 'A counterproductive "war on terror"', Middle East Online, 27 April 2008, www.middle-east-online.com/english/?id=25528=25528&format=0.

Elliott, M. (2006), 'United Kingdom: Detention without trial and the "war on terror"', *International Journal of Constitutional Law*, 4(3): 553–66.

Elworthy. S. and P. Rogers (2001), 'The United States, Europe and the Majority World After 11 September', Oxford Research Group.

Esposito, J. L. and D. Mogahed (2008), *Who Speaks for Islam? What a Billion Muslims Really Think*, Gallup Press, New York.

Feith, D. J. (2008), *War and Decision: Inside the Pentagon at the Dawn of the War on Terrorism*, Harper, London.

Ferguson, N. (2008), *Colossus: The Rise and Fall of the American Empire*, Penguin, London.

Fieldhouse, D. K. (1966), *The Colonial Empires: A Comparative Survey from the Eighteenth Century*, Weidenfeld and Nicolson, London.

Finel, B. I. and H. C. Gell (2007), 'Measuring Progress in the Struggle Against Violent Jihadism: Are We Winning?', American Security Project.

Finel, B. I. and Dehn, C. (2009), 'Are We Winning? Measuring Progress in the War on Terror: An Interim Update', American Security Project.

Forster, A. (2006), 'Breaking the covenant: Governance of the British army in the twenty-first century', *International Affairs*, 82(6): 1043–57.

Foster, J. B. (2001), 'Imperialism and "empire"', *Monthly Review*, 53(7), www.monthlyreview.org/1201jbf.htm.

Foster, J. B. (2006), 'The new geopolitics of empire', *Monthly Review*, 57(8), www.monthlyreview.org/0106jbf.htm.

Frank, A. G. (1966), *The Development of Underdevelopment*, MRP, New York.

Gallagher, J. and R. Robinson (1953), 'The imperialism of free trade', *Economic History Review*, VI(1): 1–15.

Galtung, J. (1971), 'A structural theory of imperialism', *Journal of Peace Research*, 81(8): 81–117.

Gamble, A. (2003), *Between Europe and America: The Future of British Politics*, Palgrave, Basingstoke.

Georgiadis, A. and A. Manning (2009), 'One Nation Under a Groove? Identity and Multiculturalism in Britain', CEP Discussion Papers dp0944, Centre for Economic Performance, LSE.

Githens-Mazer, J. (2008), 'Islamic radicalisation among North Africans in Britain', *British Journal of Politics and International Relations*, 10(4): 550–70.

Gove, M. (2006), *Celsius 7/7*, Phoenix, London.

Grey, S. (2006), *Ghost Plane: The Inside Story of the CIA's Secret Rendition Programme*, Hurst & Co., London.

Habermas, J. (2006), 'Religion in the public sphere', *European Journal of Philosophy*, 14(1): 1–25.

Hardt, M. and A. Negri (2000), *Empire*, Harvard University Press, London.

Harvey, D. (2003), *The New Imperialism*, Oxford University Press, Oxford.

Harvey, D. (2007), 'In what ways is "the new imperialism" really new?', *Historical Materialism*, 15(3): 56–70.

Haubrich, D. (2003), 'September 11, anti-terror laws and civil liberties: Britain, France and Germany compared', *Government and Opposition*, 38(1): 3–28.

Heuer U-J, and G. Schirmer (1998), 'Human rights imperialism', *Monthly Review*, 49(10), www.monthlyreview.org/398heuer.htm.

Hewitt, S. (2008), *The British War on Terror: Terrorism and Counter-Terrorism on the Home Front Since 9/11*, Continuum, London.

Hilferding, R. (1981), *Finance Capital: A Study of the Latest Phase in Capitalist Development*, Routledge, London.

Hobson, J. A. (1978), *Imperialism: A Study*, University of Michigan Press, Michigan.

Hoffman, B. (2008), 'The myth of grass-roots terrorism: Why Osama bin Laden still matters', *Foreign Affairs*, May/June, www.foreignaffairs.com/articles/63408/bruce-hoffman/the-myth-of-grass-roots-terrorism.

Holloway, A. (2009), 'The failure of British political and military leadership in Iraq', FirstDefence.org

Holloway, J. (1996), 'Global capital and the national state', in W. Bonefeld and J. Holloway (eds), *Global Capital, National State and the Politics of Money*, Macmillan, London.

Hopkins, A. G. (2007), 'Capitalism, nationalism and the new American empire', *Journal of Imperial and Commonwealth History*, 35(1): 95–117.

Human Rights Watch (2009), 'Cruel Britannia: British Complicity in the Torture and Ill-Treatment of Terror Suspects in Pakistan', New York.

Ignatieff, M. (2003), *Empire Lite: Nation-building in Bosnia, Kosovo, Afghanistan*, Vintage, London.

Ignatieff, M. (2003a), 'The challenges of American imperial power', *Naval War College Review*, LVI(2): 53–63.

Ikenberry, G, J. (2002), 'America's imperial ambition', *Foreign Affairs*, September/October, www.foreignaffairs.com/articles/58245/g-john-ikenberry/americas-imperial-ambition.

Ikenberry, G. J. (2004), 'Illusions of empire: Defining the new American order', *Foreign Affairs*, March/April, www.foreignaffairs.com/articles/59727/g-john-

References

ikenberry/illusions-of-empire-defining-the-new-american-order.

Ikenberry, G. J. (2005), 'Power and liberal order: America's post-war world order in transition', *International Relations of the Asia-Pacific*, 5(2): 133–52.

Johnson, C. (2006), *The Sorrows of Empire: Militarism, Secrecy, and the End of the Republic*, Verso, London.

Jones, E. (2004), 'Debating the transatlantic relationship: Rhetoric and reality', *International Affairs*, 80(4): 595–612.

Jones, P. (1997), *America and the British Labour Party: The Special Relationship at Work*, Tauris, London.

Jones, S. G. and M. C. Libicki (2008), 'How Terrorist Groups End: Lessons for Countering al Qa'ida', RAND.

Kagan, R. (1998), 'The benevolent empire', *Foreign Policy*, No. 111.

Kagan, R. (2003), *Paradise and Power: America and Europe in the New World Order*, Atlantic, London.

Kampfner, J. (2004), *Blair's Wars*, Polity, London.

Kautsky, K. (1914), 'Ultra-Imperialism', *Die Neue Zeit*, September 1914.

Kelly, P. (2005), 'Multiculturalism and 7/7: Neither problem nor solution', OpenDemocracy. net, www.opendemocracy.net/conflict-terrorism/problem_solution_2946.jsp.

Kennedy, P. (1989), *The Rise and Fall of the Great Powers*, Vintage, London.

Kepel, G. (2009), *Jihad: The Trail of Political Islam*, I. B. Tauris, London.

Kettell, S. (2004), 'Circuits of capital and overproduction: A Marxist analysis of the present world economic crisis', *Review of Radical Political Economics*, 38(1): 24–44.

Kettell, S. (2006), *Dirty Politics? New Labour, British Democracy and the Invasion of Iraq*, Zed, London.

Kettell, S. (2008), 'Who's afraid of Saddam Hussein? Re-examining the "September dossier" affair', *Contemporary British History*, 22(3): 407–26.

Kettell, S. and P. Kerr (2008), 'One year on: The decline and fall of Gordon Brown', *British Politics*, 3(4): 490–510.

Khalidi, R. (2006), 'Iraq and American empire', *New Political Science*, 28(1): 125–34.

Kiely, R. (2006), 'United States hegemony and globalisation: what role for theories of imperialism?', *Cambridge Review of International Affairs*, 19(2): 205–21.

Kiely, R., D. McCrone and F. Bechhofer (2005), 'Whither Britishness? English and Scottish people in Scotland', *Nations and Nationalism*, 33(1): 65–82.

Kirby, A. (2007), 'The London bombers as "self-starters": A case study in indigenous radicalization and the emergence of autonomous cliques', *Studies in Conflict and Terrorism*, 30(5): 415–28.

Klare, M. (2003), 'The new geopolitics', *Monthly Review* 55(3), www.monthlyreview. org/0703klare.htm.

Klausen, J. (2007), 'British Counter-Terrorism After the July 2005 Attacks', USI Peace Briefing.

Kornprobst, M. (2007), 'Comparing apples and oranges? Leading and misleading uses of historical analogies', *Millennium: Journal of International Studies*, 36(1): 29–49.

Kundnani, A. (2009), 'Spooked! How Not to Prevent Violent Extremism', Institute of Race Relations, London.

Lenin, V. I. (1963), *Imperialism, the Highest Stage of Capitalism*, Progress, Moscow.

Louis, W. M. R. and H. Bull (eds) (1989), *The 'Special Relationship': Anglo-American Relations Since 1945*, Clarendon Press, Oxford.

Luxemburg, R. (1951), *The Accumulation of Capital*, Routledge and Kegan Paul, New York.

Magdoff, H. (1978), *Imperialism: From the Colonial Age to the Present*, Monthly Review

Press, London.

Magdoff, H. and J. B.Foster (2001), '2001 after the attack ... the war on terrorism', *Monthly Review*, 53(6), http://monthlyreview.org/1101edit.htm.

Magdoff, H. and J. B. Foster (2002), 'U.S. imperial ambitions and Iraq', *Monthly Review*, 54(7), www.monthlyreview.org/1202editor.htm.

Maier, C. S. (2002), 'An American empire? The problems of frontiers and peace in twenty-first-century world politics', *Harvard Magazine*, November–December: 28–31.

Mandel, E. (1975), *Late Capitalism*, New Left Books, London.

Marsden, P. (2003), 'Afghanistan: The reconstruction process', *International Affairs*, 79(1): 91–105.

McCrisken, T. (2009), 'George W. Bush, American exceptionalism, and the Iraq War', in D. Ryan and P. Kiely (eds), *America and Iraq: Policy-Making, Intervention and Regional Politics*, Routledge, London.

McCrisken, T. (2010), 'Past is present: George W. Bush and the future of conservative US Foreign Policy', in J. Aberbach and G. Peele (eds), *The Crisis of Conservatism*, Oxford University Press, New York.

Meiksins Wood, E. (1999), 'Kosovo and the new imperialism', *Monthly Review*, 51(2), www.monthlyreview.org/699wood.htm.

Meiksins Wood, E. (2005), *Empire of Capital*, Verso, London.

Meiksins Wood, E. (2006), 'Democracy as ideology of empire', in C. Mooers (ed.), *The New Imperialists: Ideologies of Empire*, OneWorld, Oxford.

Meyer, C. (2005), *DC Confidential*, Phoenix, London.

Modood, T. and F. Ahmad (2007), 'British Muslim perspectives on multiculturalism', *Theory Culture Society*, 24(2): 187–213.

Mommsen, W. J. (1982), *Theories of Imperialism*, University of Chicago Press, Chicago.

Murphy, C. (2007), *The New Rome: The Fall of an Empire and the Fate of America*, Icon, London.

Naughtie, J. (2004), *The Accidental American: Tony Blair and the Presidency*, Macmillan, London.

Neep, D. (2004), 'Dilemmas of democratization in the Middle East: The "forward strategy of freedom"', *Middle East Policy*, 11(3): 73–84.

Niblett, R. (2007), 'Choosing between America and Europe: A new context for British foreign policy', *International Affairs*, 83(4): 627–41.

Nuttall, S. J. (2000), *European Foreign Policy*, Oxford University Press, Oxford.

Oborne, P. (2006), 'The Use and Abuse of Terror: The Construction of a False Narrative on the Domestic Terror Threat', Centre for Policy Studies, London.

Oborne, P. and S. Walters (2004), *Alastair Campbell*, Aurum, London.

O'Duffy, B. (2008), 'Radical atmosphere: Explaining Jihadist radicalization in the UK', *Political Science and Politics*, 41(1): 37–42.

Peterson, J. and H. Sjursen (eds) (1998), *A Common Foreign Policy for Europe? Competing Visions of the CFSP*, Routledge, London.

Pew (2005), 'Support for Terror Wanes Among Muslim Publics', Pew Research Center, Washington DC.

Pew (2006), 'Europe's Muslims More Moderate', Pew Research Center, Washington DC.

Pew (2006a), 'Muslims in Europe: Economic Worries Top Concerns About Religious and Cultural Identity', Pew Research Center, Washington DC.

Pew (2008), 'Unfavourable Views of Jews and Muslims on the Increase in Europe', Pew Research Center, Washington DC.

Pew (2008a), 'Global Public Opinion in the Bush Years (2001–2008)', www.pewglobal.org.

Pieterse, J. N. (2006), 'Beyond the American bubble: Does empire matter?', *Third World Quarterly*, 27(6): 987–1002.

Pilger, J. (2003), *The New Rulers of the World*, Verso, London.

Pozo-Martin, G. (2006), 'A tougher Gordian knot: Globalisation, imperialism and the problem of the state', *Cambridge Review of International Affairs*, 19(2): 223–42.

Project for a New American Century (2000), 'Rebuilding America's Defenses: Strategy, Focus and Resources for a New Century', Washington DC.

Rapkin, D. P. (2005), 'Empire and its discontents', *New Political Economy*, 10(3): 389–411.

Rashid, A. (2008), *Taliban: Islam, Oil and the New Great Game in Central Asia*, I. B. Tauris, London.

Reid, J. (2005), 'The biopolitics of the war on terror: A critique of the "return of imperialism" thesis in international relations', *Third World Quarterly*, 26(2): 237–52.

Reynolds, D. (1986), 'A "special relationship"? America, Britain and the international order since the Second World War', *International Affairs*, 62(1): 1–20.

Reynolds. D. (2006), *From World War to Cold War: Churchill, Roosevelt, and the International History of the 1940s*, Oxford University Press, Oxford.

Riddell, P. (2004), *Hug Them Close: Blair, Clinton, Bush and the 'Special Relationship'*, Politicos, London.

Rieff, D. (1999), 'A new age of Liberal imperialism?', *World Policy Journal*, 16(2): 1–10.

Robinson, W. I. (2007), 'Beyond the theory of imperialism: Global capitalism and the transnational state', *Societies Without Borders*, 2(1): 5–26.

Rogers, P. (2005), 'Endless War: The Global War on Terror and the New Bush Administration', Oxford Research Group, Briefing Paper, March.

Rogers, P. (2007), 'From Evil Empire to Axis of Evil', Oxford Research Group.

Rogers. P. and S. Elworthy (2002), 'A Never-Ending War? Consequences of 11 September', Oxford Research Group, Briefing Paper.

Rose, D. (2004), *Guantánamo: America's War on Human Rights*, Faber and Faber, London.

Rosen, S. R. (2003), 'An Empire if you can keep it', *The National Interest*, 71: 51–61.

Roy, O. (2004), *Globalised Islam: The Search for a New Ummah*, C. Hurst & Co., London.

Roy, O. (2008), *The Politics of Chaos in the Middle East*, Columbia University Press, New York.

Sageman, M. (2004), *Understanding Terror Networks*, University of Pennsylvania Press, Pennsylvania.

Sageman, M. (2008), *Leaderless Jihad: Terror Networks in the Twenty-First Century*, University of Pennsylvania Press, Pennsylvania.

Saggar, S. (2009), *Pariah Politics: Understanding Western Radical Islamism and What Should be Done*, Oxford University Press, Oxford.

Sands, P. (2009), *Torture Team: Uncovering War Crimes in the Land of the Free*, Penguin, London.

Savigny, H. (2002), 'Public opinion, political communication and the internet', *Politics*, 22(1): 1–8.

Schumpeter, J. (1918), 'Sociology of Imperialism', in *Imperialism and Social Classes* [1951], Meridian, New York.

Seldon, A. (2005), *Blair*, second edition, Free Press, London.

Senlis (2008), 'Afghanistan – Decision Point 2008', M. F. Publishing, London.

Shah, S. (2006), 'The UK's anti-terror legislation and the House of Lords: The battle continues', *Human Rights Law Review*, 6(2): 416–34.

Shawcross, W. (2004), *Allies: The United States, Britain, Europe and the War in Iraq*, Atlantic Books, London.

Sklair, L. (2001), *The Transnational Capitalist Class*, Blackwell, Oxford.

Smith, C. S. (2007), *Bad Men: Guantánamo and the Secret Prisons*, Orion, London.

Smith, J. (2005), 'A missed opportunity? New Labour's European policy 1997–2005', *International Affairs*, 81(4): 703–21.

Spence, K. (2005), 'World risk society and war against terror', *Political Studies*, 53(2): 284–302.

Steele, J. (2008), *Defeat: Why They Lost Iraq*, I. B. Tauris, London.

Stephens, P. (2004), *Tony Blair: The Price of Leadership*, Politicos, London.

Stokes, D. (2005), 'The heart of empire? Theorising US empire in an era of transnational capitalism', *Third World Quarterly*, 26(2): 217–36.

Stothard, P. (2003), *30 Days: A Month at the Heart of Blair's War*, HarperCollins, London.

Straw, J. (2002), 'Order Out of Chaos: The Challenge of Failed States', in *Re-Ordering the World*, Foreign Policy Centre.

Synnott, H. (2008), *Bad Days in Basra: My Turbulent Time as Britain's Main Man in Southern Iraq*, I. B. Tauris, London.

Todd, E. (2003), *After the Empire: The Breakdown of the American Order*, Constable, London.

Thorne, J. and H. Stuart (2008), 'Islam on Campus: A Survey of UK Student Opinions', Centre for Social Cohesion, London.

Uberoi, V. and I. McLean (2007), 'Britishness: a role for the state?', *Political Quarterly*, 78(1): 41–53.

Walker, C. (2006), 'Clamping down on terrorism in the United Kingdom', *Journal of International Criminal Justice*, 4(5): 1137–51.

Wallace, W. and C. Phillips (2009), 'Reassessing the special relationship', *International Affairs*, 85(2): 203–84.

Wallerstein, I. (1975), *World Inequality: Origins and Perspectives on the World System*, Spokesman, Nottingham.

Wishnick, E. (2002), 'Growing US Security Interests in Central Asia', Strategic Studies Institute.

Woods, R. B. (1990), *A Changing of the Guard: Anglo-American Relations, 1941–1946*, University of North Carolina Press, Chapel Hill, NC.

Woodward, B. (2002), *Bush at War*, Simon and Schuster, London.

Woodward, B. (2004), *Plan of Attack*, Simon and Schuster, London.

Youngs, T., P. Bowers and A. Oakes (2001), 'The Campaign against International Terrorism: Prospects After the Fall of the Taliban', House of Commons Research Paper 01/112.

Index

Afghan Center for Socio-Economic and
    Opinion Research, 149
Afghanistan
    British public opinion, 150–151,
        176–178
    future of, 176–179
    post-war problems in, 64–66, 95–96,
        102–103, 111–115, 132–137,
        148–149, 159–162
    Soviet invasion of, 26, 30–31
    Taliban, emergence of, 31
    US-led invasion of, 37–38, 45–46, 57
    US military surges in, 134, 147, 150,
        161
    see also Al-Qaeda; radical Islamic
        terrorism; Taliban; war on terror
Afghanistan Study Group, 114
Ainsworth, Bob, 152, 160
Al-Qaeda
    9/11 attacks, 36–37
    origins, 31
    resurgence, 65–66, 102–103
    support for, 114–115
    threat from, 138, 157–159, 176–179
    see also Afghanistan; bin Laden, Osama;
        radical Islamic terrorism
al-Maliki, Nouri, 122
Alexander, Douglas, 107, 134
Allawi, Ayad, 96
American Security Project, 115
Amnesty, 72, 155
Anti-terror legislation
    see Anti-Terrorism, Crime and Security
        Act; Counter Terrorism Bill,
        Prevention of Terrorism Bill
    see also Contest2
Anti-Terrorism, Crime and Security Act,
    38–39, 75–78
Attorney General, see Goldsmith, Lord

Beckett, Margaret, 98, 101, 105
Benn, Hilary, 105–106
Bin Laden, Osama, 31, 36–37, 46, 114

    see also al-Qaeda; radical Islamic
        terrorism
Black, Cofer, 40
Blair, Ian, 84–85, 125
Blair, Tony
    9/11 attacks, 34–39
    Afghanistan, 96–97, 103
    Brown, Gordon, 30
    Chilcot inquiry, 164
    extraordinary rendition, 89, 155
    foreign policy, early approach, 12–13,
        29–30
    Guantánamo Bay, 41, 73, 90
    Iraq
        approach to, 28, 47–49, 52–56
        invasion of, 56–59, 61–64, 80–84
        withdrawal from, 103–104
    Kosovo crisis, 28–29
    Lebanon crisis, 97–99
    radical Islamic terrorism, 78, 82–86,
        104–107
    resignation, 99–100, 106–107
    Sierra Leone, 29–30
    special relationship, 21–22, 28–29,
        34–38, 40–41, 51–53, 62–63, 72–74,
        82–84, 97–99, 103, 106–107
    see also New Labour
Blunkett, David, 37, 39, 46, 57, 63,
    75–76, 78
Boyce, Sir Michael, 51–52
Bradshaw, Ben, 40
Bremer, Paul, 58, 60
British empire, 6–10
Brown, Gordon
    Afghanistan, 112–113, 134–136,
        150–152, 160–161
    Blair, Tony, 30
    Chilcot inquiry, 164–165
    extra-legal measures, 154
    foreign policy weakness, 139–140
    Iraq war, 108–110, 123, 132, 149,
        164–165
        leadership crisis, 123–134

Obama, Barack, 147
special relationship, 108–111, 130, 132
war on terror, 107–108, 157–159
Browne, Des, 97, 110, 112, 136
Bush, George (Senior), 11–12
Bush, George W.
9/11 attacks, 32–34, 40
Brown, Gordon, 132
election, 30
Guantánamo Bay, 90
Iraq, 54–56, 62–64
Lebanon crisis, 98–99
war on terror, 46, 65, 72, 121, 137–138
see also United States, war on terror
Butler Inquiry, 62, 64

Cage Prisoners, 155
Campbell, Alastair, 35–36, 62
Camp X-Ray see Guantánamo Bay
Carleton-Smith, Mark, 135
Carlile, Lord, 125, 155
Centre for Social Cohesion, 128–129
Chakrabarti, Shami, 85, 125
Chaplin, Edward, 51–52
Charge of the Knights, 122–123
Chatham House, 81
Cheney, Dick, 26, 33, 50. 53, 137
Chilcot Inquiry, 149–150, 164–165
Chilcot, Sir John see Chilcot inquiry
Chilcott, Dominick, 53
Churchill, Winston, 7
Clarke, Charles, 78, 82, 85, 155
Clarke, Peter, 84, 126
Clarke, Richard, 37
Clinton, Bill, 12–13, 27–28
Communities and Local Government
Committee, 163
Contest2, 157–159
Cook, Robin, 12, 28, 56, 81
Counter Terrorism Bill, 124–127
Cowper-Coles, Sir Sherard, 135
Craig, Lord, 123
Cranshaw, Steve, 72
Crawford, Susan, 137
Cross, Tim, 51–53, 61

Dannatt, Sir Richard, 97, 100, 111, 135,
150
de Menezes, Jean Charles, 81
Dearlove, Richard, 153

Defence Committee, 96, 110, 150
Defense Planning Guidance, 26–27
Denham, John, 85
Demos, 111

Eden, Anthony, 9
Eisenhower, Dwight, 9
Europe, 6–14, 21–22
Evans, Jonathan, 125, 153–154, 156, 164
Extraordinary rendition, 40–41, 72–74,
87–90, 129–131, 137, 152–156
see also Guantánamo Bay; New Labour,
extra-legal measures

Falconer, Lord, 90, 125–126
Falklands war, 11
Fleischer, Ari, 36
Foreign Affairs Committee, 61–62, 66, 72,
88, 131, 165
Future of Iraq Project, 50

Garner, Jay, 50–51, 58
General Election
1997, 12
2001, 30
2005, 80–81
2010, 165–166
Georgia, war with Russia, 139
Goldsmith, Lord, 49, 54, 56, 90, 126, 136
Greenstock, Sir Jeremy, 59, 61
Guantánamo Bay, 40–41, 72–74, 90, 130,
137, 147, 152, 155, 158
Gulf war (first), 27
Guthrie, Lord, 100, 111, 155

Heath, Edward, 10–11
Hemming, Sue, 125
Home Affairs Committee, 39, 76, 85,
125–126
Hoffmann, Lord, 77–78
Hoon, Geoff, 40–41, 46, 53, 57, 60
Howells, Kim, 88
Human Rights Committee, 89, 125, 131,
155, 163–164
Human Rights Watch, 72, 155
Hussein, Saddam, 27, 66, 102
see also Iraq
Hutton Inquiry, 62
Hutton, John, 136–137, 151, 154–155

Identity Cards, 75–76, 157
Inge, Lord, 46, 100
Intelligence and Security Committee, 61–62, 73, 81, 129–130, 154, 163
International Institute of Strategic Studies, 66, 114, 121
Iran, 102–103, 139
Iraq
British withdrawal from, 100–101, 103–104, 109–111, 122–123, 132, 149
first Gulf war, 27
invasion of, 56–59
London bombings, 81–82
Operation Desert Fox, 28
post-war planning, 49–53
post-war problems, 56–66, 95–96, 102–103, 120–122
state of intelligence, 49
US approach to, 34, 46–47, 103, 120–122
see also Hussein, Saddam
Iraq Body Count, 121
Iraq Planning Unit, 52
Iraq Policy Unit, 52–53
Iraq Study Group, 103
Iraq Survey Group, 64
Islamic terrorism see radical Islamic terrorism

Jackson, Sir Mike, 51, 59, 100
Jay, Michael, 77
Joint Intelligence Committee, 49
Joint Terrorism Analysis Centre, 81
Johnson, Alan, 154
Johnson, Lyndon. B, 10
JUSTICE, 85

Karzai, Hamid, 114, 159, 161–162
Kelly, Dr David, 62
Kennedy, John. F, 9
Kosovo, 28–29

Lebanon crisis, 97–99
London bombings, 81–82

Macdonald, Sir Ken, 105, 155
Macmillan, Harold, 9
Madrid bombing, 65–66, 76–77
Major, John, 11–12

Malloch-Brown, Lord, 107, 112, 130–131, 151–152
Mandelson, Peter, 53
Manning, Sir David, 48, 49–53, 60–61
Manningham-Buller, 73–74, 104, 126
McCaffrey, Barry, 131
McChrystal, Stanley, 159
McConnell, Mike, 114
Messenger, Gordon, 135
Metcalfe, Eric, 125
Meyer, Sir Christopher, 48, 53, 81
Miliband, David, 107–110, 113, 123, 130, 136, 139–140, 147–148, 151–154, 160
Mohamed, Binyam, 152–154, 162–163
Morgan, Sally, 52
Mueller, Robert, 65
Murray, Craig, 72–73

Naik, Niaz, 32
NATO
9/11 attacks, 33
Afghanistan, 65, 97, 112–114, 133–134, 136–137, 148–150, 159–162
Bosnia, 27
creation, 8
Russia-Georgia war, 139
Kosovo, 28–29
new imperialism
alternative approach, 18–22
criticism, 17–18
emergence and features, 14–17
failure, 64–66, 71–72, 101–103, 138–140
United States, 26–28
see also Afghanistan; Iraq
New Labour
1997 general election, 12
2001 general election, 30
2005 general election, 80–81
2010 general election, 165–166
9/11 attacks, 34–41
Afghanistan, 35–38, 45–46, 76–77, 82–83, 95–103, 108–115, 132–137, 148–152, 159–162, 176–179
armed forces, relations with, 57, 96–97, 100–101, 111, 135–137
extra-legal measures, 40–41, 72–74, 87–90, 129–131, 152–156, 162–163, 174

see also Guantánamo Bay;
  extraordinary rendition; torture
foreign policy, initial approach to,
  12–13, 21–22
Iraq
  approach to, 28, 47–49
  post-war problems, 60–66
  withdrawal from, 103–104, 122–123,
    132, 149
Kosovo crisis, 28–29
Lebanon crisis, 98–99
London bombings, 81–87
Madrid bombing, 76–77
radicalisation, domestic, 77–80, 127–
  129, 157–159, 175–176, 179–183
see also anti-terror legislation
Sierra Leone, 29–30
surveillance plans, 156–157
war on terror (phrase), 105–106,
  108–111, 128, 147–148
Newton Committee, 75
Novak, Manfred, 131

Obama, Barack
  Afghanistan, 161–162
  war on terror, 146–147
Office of Reconstruction and
  Humanitarian Assistance, 50–51,
  57–59
Omand, David, 156–157
Operation Desert Fox, 28
Operation Enduring Freedom, 37
Operation Herrick, 96
Operation Moshtarak, 162
Operation Panther's Claw, 150
O'Neill, Paul, 34
Oxford Research Group, 66, 115

Pakistan, 111–112, 134, 139, 147, 149,
  151, 155, 161
Petraeus, David, 120
Powell, Colin, 31–32, 33, 89–90
Powell Doctrine, 27, 37
Powell, Jonathan, 60
Preventing Extremism Together, 85, 106
Preventing Violent Extremism, 106
Prevention of Terrorism Bill, 78–79
Project for the New American Century, 30

radical Islamic terrorism
  9/11 attacks, 36–37
  Afghanistan, 134–137, 150–152
  threat from, 20, 55–56, 65–66, 76–80,
    84–87, 104–105, 114–115, 138,
    157–159, 175
  London bombings, 81–87
  Madrid bombing, 65–66, 76–77
  origins, 25–26, 30–31
  see also Al-Qaeda; Afghanistan; New
    Labour, radicalisation
Rammell, Bill, 72
RAND, 115, 178–179
Reagan, Ronald, 11
Reid, John, 86–87, 95–97, 104–105
rendition *see* extraordinary rendition
Rice, Condoleeza, 48, 54, 87–88
Ricketts, Peter, 51–52, 64
Rimington, Dame Stella, 156
Robertson, George, 28
Roosevelt, Franklin, 7
Royal British Legion, 111
Rumsfeld, Donald, 31, 33–34, 36, 37, 40,
  47, 50, 57, 58, 60, 65, 101–102
Russia, war with Georgia, 139

Sarkozy, Nicholas, 139
Sawers, John, 59
Scarlett, John, 74, 153
Scheffer, Jaap de Hope, 113
Scheinin, Martin, 155–156
Select Committee on the Constitution, 156
Senlis Council, 114
Siddiq, Irfan, 88
Sierra Leone, 29–30
Simons, Tom, 32
Short, Clare, 57, 81
Smith, Jacqui, 107, 124–127, 156
Soviet Union
  Afghanistan, 26, 30–31
  collapse of, 11–12, 14, 26
  threat from, 8, 26
Special Immigration Appeals Commission,
  75
special relationship, 6–14, 28–29, 34–38,
  40–41, 51–53, 62–63, 72–74, 82–84,
  87–90, 97–99, 103, 107–111, 130–
  132, 147–148, 152–154, 164–165,
  174–176
St Malo agreement, 13

Stevens, Sir John, 78
Stewart, Rory, 110
Stirrup, Sir Jock, 106, 122–123, 135
Straw, Jack, 35, 60, 63–64, 66, 73–74, 82,
    88–90, 98, 155
Suez crisis, 8–9
Synnott, Sir Hilary, 59, 61

Taliban
    collapse, 38
    emergence, 31
    resurgence, 65–66, 95–97, 102–103,
        111–115, 132–137, 148–149,
        159–162, 176–179
    US approach to, 32, 34, 36–38
    see also Afghanistan
Tebbit, Sir Kevin, 60
Terrorism Act, 85
Thatcher, Margaret, 11–12
Thomas, Richard, 156
Tomb, Rex, 36
torture, 40, 72, 152–156
Triesman, Lord, 89
Turnbull, Sir Andrew, 77

United States
    9/11 attacks, 32–34, 36–38, 40

Afghanistan, 37–38, 45–46, 57, 134,
    147, 150, 161
    al-Qaeda, initial response to, 31–32
    extra-legal measures, 40–41, 72–74,
        87–90, 129–131, 137–138, 152–156
    Iraq, 46–47, 49–56, 59–60, 101–103,
        120–121
    new imperialism, 14–22, 26–28, 30
    Taliban, approach to, 32, 34, 36–38
    see also Bush, George W.; special
        relationship; war on terror

Wadham, John, 39
war on terror
    academic literature, 1–2
    impact, 2–3, 65–66, 71–72, 102–103,
        114–115, 138–140, 172–176
    meaning, 105–106
    origins, 25–32
West, Sir Alan, 107, 126
Wilson, Harold, 10–11
Whitley, Albert, 59
Wolfowitz, Paul, 26, 33–34, 47, 48, 50
World Markets Research Center, 66